Courtroom DRAMA

120 of the World's Most Notable Trials

CONTRIBUTORS

John S. Bowman

Rodney Carlisle

Stephen G. Christianson

Kathryn Cullen-DuPont

Teddi DiCanio

Colin Evans

Michael Golay

Bernard Ryan Jr.

Tom Smith

Eva Weber

Janet Bond Wood

NEW ENGLAND PUBLISHING ASSOCIATES

Edited and prepared for publication by
New England Publishing Associates, Inc.

GENERAL EDITORS
Elizabeth Frost-Knappmann,
Edward W.Knappmann, and
Lisa Paddock

EDITORIAL ADMINISTRATION
Ron Formica and Christopher Ceplenski

PICTURE EDITOR
Victoria Harlow

Courtroom
DRAMA

120 of the World's
Most Notable Trials

Elizabeth Frost-Knappman,
Edward W. Knappman,
and Lisa Paddock, Editors

Victoria Harlow, Picture Editor

VOLUME 2
ASSASSINATIONS
ESPIONAGE
MURDER
POLITICAL CORRUPTION

AN IMPRINT OF GALE

Detroit   New York   Toronto   London

Courtroom Drama:
120 of the World's Most Notable Trials

Staff

Jane Hoehner, *U·X·L Senior Editor*
Carol DeKane Nagel, *U·X·L Managing Editor*
Thomas L. Romig, *U·X·L Publisher*

Mary Beth Trimper, *Production Director*
Evi Seoud, *Assistant Production Manager*
Shanna Heilveil, *Production Associate*

Cynthia Baldwin, *Product Design Manager*
Barbara J. Yarrow, *Graphic Services Supervisor*
Tracey Rowens, *Senior Art Director*

Margaret Chamberlain, *Permissions Specialist (Pictures)*

Library of Congress Cataloging-in-Publication Data

Courtroom drama : 120 of the world's most notable trials / Elizabeth
Frost-Knappman, Edward W. Knappmann, and Lisa Paddock, editors.

    p.   cm.
   Includes bibliographical references and index.
   Summary: Covers 120 notable trials that occurred around the world,
from the Salem witchcraft cases to O. J. Simpson.
    ISBN 0-7876-1735-0 (set). — ISBN 0-7876-1736-9 (v. 1) — ISBN
0-7876-1737-7 (v. 2) — ISBN 0-7876-1738-5 (v. 3)
    1. Trials—Juvenile literature. [1. Trials.]   I. Frost
-Knappman, Elizabeth.   II. Knappmann, Edward W.   III. Paddock, Lisa.

K540.C68 1998

347'.07—dc21   97-23014
                                                   CIP
                                                    AC

This book is printed on acid-free paper that meets the minimum requirements of American National Standard for Information Sciences—Permanent Paper for Printed Library Materials, ANSI Z39.48-1984.

Published by U·X·L An Imprint of Gale Research

Printed in the United States of America

10 9 8 7 6 5 4 3 2

Contents

VOLUME 1:

THE CONSTITUTION

This historic case established the principle of judicial review that gives courts the power to decide whether acts of Congress or the president are constitutional.

The Supreme Court ruled that the Indian nations were not foreign nations under the Constitution, and therefore they were unable to sue for compensation from U.S. citizens that had taken over their land.

Dred Scott, a slave, sued for his freedom in 1846 based on the Missouri Compromise. The decision against Dred Scott ended the Missouri Compromise and paved the way for the Civil War.

Laws banning polygamy were found to be constitutional and did not violate the Mormons' right to freedom of religion.

Contents

Contents

VOLUME 2:

Contents

MURDER

Contents

VOLUME 3:

MILITARY TRIALS AND COURTS MARTIAL

RELIGION AND HERESY

Contents

Contents

Trials Alphabetically

A

B

**Trials
Alphabetically**

I

J

K

L

M

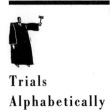

S

T

U

**Trials
Alphabetically**

Trials Chronologically

Trials Chronologically

1910–1919

1920–1929

1930–1939

1940–1949

Reader's Guide

Courtroom Drama: 120 of the World's Most Notable Trials presents twenty-five centuries of intriguing and influential trials that helped shape the course of world history. Falling into thirteen categories, the cases cover assassinations, murders, war crimes, court martials, religious crimes, espionage, treason, negligence, political corruption, freedom of speech, family law, and constitutional cases.

The earliest featured courtroom drama dates from 399 B.C. For refusing to worship the gods of the city of Athens, the philosopher Socrates was sentenced to death. The Timothy McVeigh trial, which deals with the worst act of terrorism in American history—the bombing of the Oklahoma City Federal Building in 1995—is among the more recent trials. Others are the *Jones v. Clinton and Ferguson* lawsuit brought by Paula Jones against President Bill Clinton for sexual harassment that allegedly occurred when he was governor of Arkansas. *Vacco v. Quill* and *Washington v. Glucksberg* together make up the Right to Die test cases heard by the Supreme Court in 1997.

Most of the cases in this book resulted in true trials, meaning that a court—usually a judge or a panel of judges—followed established rules and procedures and impartially examined disputes between parties over fact or law. Others are jury trials in which lawyers presented evidence to a jury that delivered a verdict.

Others are not real trials at all. The Salem witchcraft persecutions, for example, were not true trials since no attorney was present to represent the accused. Still, they were among the greatest social upheavals in colonial New England. Communist dictator Joseph Stalin's "show trials" made a mockery of justice since their verdicts were foregone conclusions.

The trials are arranged chronologically by category. There is an alphabetical listing as well. For easy reference, a Words to Know section at the beginning of each volume defines key terms. More than 120 sidebars provide related information while 172 photos enliven the text. A cumulative index concludes each volume.

Special Thanks

Our special thanks go to the following people for their help in preparing this book:

Colin Evans, for writing the essays on *Jones v. Clinton and Ferguson,* the Markus Wolf trials, the Right to Die case, the Steven Biko Inquest, the Roh Tae-woo and Chun Doo-hwan trials, and the Timothy McVeigh trial; Victoria Harlow, for obtaining all of the illustrations; Ron Formica, for trustworthy and meticulous editorial assistance; Tom Romig, for developing this three-volume set and asking us to prepare it; Jane Hoehner, for her high spirits, flexibility, and editorial advice; Rachael Kranz, for the lively sidebars; Carl Rollyson, for suggestions and support; Christopher Ceplenski, for general assistance and help in preparing the index; Amanda Frost-Knappman, for her independence, which allowed her parents to complete this project; John S. Bowman, for the Martin Guerre Trials and Reichstag Fire Trial essays; Rodney Carlisle, for the Peter Wright (Spycatcher) Trials and Boston Massacre Trials essays; Stephen G. Christianson, for the William "Big Bill" Haywood Trial, *Marbury v. Madison, Cherokee Nation v. Georgia,* Dred Scott Decision, *Reynolds v. U.S., Plessy v. Ferguson, Brown v. Board of Education, U.S. v. Nixon, Bakke v. University of California . . . Appeal, New York Times Company v. Sullivan, U.S. v. Cinque, U.S. v. Berrigan,* Harry Thaw Trials, Leo Frank Trial, Haymarket Trial, The Triangle Shirtwaist Fire Trial, Samuel Chase Impeachment, President Andrew Johnson Impeachment Trial, Aaron Burr Trial, John Brown Trial, and Tokyo Rose Trial essays; Kathryn Cullen-DuPont, for the *Packard v. Packard, Buck v. Bell, Roe v. Wade,* Anne Hutchinson's Trials, Mary Dyer Trials, *U.S. v. Susan B. Anthony,* The Trials of Alice Paul and Other National Woman's Party Members, *In the Matter of Karen Ann Quinlan,* and Hester Vaughan Trial essays; Teddi DiCanio, for the Alien and Sedition Acts, The "Great Negro Plot" Trial, Major John Andre Trial, and Salem Witchcraft Trials essays; Colin Evans, for the Sirhan Bishara Sirhan Trial, Edith Cavell Trial, *O'Shea v. Parnell and O'Shea, In the Matter of Baby M,* Chicago Seven Trial, Oscar Wilde Trials, Clarence Earl Gideon Trials, Ernesto Miranda Trial, Los Angeles Police Department Officers' Trials, *Bounty* Mutineers Court-Martial, William Calley Court-Martial, Samuel Sheppard Trials,

Angela Davis Trial, Guildford Four Trial, *Titanic* Inquiry, *Silkwood v. Kerr-McGee,* Oliver North Trial, Manuel Noriega Trial, Thomas More Trial, Mary Queen of Scots Trial, Walter Raleigh Trials, Gunpowder Plot Trial, Charles I Trial, Roger Casement Trial, and John Demjanjuk Trial essays; Michael Golay, for the Charlotte Corday Trial, Red Brigades Trial, Joan of Arc Trial, Giordano Bruno Trials, Galileo Galilei Trial, Louis XVI and Marie Antoinette Trials, Alfred Dreyfus Trials, The Moscow Purge Trials, József Cardinal Mindszenty Trial, The Nuremberg Trial, and Klaus Barbie Trial essays; Edward W. Knappman, for the John Peter Zenger Trial and John Thomas Scopes Trial (The "Monkey" Trial) essays; Bernard Ryan Jr., for the Alger Hiss Trials, Trial of Julius and Ethel Rosenberg and Morton Sobell, *Schenck v. U.S. Appeal, Ulysses* Trial, Hollywood Ten Trials, The Scottsboro Trials, Sacco-Vanzetti Trial, Bruno Richard Hauptmann Trial, Baader-Meinhof Trial, O. J. Simpson Trial, The Teapot Dome Trials, Socrates Trial, Martin Luther Trial, Vidkun Quisling Trial, Henri Philippe Pétain and Pierre Laval Trials, Ezra Pound Trial, Jiang Qing and the Gang of Four Trial, Tiananmen Square Dissidents Trial, Tokyo War Crimes Trial, and Adolf Eichmann Trial essays; Tom Smith, for the Alexander II's Assassins Trial, Rosa Luxemburg's Assassins Trial, Indira Gandhi's Assassins Trial, Argentina's "Dirty War" Trial, Jean-Bédel Bokassa Trial, Isabel Perón Trial, Milovan Djilas Trial, Cuban Revolutionary Tribunals, Václav Havel Trials, and Anatoly Shcharansky and Alexandr Ginzburg Trials essays; Eva Weber, for the Archduke Franz Ferdinand's Assassins Trial, Anti-Hitler Conspirators Trial, Assassins of Gandhi Trial, Jomo Kenyatta Trial, The Sharpeville Six Trial, and Nelson Mandela Trial essays; and Janet Bond Wood, for the Leon Trotsky's Assassin Trial and Jesus of Nazareth Trial essays.

Comments and Suggestions

We welcome your comments on this work as well as your suggestions for trials to be featured in future editions of *Courtroom Drama: 120 of the World's Most Notable Trials.* Write: Editors, *Courtroom Drama,* U•X•L, 835 Penobscot Bldg., Detroit, Michigan 48226-4094; Call toll-free: 1-800-877-4253; or fax: (313)877-6348.

Words to Know

Note: References to other defined terms are set in **bold**

A

Abortion: a medical term meaning the termination of a fetus or pregnancy

Accessory after the fact: one who obstructs justice by giving comfort or assistance to the felon (*see* **felony**), knowing that the felon has committed a crime or is sought by authorities in connection with a serious crime

Accessory before the fact: one who aids in the commission of a felony by ordering or encouraging it, but who is not present when the crime is committed

Accomplice: a person who helps another to commit or attempt to commit a crime

Acquit: to find a criminal defendant not guilty

Affirmative action: preferences given to one group over another to ease conditions resulting from past discrimination

Alibi: a Latin term meaning "elsewhere"; a criminal defense which shows that the defendant was unable to commit an act because he or she was at some other place

Alimony: an agreement or court order for support payments to either husband or wife after their marriage has ended

Amicus curiae: a Latin term meaning "friend of the court;" a person or organization not party to the lawsuit who provides the court with information

Annulment: to make void; to wipe out the effect of an action or agreement, such as an annulment of a marriage so that it never existed legally

Anti-Semitism: discrimination against or dislike of Jewish persons

Apartheid: a governmental policy of strict racial discrimination and **segregation**

Appeal: a legal request for a new trial or reversal of conviction

Appellant: a party which appeals a decision or a case to a higher court

Appellate jurisdiction: the power of a higher court or other tribunal to review the judicial actions of a lower court

Appellee: the party opposing the party which appeals a decision or case to a higher court; the opponent of the appellant

Arraignment: the procedure by which a criminal defendant is brought before the trial court and informed of the charges against him or her and the pleas (guilty, not guilty, or **no contest**) he or she may enter in response

Asylum: any place that provides protection or safety

Authoritarian: not questioning authority

B

Bench warrant: an order from the court giving the police or other legal authority the power to arrest an individual

Bigamy: having more than one legal spouse

Brief: a written argument a lawyer uses in representing a client

C

Cartel: an association between countries or other financial interests to fix prices of a resource or product to create a **monopoly**

Change of venue: the removal of a lawsuit from a county or district to another for trial, often permitted in criminal cases where the court finds that the defendant would not receive a fair trial in the first location because of adverse publicity

Circumstantial evidence: indirect evidence which can lead a jury or judge to conclude the existence of a fact by inference

Civil disobedience: breaking a law in order to draw attention to its unfairness

Civil liberties: rights reserved for individuals that are protections from the government

Civil rights: rights that civilized communities give to people by enacting positive laws

Claimant: the party, customarily the **plaintiff,** asserting a right, usually to money or property

Class action: a lawsuit a person brings on behalf of all members in a group sharing a common interest

Clemency: the act, usually by a chief executive such as a president or governor, of forgiving a criminal for his or her actions, as when **pardon** is granted

Co-conspirator: one who engages in a **conspiracy** with others; the acts and declarations of any one conspirator are admissible as evidence against all his or her co-conspirators

Cold war: the period of tense relations, from 1945–1990, between the former Soviet Union (and its Eastern allies) and the United States (and its Western European allies)

Common law: principles and rules established by past judicial decisions

Communism: an economic system in which all property and means of production are owned by the community or society as a whole, and all members of the community or society share in the products of their work

Communist Party: the political party that believes, supports, and advances the principles of **Communism**

Community property: everything acquired by a wife or husband after marriage, except for gifts and inheritances

Commutation: change or substitution, such as when one criminal punishment is substituted for another, more severe one

Compensatory damages: monetary damages the law awards to compensate an injured party solely for the injury sustained because of the action of another

Conspiracy: the agreement of two or more people to jointly commit an unlawful act

Contempt of court: an act that obstructs or attempts to obstruct the administration of justice, such as when someone fails to follow a specific court order

Coroner: a public official who investigates the causes of death

Coroner's inquest: an examination by the coroner, often with the aid of a jury, into the causes of a death occurring under suspicious circumstances

Corpus delicti: proof that a crime has been committed, which ordinarily includes evidence of the criminal act and evidence of who is responsible for its commission

Coup: the sudden, forcible, sometimes violent overthrow of a government

Court of chancery: courts that follow rules of **equity,** or general rules of fairness, rather than strictly formulated **common law;** distinctions between courts of equity and courts of law have essentially disappeared at both the state and federal levels

Cross-examination: questioning a witness, by a party or a lawyer other than the one who is called the witness, about testimony the witness gave on **direct examination**

D

Declarative judgment of relief: a binding decision of the rights and status of parties that does not require any further action or relief

Defamation: speech (**slander**) or writings (**libel**) that damages the reputation of another

Deliberations: any method used to weigh and examine the reasons for and against a verdict, usually by a jury

Deposed: one who is removed from a high office of government

Direct evidence: testimony at trial by a witness who actually heard the words or saw the actions in question

Direct examination: initial questioning of a witness by the lawyer who called him or her

Dissent: a legal opinion of one or more judges in a case who disagree with the legal opinion of the majority of judges; to disagree with

Dissenter: one who voices disagreement with the opinion of the majority

Dissident: one who expresses disagreement with the policies of a government or other ruling authority

Diversity jurisdiction: one basis for granting federal courts the power to hear and determine cases, applicable to cases arising between citizens of different states or between a citizen of the United States and a citizen of a foreign country

DNA: deoxyribonucleic acid; a molecule that appears in all living cells, and is the "building block" of life

Double jeopardy: in criminal law, the Constitutional prohibition against putting a person on trial more than once for the same offense

Due process: relevant only to actions of state or federal governments and their officials; it guarantees procedural fairness when the state deprives an individual of property or liberty

E

Emancipated: freedom from control by another

Equity: legal principle of general fairness and justice

Ex parte: a Latin term meaning "without a party"; a judicial proceeding brought for the benefit of one party without the participation of the opposing party

Excommunicated: one who is expelled from membership in a church by church authority

Executive priviledge: the right of the executive branch to keep matters confidential

Exile: being ordered to leave one's country and being prohibited to return

Expert witness: a witness, such as a psychiatrist or ballistics expert, with special knowledge concerning the subject he or she will testify about

Extenuating circumstances: factors which would reduce a defendant's criminal punishment

Extortion: a criminal offense, usually punished as a felony, consisting of obtaining property from another through use or threat of force, or through illegitimate use of official power

Extradition: the surrender by one state or country of an individual accused or convicted of an offense outside its borders and within those of another state or country

F

Fascism: a system of government (first established by Benito Mussolini in Italy in 1922) usually characterized by one ruling political party led by a strong leader that forcibly holds down any opposition, controls its people very closely, and advocates war

Fascists: individuals who believe, support, and advance the priciples of **fascism**

Felony: high crimes, such as burglary, rape, or homicide, which unlike **misdemeanors,** are often punishable by lengthy jail terms or death

G

Gag order: a court order restricting attorneys and witnesses from talking about or releasing information about a case; also, an order to restrain an unruly defendant who is disrupting his or her trial

Genocide: the intentional and systematic destruction, in whole or in part, of a racial, ethnic, or religious group

Grand jury: traditionally consisting of twenty-three individuals empaneled to determine whether the facts and accusations presented by prosecutors in a criminal proceeding require an **indictment** and trial of the accused

Guardian ad litem: a person appointed by the court to represent the interests of a child or one not possessing legal capacity in legal proceedings

Guerilla: a member of a small military force who make surprise attacks against an enemy army

H

Habeas corpus: a Latin term meaning "you have the body"; a procedure for a judicial ruling on the legality of an individual's custody. It is used in a criminal case to challenge a convict's confinement, and in a civil case to challenge child custody, deportation, and commitment to a mental institution (see **Writ of** *habeas corpus*)

Hearsay: a statement, other than one made by a witness at a hearing or trial, offered to prove the truth of a matter asserted at the hearing or trial

House arrest: confinement under guard to quarters other than a prison

Hypocrisy: pretending to be what one is not

I

Immunity: exemption from a duty or penalty; witnesses are often granted immunity from prosecution in order to compel them to respond to questions they might otherwise refuse to answer based on the Fifth Amendment's privilege against self-incrimination

Impeach: to charge a public official with a wrongdoing while in office

Impeachment: criminal proceedings against a public official, such as a president or a supreme court justice, accused of wrongdoing while in office

In re: a Latin term meaning "in the matter of"; used to signify a legal proceeding where there are no adversaries, but merely a matter, such as an estate, requiring judicial action

Indicted: when someone is charged with a crime by a **grand jury**

Indictment: a formal written accusation drawn up by a public prosecuting attorney and issued by a grand jury against a party charged with a crime

Injunction: a judicial remedy requiring a party to cease or refrain from some specified action

Interspousal immunity: a state common law rule, now largely abolished, prohibiting tort actions, or lawsuits concerning certain civil wrongs, between husbands and wives

J

Judicial notice: recognition by a court during trial of certain facts that are so universally acknowledged or easily verifiable (for example, historical facts, geographical features) that they do not require the production of evidence as proof of their existence

Jurisdiction: a court's authority to hear a case

L

Libel: a method of **defamation** expressed by false and malicious publication in print for the purpose of damaging the reputation of another

M

Manslaughter: unlawful killing of another without malice or an intent to cause death. It calls for less severe penalties than murder. Most jurisdictions distinguish between voluntary, or intentional, manslaughter and involuntary manslaughter, such as a death resulting from an automobile accident

Martial law: the law enforced by military forces in substitution for the ordinary government and adminstration of justice when a state of war, rebellion, invasion, or other serious disturbance exists

Martyr: a person who chooses to suffer or die rather than give up his or her faith or principles

Marxism: economic and political philosophy founded by Karl Marx, also known as Socialism

Misdemeanor: any criminal offense less serious than a felony. It is generally punished by a fine or jail (not a penitentiary) and for a shorter period than would be imposed for a felony

Mistrial: a trial terminated and declared void before a verdict is reached because of serious error in procedure or other major problem

Monopoly: an organization, such as a corporation or **cartel,** that has exclusive control of a service or product in a given market

Mutiny: an act of defiance or resistance to a lawful authority, usually by a member or members of one of the armed forces against a higher ranking officer or officers

N

Nationalized: the transfer of ownership or control of land, resources, and industries from private interests to the government

No contest: a type of plea available in a criminal case that does not require a defendant to admit responsibility to the charge, however, the consequences are the same as a guilty plea

O

Opportunism: acting in a way to further one's own interest without any regard to the consequences

P

Pacifist: one who opposes war or the use of force to settle disputes

Pardon: an act, usually of a chief executive such as a president or governor, that relieves a convict from the punishment imposed for his or her crime

Parole: a conditional release of a prisoner after he or she has served part of a sentence

Patriotism: love and loyal support for one's own country

Perjury: the criminal offense of making false statements or lying while under oath

Pernicious: having the power of killing, destroying, or injuring

Plaintiff: the party who initiates a lawsuit, seeking a remedy for an injury to his or her rights

Police power of the state: the power of state and local governments to impose upon private rights restrictions that are necessary to the general public welfare

Precedent: a court decision which serves as a rule for future cases involving similar circumstances

Pro bono: a Latin term meaning "for the good of the people"; when an attorney takes a case without charging a fee

Pro se: a Latin term meaning "for oneself"; representing oneself without an attorney

Prosecution: the act of conducting a lawsuit or criminal case

Prosecutor: a person who handles the **prosecution** of persons accused of crime

Punitive damages: compensation above actual losses awarded to a successful plaintiff who was injured under circumstances involving malicious and willful misconduct on the part of the defendant

R

Reasonable doubt: the degree of certainty required for a juror to find a criminal defendant guilty. Proof of guilt must be so clear that an ordinary person would have no reasonable doubt as to the guilt of the defendant

Redress: to correct or compensate for a fault or injustice

Regime: a political system in power

Repression: strict control of another

Reprieve: a temporary relief or postponement of a criminal punishment or sentence

Republicanism: belief in a republican form of government in which all power rests with the citizens who are entitled to vote, as in the United States

Resistance fighters: members of an organization that secretly work against a government or army in power

S

Sedition: a form of treason consisting of acts intending to overthrow or disrupt the government

Segregation: practice of separating groups of people in housing, public accomadations, and schools based on race, nationality, or religion

Show trial: a trial whose outcome has been decided before it starts

Slander: false and malicious words spoken with the intent to damage another's reputation

Stalemate: any situation making further action impossible; a deadlock

Subpoena: a Latin term meaning "under penalty"; a written order issued by a court authority requiring the appearance of a witness at a judicial proceeding

T

Temporary insanity: a criminal defense which asserts that, because the accused was legally insane at the time the crime was committed, he or she did not have the necessary mental state to commit it, and is therefore not legally responsible

Totalitarian: a government in which one political party or group has complete control and refuses to recognize any other political party or group

Tribunal: an officer or body having authority to judge a case

U

Unanimous: complete agreement

Words to Know

V

Voir dire: a Latin term meaning "to speak the truth"; the examination of possible jurors by lawyers to determine their qualifications to serve

W

Writ of *habeas corpus:* a procedure used in criminal law to bring a petitioning prisoner before the court to determine the legality of his or her confinement (*see **Habeas corpus***)

Writ of *mandamus:* an order issued by a court, requiring the performance of some act or duty, or restoring rights and privileges that have been illegally denied

Picture Credits

The photographs and illustrations appearing in *Courtroom Drama: 120 of the World's Most Notable Trials* were received from the following sources:

On the cover, clockwise from upper left: Crowds at the Bruno Richard Hauptmann Trial (**National Archives and Records Administration**); Salem Witchcraft Trials (**The Library of Congress**); John Demjanjuk (**AP/Wide World Photos**). On the back cover: Scottsboro Trial defendant Haywood Patterson (**National Archives and Records Administration**).

United States Supreme Court. Reproduced by permission: 4, 31, 37, 120, 212; **The Library of Congress:** 6, 11, 12, 16, 17, 25, 106, 107, 108, 113, 124, 138, 158, 173, 174, 178, 184, 191, 192, 198, 252, 253, 256, 303, 336, 342, 382, 387, 425, 518, 524, 531, 532, 580, 604, 642, 643, 649, 650, 651, 669, 695, 700, 701, 707, 749; **Utah State Historical Society. Reproduced by permission:** 24; **Reproduced by permission of Elizabeth Frost-Knappman:** 41; **Official White House photo:** 44; **Photograph by Bettye Lane. Reproduced by permission:** 48, 98; **AP/Wide World Photos. Reproduced by permission:** 55, 142, 149, 211, 222, 228, 235, 236, 337, 369, 374, 412, 440, 448, 468, 498, 500, 504, 543, 760, 783, 789, 794, 833; **Illinois State Historical Society. Reproduced by permission:** 72, 406, 407; **Virginia State Library & Archives. Reproduced by permission:** 85; **Mrs. A. T. Newberry. Reproduced by permission:** 86; **Reproduced by permission of Sarah Weddington:** 90; **National Archives and Records Administration:** 114, 197, 298, 324, 328,

Picture Credits

399, 401, 424, 432, 581, 705, 751, 806, 808, 819; **Hearst Newspaper Collection, University of Southern California. Reproduced by permission:** 130; **The Supreme Court Historical Society. Reproduced by permission:** 137; **Massachusetts Art Commission. Reproduced by permission:** 164; **Hulton-Deutsch Collection. Reproduced by permission:** 205, 316, 454, 460, 474, 492, 725, 739, 744, 756, 770, 775, 825, 837; **Connecticut State Police. Reproduced by permission:** 216; **U.S. Department of Justice:** 237; **U.S. Navy Hydrographic Office:** 260; **The Bettmann Archive. Reproduced by permission:** 292; **United States Air Force. Reproduced by permission:** 358; **Georgia Department of Archives and History. Reproduced by permission:** 417; **The Maryland Historical Society. Reproduced by permission:** 514; **Ronald Reagan Library. Reproduced by permission:** 537; **Columbus Ledger-Enquirer. Reproduced by permission:** 594; **Archive Photos, Inc. Reproduced by permission:** 499, 660, 665.

Courtroom
DRAMA

**120 of the World's
Most Notable Trials**

ASSASSINATIONS

Alexander II's Assassins Trial: 1881

Defendants: Nikolai Rysakov, Timothy Mikhailov, Gesya Helfmann, Nikolai Kibalchich, Andrei Zhelyabov, and Sofia Perovskaya

Crimes Charged: Murder of the head of state, the tsar; membership in a secret society dedicated to overthrowing the government

Chief Defense Lawyers: Court-appointed lawyers for all defendants, except Zhelyabov, who conducted his own defense. The historical records contain the last name of only one defense lawyer, Gerard, the attorney for Kibalchich.

Chief Prosecutors: Assistant Prosecutor Muravieff (the historical records do not report his first name)

Judges: Senator Fuchs, presiding over a ten-member panel (the historical records do not report his first name)

Place: St. Petersburg, Russia

Dates of Trial: March 26–29, 1881

Verdicts: Guilty on twenty charges of "tsaricide"; not guilty on some of the lesser charges

Sentences: Death

SIGNIFICANCE: The assassination of Alexander II ended government reforms in nineteenth-century Russia. The execution of his killers crippled the revolutionary party known as "The People's Will."

From the moment he inherited the throne in 1855, Tsar Alexander II moved the Russian Empire forward. During his rule, individual regions began to govern themselves. He improved education and upgraded the armed forces. He reformed the judicial system, introducing new ideas such as the jury. Alexander II's greatest act was to free the serfs, ending a system of forced labor that had bound more than twenty million peasants.

Despite these reforms, some Russians felt that the "Tsar Liberator," as Alexander II was known, had not gone far enough. Peasants still paid heavy taxes, and the police could be unexpectedly brutal. Since there was no legislature or parliament, the tsar's complete power made him a symbol of tyranny to young rebels who wanted swifter change.

Alexander II, shortly before he was assassinated on March 1, 1881.

"The People's Will" Plots Alexander's Death

The most violent revolutionary group of the time called itself "The People's Will." Although few in number, members of The People's Will aimed to destroy the monarchy and provide the lower classes with some of the country's wealth. Believing that by assassinating the tsar they could encourage peasants to rebel, members of The People's Will officially condemned Alexander II to death.

By 1879, assassins had tried three times to kill the tsar. Although The People's Will was better organized than groups that had previously attempted to kill the tsar, at first the new group was no more successful. The revolutionaries spent months laying explosives along a rail line to the tsar's summer home in the Crimea—a southern peninsula warmed by the Black Sea—but they succeeded only in blowing up the wrong train. One terrorist, dressed as a carpenter, exploded a bomb in the basement of the tsar's Winter Palace, destroying the royal dining room and killing eleven people. Alexander, who was in another part of the palace, was unharmed.

In 1881, the group decided to kill the tsar during one of his Sunday outings. Assassins rented a small cheese shop along his usual route. The plotters began digging an underground passage from which they planned to blow up the tsar as he passed overhead. Four bomb throwers stood in the streets in case the attempt failed.

Suspicious policemen inspected the cheese shop, but they failed to find the tunnel. Still, on February 27 they arrested Andrei Zhelyabov, the plot's main organizer. The other conspirators began to wonder if their plan was about to collapse.

Bomb Kills Alexander

On the afternoon of March 1, the tsar left the Winter Palace to review a weekly parade of his troops. A chemical-filled canister exploded, injuring the horses and some passersby, but the tsar was unhurt. He got out of his carriage, examined the damage, asked about those who had been injured, and reprimanded Nikolai Rysakov, whom a crowd had grabbed. A second terrorist, Agnate Grinivetsky, stood close by, watching.

As Alexander walked past, Grinivetsky set off a second bomb. The blast seriously injured Grinivetsky and mortally wounded the tsar. "Home to die," muttered the tsar as staff eased his mangled body into a carriage. "It's cold." Within an hour, thousands of Russians kneeling in prayer outside the Winter Palace learned that the tsar was dead.

Grinivetsky died of his wounds that evening, as police kept Rysakov talking about his fellow conspirators. Police arrested Gesya Helfmann, but not quickly enough to prevent her roommate, Nikolai Sablin, from committing suicide during the raid. When a third bomb thrower, Timothy Mikhailov, arrived at the Helfmann-Sablin apartment, police arrested him too. The leadership of The People's Will suffered a more serious blow the following week, when police captured Sofia Perovskaya on the street. Perovskaya, Zhelyabov's lover and the well-educated daughter of a former St. Petersburg governor, had organized the assassination plot after Zhelyabov's arrest.

Arrests continued. Authorities were eager for a quick trial and charged six people with the tsar's murder: Rysakov, Mikhailov, Helfmann, Perovskaya, Zhelyabov, and former engineering student Nikolai Kibalchich, who had taken charge of the organization's bomb-making.

Six Tried for "Tsaricide"

The defendants faced twenty-four charges, including "murdering the tsar" and membership in a secret revolutionary society. The authorities also charged them with trying to blow up the royal train and the cheese shop plot. A ten-member panel drawn from various social classes would decide their fate. Press coverage was censored.

When court opened on March 26, a guard with a drawn sword stood in the center of the room alongside a table full of captured explosives. A portrait of the tsar, draped in black cloth, stared down as the prosecutor described the assassination.

Defendant Helfmann refused to testify. So did Mikhailov, who the others said had not taken part in the assassination. Kibalchich, the explosives expert, corrected the prosecutor for stating that the cheese shop bomb would have killed many civilians.

Most of the defendants had court-appointed lawyers. Only Kibalchich's attorney, Gerard, put up a fight. Andrei Zhelyabov—acting as his own attorney—caught witnesses in lies, and turned every question into an explanation of his cause. He freely admitted his part in the plot to kill the tsar, but he insisted that the failure of peaceful means of changing society had forced him to do so.

When the trial ended after three days, Rysakov tried to save himself. Although he had clearly thrown a bomb at the tsar, Rysakov denied ever having approved of terrorism. The court showed surprise at Kibalchich's final statement, when he asked that his plans for a rocket-powered "flying machine" be given to his attorney.

Assassins Hang

Russia had abolished the death penalty more than one century earlier. However, the assassination of Alexander called for an exception and the prosecutor demanded it. Final arguments in the case ended after midnight on March 29, and the court returned at 3 A.M. with its verdicts. The panel found Rysakov, Helfmann, and Mikhailov innocent of having plotted to mine the cheese shop tunnel. On twenty remaining charges relating to the

THE EDICT OF EMANCIPATION

Alexander II, tsar of Russia, made history in 1861 when he signed the Edict of Emancipation. In so doing, he freed the serfs, who made up one-third of Russia's population. The serfs were peasants who worked on the estates of large landowners. They could not leave the estates on which they were born. When Alexander II ended serfdom, the former serfs were free to own their own plots of land—at least in theory. In practice, most serfs ended up working for the same landowners as before, similar to what happened to African-American enslaved men and women after emancipation in the United States in 1865.

tsar's murder, however, the ten members found all six defendants guilty. After an argument over whether minors like nineteen-year-old Rysakov were eligible for the death penalty, the court sentenced all six defendants to death.

Only Mikhailov and Rysakov appealed their sentences to the new tsar, Alexander III. He rejected both. The new tsar also approved the execution of Perovskaya, whose noble background required that her sentence be confirmed by the monarch. On the same day, Helfmann revealed that she was pregnant, and the court postponed her sentence.

On April 2, guards took the other five revolutionaries from their cells. With signs reading "TSARICIDE" hung around their necks, they were hanged one by one as 80,000 people looked on. Tsar Alexander III granted Helfmann's plea for mercy, and the court changed her sentence: Instead of death she would serve a lifetime of hard labor in prison. She gave birth in her cell to a daughter, but the child was taken away from her. Helfmann died in prison in February 1882.

The terrorists were not the only ones punished. A general and two policemen who had failed to detect the cheese shop tunnel languished in exile near the Arctic Circle. Police continued to arrest members of The People's Will. At the 1882 trial of the fourth bomb thrower, Emilianov, the accused made a surprising confession. After he had watched the fatal bomb explode, he rushed to help the tsar, still carrying his own bomb under his arm.

ASSASSINATIONS

The executions of those convicted of "tsaricide" did not bring about the expected social uprising. In fact, many peasants resented the killing of the tsar, whom they considered their protector for having abolished serfdom. Alexander III did not carry out his father's plans for further change. Instead, the new tsar imposed a brutal regime that did away with many of Alexander II's reforms. Nearly forty more years of tsarist rule would pass before the revolutionaries of the nineteenth century would do away with the tsars forever.

Suggestions for Further Reading

Engel, Barbara Alpen and Clifford N. Rosenthal. *Five Sisters: Women Against The Tsar.* New York: Alfred A. Knopf, 1987.

Tessendorf, K. C. *Kill the Tsar!* New York: Atheneum, 1986.

William "Big Bill" Haywood Trial: 1907

Defendant: William Dudley Haywood

Crime Charged: Conspiracy to commit murder

Chief Defense Lawyers: Clarence Darrow, Fred Miller, John Nugent, Edmund Richardson, and Edgar Wilson

Chief Prosecutors: William E. Borah, James H. Hawley, Charles Koelsche, and Owen M. Van Duyn

Judge: Fremont Wood

Place: Boise, Idaho

Dates of Trial: May 9–July 28, 1907

Verdict: Not guilty

SIGNIFICANCE: The government used the courts and the military in an attempt to destroy the left-wing labor movement during a time of public unrest. The public applauded William Haywood's acquittal as a victory for organized labor and a defeat for big business.

Born in 1869, William Dudley Haywood, known as "Big Bill," grew up in the rough-and-tumble world of the Wild West. Discoveries of gold, copper, silver, and other valuable metals brought in big mining companies. Conditions in the mines were poor: miners performed back-breaking labor for long hours and low pay in dark, cramped, and almost airless spaces. In the late nineteenth century, union leaders found miners eager to organize.

Haywood soon rose through the Western labor movement and became an executive officer of the Western Federation of Miners. He was one of labor's recognized radicals. Haywood also belonged to the Socialist Party and was active in the anarchist International Workers of the World, known as the "Wobblies," which wanted to do away with all organized government. Haywood publicly backed strikes and even violence as means of furthering the workers' cause. Haywood's radicalism made him an enemy of big business and the federal government.

Chief defense lawyer Clarence Darrow.

Governor Killed

Idaho's Coeur d'Alene region is the site of some of the world's richest lead and silver deposits. In 1892, Haywood's Western Federation of Miners led a general strike against the mining companies in the area. The owners hired nonunion workers ("scabs") to replace the strikers, protecting them with armed Pinkerton guards. On July 11, 1892, armed union miners dynamited a mine, battled the guards, and kicked out the scabs. As a result, state and federal troops flooded the area, imposing martial law. More strikes in 1894 and 1899 prompted federal troops to enter the area. In the process, the legal rights of strikers fell by the wayside as hundreds of men went to jail without bail in stockades nicknamed "bull pens." Governor Frank Steunenberg, who won re-election in 1898 and who had invited federal troops into the region, had seemed to be in favor of labor unions when running for office. Now he was a marked man. Years later, on December 30, 1905, after his term as governor was over, he died when a bomb exploded in the front yard of his house in Caldwell, Idaho.

Haywood Arrested

Two days later, the police arrested miner Harry Orchard for Steunenberg's murder. Orchard confessed, telling the police that Haywood and Charles H. Moyer, another executive officer of the Western Federation, paid him to kill Steunenberg. Police took Haywood, Moyer, and another union member named George Pettibone to Boise, Idaho, to stand trial.

The famous criminal lawyer Clarence Darrow went to Boise to defend Haywood. Haywood's trial for conspiracy to commit murder began on May 9, 1907.

The prosecution's star witness was Harry Orchard, the confessed assassin. However, Orchard had had a long criminal career, and he admitted that he had lied many times in the past "whenever it suited my purpose." Still, Orchard stuck with his story that Haywood and Moyer wanted him to murder Steunenberg. Darrow suspected that it was the mining companies that had paid Orchard and said so to the jury.

When the prosecutors called Haywood to the witness stand, he denied hiring Orchard to kill Steunenberg. He admitted that he hated the former governor, but he added: "I felt toward him much as I did toward . . . others who were responsible for martial law and the bull pen in the Coeur d'Alene."

A Jury of Farmers

Darrow questioned more than eighty character witnesses who knew Orchard and who testified that he did not always tell the truth. Darrow then went on to declare that the real issue in the case was big business's effort to finish off Haywood and the unions. Addressing the jury, Darrow said:

> Gentlemen, it is not for him alone that I speak. I speak for the poor, for the weak, for the weary, for that long line of men who, in darkness and despair, have borne the labors of the human race. The eyes of the world are upon you, upon you twelve men of Idaho tonight. . . . If you kill him your act will be applauded by many. If you should decree Bill Haywood's death, in the railroad offices of our great cities men will applaud your names. If you decree

his death, amongst the spiders of Wall Street will go up paeans of praise for these twelve good man and true.

Because the jury consisted of Idaho farmers, Darrow made it sound as if all farmers and miners were brothers united against the corporations. Prosecutor William Borah tried to get the jury to focus on the real issue, whether Haywood was a party to Steunenberg's murder. Borah also used Darrow's political appeal to the jury against the defendant. The prosecutor knew that the unpopular aspect of the union movement was its connection with anarchists, Wobblies, and others trying to overthrow the government. Knowing that Haywood's connection with these elements was well publicized, Borah played on the threat of social revolution:

We see anarchy, that pale, restless, hungry demon from the crypt of hell, fighting for a foothold in Idaho! Should we compromise with it? Or should we crush it? . . . I only want what you want, the gates to our homes, the yard gate whose inward swing tells of the returning husband and father, shielded and guarded by the courage and manhood of Idaho juries!

Haywood Goes Free

By the end of the trial, the jury had seen one of Clarence Darrow's great performances, however, the prosecution had offered speeches that were nearly as good. Judge Wood reminded the jury that while they might not be sure of Haywood's innocence, they must find him not guilty unless they thought—beyond a reasonable doubt—that he committed the crime. The judge also attacked the prosecution's failure to bring forward other evidence to support Orchard's claims. Whether it was the result of Darrow's speeches or the judge's instructions, on July 28, 1907, the jury returned a verdict of not guilty. Haywood went free, but Orchard spent the rest of his life in prison.

Haywood returned to his radical activities, keeping up his support for the Wobblies. When World War I broke out, public opinion and the government turned against the Wobblies and other radical groups, who some thought were unpatriotic for backing world labor rather than an American victory.

BIG BILL'S CHILDHOOD

"Big Bill" Haywood grew up in the poor mining camp of Ophir, Utah, an area so wild that he remembered seeing a gun duel at age seven on his way to school. When he was fifteen, he saw the lynching of an African American man, which led to his resolve to oppose racial injustice. Later that year, he began work in the Ohio Mine in Nevada's Eagle Creek Canyon. Despite the fact that the miners worked long hours at back-breaking labor, Haywood later recalled that they were all "great readers. . . . I did not have many books of my own, but the miners all had some. One had a volume of Darwin; others had Voltaire, Shakespeare, Byron, Burns, and Milton. . . . We all exchanged books and quite a valuable library could have been collected among these few men."

Haywood Tried Again

In 1918, the government again brought Haywood to trial. He faced charges of treason, and this time the jury found him guilty, sentencing him to twenty years in prison. While he was out on bail, Haywood fled the United States for the Soviet Union, where the Communist regime granted him asylum. He lived there until his death in 1928, when the Soviets honored him with a burial in the Kremlin, the historic center of government in the city of Moscow.

Suggestions for Further Reading

Carlson, Peter. *Roughneck.* New York: W.W. Norton & Co., 1983.

Dubofsky, Melvyn. *"Big Bill" Haywood.* New York: St. Martin's Press, 1987.

Haywood, William. *Bill Haywood's Book.* Westport, CT: Greenwood Press, 1983.

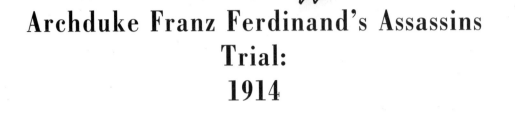

Archduke Franz Ferdinand's Assassins Trial: 1914

Defendants: Gavrilo Princip, Nedeljko Čabrinovič, Trifko Grabež, Danilo Ilič, Vaso Eubrilovič, Cvetko Popovič, Nedjo Kerovič, Mihajlo Jovanovič, Jakov Milovič, along with sixteen others accused of either helping the conspirators hide or smuggle weapons and/or of failing to report them to the authorities when they heard about the assassination plans

Crimes Charged: High treason, accomplices to high treason

Chief Defense Lawyers: Dr. Max Feldbauer, Wenzel Malek, Dr. Srecko Perišič, Dr. Konstantin Premužič, Franz Strupl, and Dr. Rudolf Zistler

Chief Prosecutors: Dr. Franjo Švara, assisted by Rudolph Sark

Judges: President of the Court Luigi von Curinaldi, assisted by Bogdan Naumowicz and Dr. Mayer Hoffmann

Place: Sarajevo, Bosnia

Dates: October 12–28, 1914

Verdicts: Guilty for sixteen of the accused, acquittals for nine

Sentences: Death by hanging for Danilo Ilič, Nedeljko Eubrilovič, Nedjo Kerovič, Mihajlo Jovanovič, and Jakov Milovič. (On appeal, Kerovič's sentence was changed to twenty years and Milovič's to life imprisonment.) For Princip, Eabrinovič, and Grabež, twenty years' hard labor; for Vaso Eubrilovič, sixteen years' hard labor; and for Popovič, thirteen years—all five to be subjected to solitary confinement in a dark cell on each June 28. The other six received sentences from three years to life.

SIGNIFICANCE: The trial was less significant than the killing itself. The murder of Franz Ferdinand had given Austria an excuse to declare war on Serbia, lighting the fuse for World War I.

Today in Sarajevo, the capital city of Bosnia-Herzegovina, many people regard Gavrilo Princip, the murderer of Archduke Franz Ferdinand, as a national hero. In 1914, Bosnia-Herzegovina, as well as much of the territory later known as Yugoslavia, belonged to the Austro-Hungarian Empire. That people could honor the killer of the man who was next-in-line to be emperor speaks volumes about the region's warring history.

Archduke Franz Ferdinand, the eldest son of Karl Ludwig.

The Assassination

In 1913, the Austrian governor of Bosnia, General Oskar Potiorek, faced a rebellion by the Serbian population, which the Austro-Hungarian Empire ruled. He fought the uprising by suspending the province's parliament, censoring the press, and increasing police activity. He then invited Archduke Franz Ferdinand, the heir to the Habsburg throne and inspector general of the Austrian Army, to observe military exercises during a one-day visit to Sarajevo on June 28, 1914. On that date in 1389 the Serbs had lost their independence after being defeated by the Turks in the battle of Kosovo, and they had remained a captive province for five hundred years.

Spotting the newspaper announcement of the archduke's visit, a young Bosnian Serb named Gavrilo Princip became enraged. He decided to murder the archduke and asked an acquaintance, Nedeljko Čabrinovič, to help him. Joined by a third conspirator, Trifko Grabež, the men stockpiled guns and bombs from the Black Hand, a secret Serbian nationalist group. When Princip, who was living in the Serbian capital of Belgrade, secured the guns, he wrote to Danilo Ilič, asking him to find several more plotters in the city of Sarajevo. Ilič, a radical intellectual, lined up three more schemers: Mehmed Mehmedbašič, a Muslim carpenter, and Vaso Čubrilovič and Cvetko Popovič, both high school students.

As the archduke's visit drew near, Ilič began to have doubts about the plan and tried unsuccessfully to discourage Princip and Grabež. In the end, Ilič went ahead and forged the plan. The newspaper had reported where and when the archduke's motorcade would appear, so Ilič stationed the conspirators along that route. The first two youths would attack first. If they missed their target, the next two would take aim. If they too failed, the last two men would try to blow up the archduke's car. Ilič passed out the guns and bombs. The conspirators mingled with the crowd. The first two plotters, Mehmedbašič and Čubrilovič, froze as the motorcade passed by. The next three, Popovič, Princip, and Grabež, also held back. Only Čabrinovič heaved his bomb at the archduke. It bounced off his car and fell under the following automobile, wounding twelve people. The archduke's car left immediately. Čabrinovič tried unsuccessfully to kill himself by taking a cyanide capsule and jumping into a nearby river. There police captured him. All the other conspirators fled except Princip, who decided to wait for a second chance at killing the archduke.

After they visited the town hall, the archduke and his wife drove to the hospital to see an aide who was wounded by the bomb. On the way, the driver of the lead car made a wrong turn, slowing to turn around in the very spot Princip was waiting. The car escorting the royals came to a stop in front of Princip, who raised his pistol and shot the archduke and his wife. Both died soon after. Police immediately seized Princip.

The Investigation

The interrogation of Princip and Čabrinovič, along with police investigations, led to the arrests of twenty-three more suspects. Mehmedbašič escaped to Montenegro, which is a Serbian region at the southern end of the Dinaric Alps. On July 13, Austrian Foreign Minister Count von Berchtold received a secret cable from an aide in the city of Sarajevo. The cable implied that the conspirators had carried out their plot with the aid of Serbian officials.

During August, the major powers of Europe chose sides over this incident and went to war even before the investigation in Sarajevo ended. When Serbian officials suggested that the trial be delayed until after the war ended, Count von Berchtold objected. Austria's aim was not so much to try the assassins, but to assign Serbia moral responsibility for starting a world war.

The Trial

The trial of twenty-five defendants opened on October 12 in a room of the military prison. Instead of a jury, a panel of three judges would decide the defendants' fates. A number of factors came into play in determing the charges against them. Although murder carried a death sentence, being an accessory to murder did not. Also, five of the conspirators were "schoolboys"—nineteen years of age and younger. As "boys" they could not receive the death penalty under the Austrian criminal code. However, the seriousness of the crime necessitated more than one execution, so the charge became high treason, punishable by death.

It was a "show trial," conducted in too short a time to examine such a complicated case. Officials announced the trial would be open to the public, yet they admitted only a few people (all supporters of Austria). Only six journalists covered the trial.

Defense lawyers were silent as prosecutors grilled the defendants about the details of the plot, their lives, their political views, and, especially, their membership in secret revolutionary societies. Strategies to prove greater Serbian involvement in the plot failed.

Archduke Franz Ferdinand's Assassins Trial: 1914

The men accused of murdering Archduke Franz Ferdinand and his wife. Front row (left to right): Trifko Grabež, Nedeljko Čabrinovič, Gavrilo Princip, Danilo Illč, and Vaso Čubrilovič. Second Row: Misko Jovanovič and Jakov Milovič.

THE AUSTRO-HUNGARIAN MONARCHY

The Austro-Hungarian Monarchy, also known as the Habsburg Empire, lasted from 1867 to 1918, when it collapsed as the result of the events set off by the assassination of Archduke Franz Ferdinand. The empire was divided into two halves. Lands west of the Leitha River, known as Cislethania, included the countries and regions that today are known as Austria, Bohemia (part of Czechoslovakia), Moravia (also part of Czechoslovakia), Austrian Silesia, Slovenia (part of the former Yugoslavia), and Austrian Poland. The eastern part of the empire, Translethania, included Hungary, Transylvania (part of Romania), Croatia (part of the former Yugoslavia), and part of Dalmatia (also part of the former Yugoslavia). The Habsburg ruler was considered the emperor of Austria—which supposedly gave him the right to rule Cislethania—and the king of Hungary—which supposedly gave him the right to rule Translethania. However, each of the two states had its own parliament and ministers for domestic affairs. A common cabinet dealt with foreign affairs, common finances, and common defense.

At the end of the trial, the defense lawyers tried half-heartedly to excuse their clients on grounds of poor upbringing, bad companions, and pro-Serbian propaganda. Only Dr. Rudolf Zistler questioned the high treason charge. The court reprimanded him and allowed the charge to stand.

On October 28, the court announced its verdict, finding sixteen defendants guilty and nine not guilty for lack of evidence. The guilty received their sentences immediately: Five of them faced hanging. (Two of these sentences were later reduced on appeal.)

The Aftermath

Sentenced to twenty years of hard labor, Princip, Čabrinovič, and Grabež traveled to Bohemia, a region that later became known as western Czechoslovakia. All three died by April 28, 1918, probably of tuberculosis—a lung disease made worse by extreme cold, starvation, and poor medical care. After the war and the collapse of the Austro-Hungarian Empire, the new nation of Czechoslovakia sent back to the new Yugoslavia the remains of the three assassins.

The second act of the Sarajevo drama opened on April 2, 1917, in Salonika, in Macedonia, now a part of northern Greece but then under control of the Austro-Hungarians. Police arrested the Black Hand leader Apis on the orders of Alexander, Prince Regent of Serbia, who feared that Apis was plotting to assassinate him. Police also arrested Mehmedbašič. When their trial opened on April 2, Apis confessed that he had participated in the archduke's assassination. In exchange, he was to go free. However, the trial was rigged. The court found Apis guilty and he was executed on June 26, 1917.

In the years that followed, many ideas emerged as to who was ultimately responsible for the Sarajevo assassination. No facts support a conspiracy among those at the top levels of government. The assassination of Franz Ferdinand was the work of a group of powerfully nationalistic young Serbs operating on their own. They were clearly amateurs, and the success of their plans owed much to pure luck. This blind luck led, in turn, to a series of historical events that were to cast dark shadows across the rest of the twentieth century.

Suggestions for Further Reading

Brook-Sheperd, Gordon. *Archduke of Sarajevo: The Romance and Tragedy of Franz Ferdinand of Austria.* Boston, MA: Little Brown, 1984.

Gilfond, Henry. *The Black Hand at Sarajevo.* Indianapolis: Bobbs-Merrill, 1975.

Morton, Frederic. *Thunder at Twilight, Vienna 1913/1914.* New York: Charles Scribner's Sons, 1989.

Owings, W. A. Dolph. *The Sarajevo Trial* (2 vols.). Translation and editing by W. A. Dolph Owings, Elizabeth Pribic, and Nikola Pribic. Chapel Hill, NC: Documentary Publications, 1984.

West, Rebecca. *Black Lamb and Grey Falcon, A Journey through Yugoslavia.* New York: Penguin, 1982.

Rosa Luxemburg's Assassins Trial: 1919

Defendants: Otto Runge and Kurt Vogel

Crimes Charged: Attempted manslaughter (Runge), illegal disposition of a corpse (Vogel)

Chief Defense Lawyer: Name not recorded

Chief Prosecutor: Paul Jörns

Place: Berlin, Germany

Dates of Trial: May 8–14, 1919

Verdicts: Guilty

Sentences: Runge: two years' imprisonment, four years' loss of civil rights, dismissal from the army; Vogel: twenty-eight months' imprisonment

SIGNIFICANCE: The poor prosecution of Luxemburg's killers created a controversy that haunted German politics during the years following World War I.

Rosa Luxemburg was one of the most hated and admired figures in German politics during her lifetime. Born in Poland in 1870, she lived in Zurich, Switzerland, from 1889 to 1898. There she helped to start the Polish Social Democratic Party, which was the beginning of the Polish Communist Party. In 1898, she moved to Berlin, Germany.

The Spartacus League

As World War I approached, Luxemburg sympathized with the working people of the world, who would suffer during the clash of arms. When Germany entered the war in 1914, the German Socialist Party (SPD) agreed to support the war effort. (The Socialists believed that the government should own factories, coal mines, railroads, and the like.) Disgust with their decision to enter the war led to a split within the party. Luxemburg and Dr. Karl Liebknecht—a representative in the German Parliament—started a new organization called the Spartacus League. Many in the league wanted to overthrow the government.

Both Luxemburg's and Liebknecht's antiwar work meant that they spent the war in government prisons. When the war ended and Luxemburg left jail in November 1918, she immediately resumed her revolutionary work.

In December 1918, she and the other Spartacists became allies of the German Communist Party (KPD). At this time, the Russian Communists (Bolsheviks) were taking power during the Russian Revolution of 1917–1920. Some Spartacists in Germany felt the time had come to overthrow the present government in their country, too. However, Luxemburg did not feel that Germany was ready for upheaval. She advised her group to wait. She lost, however, to the radicals who wanted to boycott the upcoming national election and take up arms.

On January 6, 1919, a mass demonstration took place to protest the government's dismissal of the chief of police. The protest itself was peaceful, but Communist radicals saw it as a chance to bring about the long-awaited revolution. The KPD declared the government unlawful, occupied several public buildings, and waited for the public to revolt.

Polish-born Rosa Luxemburg (pictured here around 1886) was murdered along with Karl Liebknecht during the 1919 Berlin revolt.

Luxemburg and Liebknecht Killed

The people did not revolt, but the government acted immediately. Volunteer units called *Freikorps* attacked the revolutionaries, ruthlessly crushing the "revolt" in three days of street fighting. Luxemburg and Liebknecht went into hiding, but someone betrayed them. On January 15, 1919, a volunteer unit of the Horse Guards arrested them and took them to the regiment's headquarters in the Hotel Eden.

The international press mistakenly reported that the Freikorps had taken the Spartacist leaders from the hotel "for their own safety." Later the government issued a new story: an angry mob had beaten Liebknecht while the Freikorps were taking him to a waiting car. On the way to Moabit Prison, the car had a flat tire. While waiting for another car to arrive, Liebknecht's guards had shot their prisoner when he had tried to flee into the woods.

The government claimed that an angry group had also beaten Luxemburg, in the hotel lobby. Guards had rushed her into a waiting car. A mob had stopped them demanding to know who their prisoner was. When the soldiers had admitted that their prisoner was Luxemburg, a man jumped on the running board of the car and shot her in the head. The guards then dragged Luxemburg's body out of the car and carried it away. The story was that either her friends had rescued her or her enemies had thrown her into a canal.

In truth, Liebknecht's body turned up in a morgue, but Luxemburg's was missing. On January 23, officials said that her corpse had surfaced in the Landwehr Canal. They claimed they were hiding her body to prevent Spartacists from taking revenge. A week later, a rumor circulated that Luxemburg was alive, waiting for the revolution that would allow her to come out of hiding.

Newspaper Exposes Truth

Because Chancellor Friedrich Ebert had requested Freikorps volunteers to crush the Spartacist revolt, some people began to suspect the government was the culprit. Suspicions grew when the Horse Guards took charge of the investigation.

Finally the Spartacist newspaper, *Die Rote Fahne,* exposed the truth. Leo Jogiches, with whom Luxemburg had once been in love, had learned that Luxemburg and Liebknecht had not died at the hands of the people. Instead, a trooper named Otto Runge had clubbed the prisoners with his rifle as they left the hotel. The Horse Guards drove the bleeding Liebknecht to a garden, then asked him if he could walk. When he did manage to take a few steps, they shot him for "trying to escape." They left his body at the nearest mortuary, identified only as an unknown corpse.

No mob had stopped Luxemburg's car. Runge had clubbed her until she lost consciousness, then threw her into a car. Then Lieutenant Kurt Vogel shot her in the head and ordered some soldiers to dump her body into the canal. Later that night at the hotel, the Horse Guards carelessly allowed a photographer to capture them celebrating their work. Jogiches obtained the photograph and published it.

After he exposed the killers, police arrested Jogiches and murdered him. By then, however, the public knew the true story. Police arrested Runge, Vogel, and six other officers.

Two soldiers testified that Vogel had shot Luxemburg while he was standing on the running board of the car. Vogel had also ordered them to throw her body into the canal. Vogel denied both claims. Runge confessed to having hit both prisoners with his rifle. Other witnesses suggested that hush-money had changed hands.

Rosa Luxemburg's Assassins Trial: 1919

Rosa Luxemburg's murderers celebrate by toasting her death at the Eden Hotel on January 16, 1919. Otto Runge sits at the table, third from the left.

Court Gives Killers Token Jail Terms

On May 14, the court declared that it could not determine who had performed the killings. It found five officers innocent of the murders, including Captain Horst von Pflugk-Harttung, whom the press had identified as Liebknecht's killer. Lieutenant Rudolf Liepmann, one of Liebknecht's guards, served only six weeks of confinement in his barracks for having given Runge false identity papers.

Only Vogel and Runge were convicted of serious charges. The court found Vogel innocent of murder. It convicted him of improperly disposing of a corpse and submitting a false report on the incident.

Vogel, who had obtained a false passport before the trial, faced two years and four months in prison. Three days later, he escaped to Holland. Surprisingly, the Germans later gave Vogel a pardon, which fueled suspicion that Luxemburg was the victim of a state-sponsored murder.

Runge was sentenced to two years' imprisonment for attempted manslaughter, assault, misuse of his weapon, and using false documents. The army also dismissed him. The court concluded that Runge had acted freely, without pressure from higher authorities.

On May 31, a little more than two weeks after the sentencing, someone discovered Luxemburg's corpse in a canal lock. Officials hid her body in an army base, but the discovery did not remain a secret. Luxemburg was publicly buried on June 13.

Like Vogel, Runge obtained false identity papers, but he remained in prison. Angry at his superiors for going back on their promises to protect him, he told his story to the press in 1921. Runge called his trial "a comedy," during which the accused officers lived in unlocked cells, enjoying wine, music, and women. Runge accused prosecutor Jörns of persuading him to confess and accept a four-month sentence in exchange for future help. Runge said officials had threatened him with death if he did not give his confession properly.

Aftermath

The officers had ten years to appeal the court's decision. Meanwhile the radical press harassed those responsible for the murders and the cover-up that followed. In 1928, the *Daily Tagebuch* accused prosecutor Jörns of helping the killers rather than prosecuting them. Jörns twice sued editor Josef Bornstein for libel (knowingly printing false statements), but he lost both times. On February 14, 1930, a Berlin court found that Bornstein

KAISER WILHELM II

Wilhelm II (1859–1941) was the emperor (kaiser) of Germany
and the king of Prussia during World War I. He came to the
throne in 1888 at the age of twenty-nine. Wilhelm was distanced
from his liberal-minded parents at an early age by his belief in
the divine nature of kingship, his impulsiveness, and his love of
military display. His first speech as emperor was not to the people of Germany, but "To My Army." He annonced, "We belong
to each other, I and the Army. We were born for each other." He
told young recruits, "If your emperor commands you to do so
you must fire on your father and mother."

had proved that Jörns had not taken the right attitude toward the murderers. (Jörns later continued his career as a prosecutor during the Nazi
regime.)

Rosa Luxemburg became a hero to some people for her courage.
Others hated her for opposing the Bolsheviks during the Russian Revolution because of their use of terror. Surprisingly, disagreement over Luxemburg's place in political history has lasted longer than the debate over
her murder.

In 1962, the German press interviewed Waldemar Pabst, a captain
who had questioned Luxemburg and Liebknecht after their capture. Pabst
claimed that the murders had taken place with the full support of Gustav
Noske, the government's chief military officer. When the West German
government information office agreed with Pabst's claim, further controversy arose.

Suggestions for Further Reading

Ettinger, Elzbieta. *Rosa Luxemburg: A Life.* Boston: Beacon Press,
    1986.

"Liebknecht Cool In Facing Death." *The New York Times.* January
    19, 1919: 4.

Lutz, Ralph. "The Spartacan Uprising In Germany." *Current History Magazine* (April 1921): 78.

Leon Trotsky's Assassin Trial: 1940–1943

Defendant: Ramon Mercader (aliases Frank Jacson, Jacques Mornard)

Crime Charged: Murder

Chief Defense Lawyer: Octavio Medellin Ostos

Chief Prosecutor: Ligorio Espinosa y Elenes

Judge: Manuel Riviera Vazquez (presiding over a three-judge panel)

Place: Mexico City, Mexico

Dates of Trial: August 22, 1940–April 16, 1943

Verdict: Guilty

Sentence: Nineteen years, six months for murder; six months for illegal possession of firearms

SIGNIFICANCE: Lazaro Cardenas, then president of Mexico, said: "[This] recent crime . . . will be censured throughout all time by history as dishonorable for those who inspired it and foul for those who actually perpetrated it." Still, even he could not know at the time that the significance was finding out that Joseph Stalin had inspired the crime committed by a Communist nobody.

Leon Trotsky, along with Vladimir Ilyich Lenin, was a leader of the Russian Revolution of 1917. The two men helped to establish the Communist Soviet Union in 1917. That year, Lenin made Trotsky chief of foreign affairs in the new Soviet government. In 1918, Trotsky became head of the war department. After Lenin died of a stroke in 1924, Trotsky and

Joseph Stalin fought for control of the Communist Party. Trotsky lost to the more ruthless Stalin. In 1927, Stalin expelled Trotsky from the party, and deported him to Turkey in 1929.

Stalin then staged a series of show trials that lasted throughout the 1930s. Most of the defendants fingered Trotsky as part of a plot to destroy the Communist Party or overthrow the government. The court declared each defendant guilty and had them either imprisoned or shot.

Stalin even sent his secret police (the GPU) to hunt down his old enemies and carry out assassinations in all parts of the world. He arranged for the murders of most of Trotsky's colleagues, many of his friends, and even his son. Trotsky himself fled Turkey for France, then Norway, before finally finding a safe haven in Mexico in 1937.

The Assassination

At first Trotsky lived in the home of the famous artists Diego Rivera and Frida Kahlo. Then, in 1939, Trotsky moved to a nearby walled and guarded estate on the edge of Mexico City. With him were his wife, Natalya, his grandson, Seva, and his friends the Rosmers, a French Communist couple. Although Stalin had removed him from the Soviet history books, Trotsky remained influential in the international Communist movement. Politicians, writers, and philosophers visited him from many parts of the world. At all times, though, Trotsky had his house guarded against intruders, admitting only those whom he or his friends knew.

Among the tight-knit circle at the house was a New York-born Communist, Sylvie Agelof, who in 1939 had become one of several secretaries and messengers Trotsky used. Her lover, Frank Jacson, often drove her to and from the house. Sylvie had met Jacson at a Communist meeting in France in 1938. She believed that his real name was Jacques Mornard. He said he was using a false name because he was a citizen of Belgium traveling on a Canadian passport in order to avoid being drafted into the Belgian army. For some months, Jacson could not meet Trotsky, but he seemed happy to do small favors for those who lived at the villa.

During the night of May 24, a group of Mexicans loyal to Stalin attacked the compound with machine guns. Yet they failed to kill Trotsky or anyone else living there. Four days later, Jacson met Trotsky in the villa garden. Gradually, Trotsky allowed Jacson inside the compound. Jacson had convinced Trotsky that he was writing a serious article in support of Trotsky's version of Communism, and Trotsky agreed to read it.

On August 20, Jacson took Trotsky his article, and the two went into Trotsky's study. As the old revolutionary bent over the paper on his desk,

Jacson reached under his overcoat and withdrew a small ice axe used in mountain climbing. Lifting it high, he swiftly sank it into Trotsky's head. Instead of falling forward, Trotsky lunged at his attacker and bit his hand. His screams brought the guards and his wife.

The guards caught and beat Jacson but obeyed Trotsky's request that they spare him so that he would reveal information. At the hospital Trotsky underwent surgery, then lapsed into a coma. He died the next day. Jacson, too, went to the hospital under police guard. Police arrested Sylvie Agelof, and held her as a possible accomplice. (She was soon released and no one again suspected her of being part of the assassination plot.) On August 26, police moved Jacson to a cell in a police station.

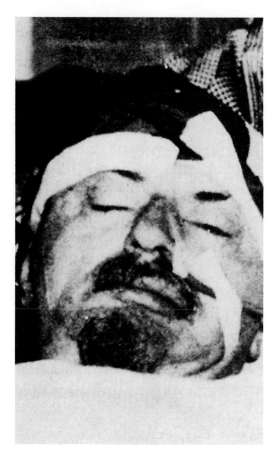

Leon Trotsky lies near death.

The Investigation

At the time of Jacson's arrest, he was carrying a three-page letter signed "Jac." In it he asked that the letter be published if anything should happen to its author. The letter stated that he came from a Belgian family, that he had been a journalist in Paris, and that he had joined a pro-Trotsky organization because of his passion for justice. It went on to say that he had become unhappy with Trotsky because of Trotsky's failures as a leader of the Communist Party.

The chief of the Mexican police took charge of the murder investigation. Under questioning, Jacson claimed to be Jacques Mornard Vandendreschd. He told a story of an idealistic young man who had been a follower of Trotsky. He said his pro-Trotsky group had chosen him for important missions, including one to the Soviet Union to assassinate Stalin. The Mexican authorities soon found flaws in his tale. Nonetheless, Jacson still insisted his name was Mornard.

In September 1940, a judge had two psychologists examine Jacson. Their report, after six months of examination, did not find that Jacson was sorry for his crime.

The Trial

At the trial, the prosecutor tried to find out the true identity of Jacson/Mornard and who was behind his actions. The prosecution maintained that Jacson was acting as a Soviet agent. The defense responded that this could not be proven.

World newspapers and radio paid little attention to the trial, mostly because World War II (1939–1945) was raging, dwarfing the trial. Moreover, Stalin was then a necessary ally to the West.

The trial dragged on for months. Finally, in February 1943, the two sides presented their closing arguments. By then, Jacson had changed his story. He now said he had killed in self-defense. Through his attorney, he claimed that Trotsky had called him "nothing but a military idiot," then attacked him. Jacson said the confession he had given to the police had been untrue. He sent notes to reporters saying, "The statements being read had been extorted from me by policemen while I was wounded and semi-conscious in the police jail."

The prosecution never proved that Jacson was acting on behalf of the Soviets. However, the court found him guilty of murder. Mexico did not have the death penalty, so the prosecutor asked for a sentence of twenty-three years. On April 16, 1943, the court sentenced Jacson to twenty years in prison. In its 118-page written decision, the court found that Jacson's attitude was one of "falseness," and that he had come to Mexico "with the sole object of killing Trotsky." During radio broadcast of the decision, Jacson threw his hat over the microphone to interrupt the transmission.

Imprisonment

In prison, Jacson lived in comfortable quarters. He taught inmates how to read and began a program to teach radio and television repair in the prison.

JOSEPH STALIN: THE MAN BEHIND TROTSKY'S DEATH

Joseph Vissarionovich Stalin was the head of the Soviet Union from 1924 until 1953. He built up the Soviet Union as a rival to the United States for world leadership. In 1922, Stalin became general secretary of the Soviet Communist Party. In 1929, after a long political battle, he exiled Leon Trotsky, his major rival for leadership. Later he had Trotsky murdered. Stalin also engineered the killings of Grigori Zinoviev, Lev Kamenev, Nikolai Bukharin, Alexei Rykov, and others who stood in the way of his becoming dictator. Stalin was best known for rapidly developing Soviet industry (under the "Five Year Plans" beginning in 1928) and agriculture, killing millions of peasants to take—"collectivize"—their lands.

Eventually, he took charge of the prison's entire electrical system, earning good money.

Before Jacson came up for parole, officials had learned his true identity. Records from Spain indicated that Jacson/Mornard was really Jaime Ramon Mercader, a Spanish Communist. In 1954, Jacson hired a lawyer to fight for his parole, but lost. In 1956, a second parole request was denied on grounds that he had "no moral regrets" about murdering Trotsky. Jacson never admitted his true identity or gave any factual information about himself. When Jacson left prison on May 6, 1960, two guards met him from the Czechoslovakian embassy in Mexico City, and put him aboard a plane to Moscow. The name on his passport was Jacques Vandendreschd.

Aftermath

By this time, much of the story of Jacson's life had emerged. He had been born in Spain in 1913 to a Spanish father and a Cuban mother. He had joined the Stalinist Communist Party. In 1935, officials arrested him in Barcelona, Spain, and tried him on charges of organizing an underground Communist group. Released, he continued his work in the Communist Party. Soviet intelligence then hired him. Stalin's secret police trained him in Moscow and sent him to Mexico to murder Trotsky. Because Ramon Mercader succeeded where so many others had failed, Stalin awarded him the Order of the Hero of the Soviet Union while he was still in prison. He spent the years after his release in Prague, Czechoslovakia, where he worked as an electrical technician. On October 18, 1978, Ramon Mercader died in Havana, Cuba, where he had gone for treatment of cancer. His grave in Moscow bears the words, "Hero of the Soviet Union."

Suggestions for Further Reading

Glotzer, Albert. *Trotsky: Memoir & Critique.* Buffalo, NY: Prometheus Books, 1989.

Payne, Robert. *The Life and Death of Trotsky.* New York: McGraw Hill Book Company, 1977.

Wyndham, Francis and David King. *Trotsky: A Documentary.* New York: Praeger, 1972.

Anti-Hitler Conspirators Trial:
1944

Defendants: Field Marshall Erwin von Witzleben, General Erich Hoepner, Major General Helmuth Stieff, Lieutenant Albrecht von Hagen, General Paul von Hase, Lieutenant Colonel Robert Bernardis, Captain Friedrich Klausing, and Lieutenant Peter, Count Yorck von Wartenburg

Crimes Charged: High treason and sedition, for participation in a conspiracy in the summer of 1944 by "a small clique of disaffected officers" to assassinate Hitler for the purpose of ending the Nazi regime; to seize power over the armed forces and the State; and to end the war by means of "disgraceful" pacts with the enemy

Defense Lawyers: Dr. Weissmann, Dr. L. Schwarz, Dr. Neubert, Dr. Gustav Schwarz, Dr. Kunz, Dr. Falck, Dr. Boden, and Hugo Bergmann

Prosecutors: Public Prosecutor Dr. Lautz and Dr. Görisch

Judges: Roland Freisler, Chief Justice of the People's Court, leading a panel consisting of General Hermann Reinecke, Counselor Lemmle, Dr. Köhler, Senate President Günther Nebelung, and "the People," represented by Hans Kaiser, gardener; Georg Seuberth, businessman; Kurt Wernicke, engineer; and Emil Winter, baker

Place: Berlin, Germany

Dates of Trial: August 7–8, 1944

Verdicts: Guilty

Sentences: Death penalty; loss of civil rights

SIGNIFICANCE: Since the Nazis showed themselves to be capable of executing anyone without judicial proceedings, the intent of the tribunal was humiliation, vengeance, and Nazi propaganda. By means of his courtroom antics, Chief Justice Roland Freisler sought to portray the defendants as fools as well as traitors.

"**S**ince the generals have achieved nothing so far, it is now for the colonels to take over." With these words German Colonel Claus, Count Schenk von Stauffenberg indicated his intent to assassinate Adolf Hitler during World War II.

Opposition to Hitler and his Nazi regime had existed among some in the military, the nobility, and the church, and among thinkers, intellectuals, Communists, Socialists, and other segments of German society since Hitler seized power in 1933. From 1937 to 1944, Hitler survived at least ten attempts on his life—three made by military officers. Stauffenberg's unsuccessful attempt of July 2, 1944, was the last and most dramatic before Hitler ended his own life on April 30, 1945. Hitler's final days were the final days of the Nazi Third Reich.

German Resistance

German resistance to the Nazis took many forms, from helping runaways, printing and distributing underground pamphlets and newspapers, and sometimes going on strike or engaging in other economically damaging activity, to relatively minor acts such as failing to use the "Heil Hitler" greeting, or tuning into British Broadcasting Corporation (BBC) radio broadcasts. All were punishable crimes. The most intensive resistance occurred in four areas: the Kreisau Circle, the Foreign Office, the military intelligence service (the *Abwehr*), and the army.

The Kreisau Circle, an association of thinkers, politicians, and others, drew up plans for a post-Hitler Germany. They even imagined setting up a second, shadow government. Foreign Office resisters participated in diplomatic missions where they warned the Allies about Hitler's plans for attack; they also assembled a list of Nazi crimes. Those in the Abwehr provided the enemy with military and technical secrets, supplied false information to Hitler, and forged documents that helped Jews to escape. The widespread army network, led by retired officers, began planning a seizure (*putsch*) of military and political power in Germany before the outbreak of World War II. They had been disgusted by the tricks Hitler used to make himself commander in chief and by his mismanagement of this office. The army officers were deeply troubled by the monstrous treatment of civilians and prisoners of war in Nazi-occupied areas of Poland and Russia. Most of all, they were concerned about the possibility that Hitler would bring total ruin upon the nation. The assassination of Hitler became part of the plan only later. At first, their loyalty oath to Hitler, their wish to hold onto some of the territory he had won, and their fear that Communism might fill the vacuum left by Hitler's passing all prevented them from taking action.

Courtroom Drama

The Plot: Operation Valkyrie

Time was running out when Stauffenberg finally made an attempt to kill Hitler. British and American forces had already landed on the Normandy beaches, located in northwestern France along the English Channel. After recovering from serious wounds he had suffered during Germany's battles in North Africa—he had lost an eye, his right hand, and two fingers of his left hand—Stauffenberg became chief of staff to the head of the reserve army in Berlin. Working secretly with other officers there, he helped to plan Operation Valkyrie, a detailed plot to seize power that involved the assassination of Hitler.

On July 20 at Hitler's East Prussia fortress, Stauffenberg slipped a briefcase holding a bomb under a table at a staff meeting and slipped away. He witnessed the explosion from some distance away and rushed off to fly back to Berlin. Miraculously, the bomb injured Hitler only slightly, but the confusion about whether he had lived or died in the explosion threw the attempted putsch into chaos. Upon his arrival at headquarters in Bendlerstrasse, Stauffenberg took charge and tried to rally the plotters back into action. However, in the end, he and the others were overpowered by troops led by General Friedrich Fromm, Stauffenberg's superior officer. Fromm had seemed to support the plot. But just hours after it failed, he announced the guilty verdict of a court martial (though there is no evidence one had taken place) and ordered the immediate execution by firing squad of Stauffenberg and three others.

The First Trial

The Nazis prevented further executions that night, deciding instead to try the other conspirators at a show trial. These trials were to take place in the People's Court, a court the Nazis had set up for trying enemies of the Nazi State. To make it possible for the accused officers to be tried in a civilian court, the Nazis first expelled the conspirators from the army in a military "Court of Honor." Accused individuals could not appear in this "court" or defend themselves in any way. Their dismissals were based solely on a "mere excerpt" from the investigators' files and took only a few minutes. The August 4 session of this body expelled twenty-two officers, some of whom were already dead. In all, fifty-five officers were expelled from the military this way.

Presiding over the People's Court was the notorious Roland Freisler, a sadist (one who gets pleasure out of hurting others) who acted as judge, prosecutor, inquisitor, avenger, and jury all rolled into one. Intent on shaming the defendants in every way possible, he had them appear in ill-

OPPOSITE PAGE

Adolf Hitler shakes hands with General Fromm at the Wolfsschanze on July 15, 1944. Just five days later, high ranking military officers tried to assassinate Hitler. To the left of Fromm is Graf Stauffenberg, one of the conspirators. German field marshall Wilhelm Keitel stands next to Hitler.

ASSASSINATIONS

Adolf Hitler examines bomb damage in 1944. Within months, Hitler came very close to being killed by a bomb planted in his headquarters— a plan devised by senior officers in the German military.

fitting clothes, without belts or suspenders, and without false teeth. (The August 7–8 trial of Field Marshall Erwin von Witzleben and the others was filmed for propaganda purposes, as was their execution. Hitler was said to have enjoyed viewing the film.)

To maintain the mask of legality, Freisler asked the defense lawyers, all of whom he had personally appointed, to speak. Witzleben's representative, Dr. Weissmann, answered his own question, "Why conduct a defense at all?" with the words, "It is part of the defense's task to help the court find a verdict. Undoubtedly . . . it will prove impossible for even the best counsel to find anything to say . . . in mitigation of the accused." The other defense attorneys all complained about their "thankless task." When allowed to speak near the end of the trial, most of the defendants asked for an honorable death by firing squad rather than by hanging. This request was denied, and later the same day they died from slow strangulation while suspended from meat hooks.

More Trials, Other Verdicts

This trial was the first of many. By the time it was all over, more than two hundred were dead as a result of the July 20 plot. Twenty-two of the dead were generals (thirteen of whom committed suicide) and fifty were members of the nobility. Nazi officials arrested thousands more, including the families of the accused and anyone else they might have reason to fear in the future. Many went to concentration camps. Near the end, many were executed without trial. Freisler himself died from injuries suffered in an air raid which interrupted yet another trial in the People's Court.

After the war, the German Federal Court of Justice reviewed the actions of the military conspirators. This court came to the conclusion that they indeed had had both the right and the duty to resist Hitler under the criminal laws of their day. Their actions were justified, the Federal Court concluded, by "the crimes of the [Nazi] regime, which went so far as . . . to annul the basis of justice; the tyranny imposed by the terroristic rulers on their own people; and the preparation for and waging of a criminal war of aggression. . . ." This opinion concluded, "It is clear that the right of resistance exercised in a state of emergency must be exercised uncompromisingly." Thus the traitors were officially recognized as patriotic and self-sacrificing martyrs.

Suggestions for Further Reading

Balfour, Michael. *Withstanding Hitler in Germany 1933–45.* London: Routledge, 1988.

OPPOSITION TO ADOLF HITLER

Throughout Adolf Hitler's leadership of Germany, there were many different types of opposition to both Hitler and the National Socialism he represented. Members of the Communist and Socialist parties hated Hitler on political grounds: they knew that he wanted to destroy the trade unions, end the rights of workers, deny equal rights for women, and persecute minorities. Jewish groups, of course, were alarmed by Hitler's pathological hatred of their ethnicity. Many religious groups resisted Hitler and National Socialism on both humanitarian grounds and because of Hitler's own actions against religion. Most surprising, perhaps, was the opposition to Hitler that came from the German aristocracy, who made up the higher ranks of the German military. This group was conservative, anti-Communist, often anti-Jewish, and to some extent sympathetic to many of Hitler's ideas. However, it nonetheless saw Hitler as a lower-class upstart (one who suddenly comes into wealth or power) whose policies would ruin Germany. In 1944, with the war going badly for Germany, the aristocracy was particularly unsympathetic.

Gill, Anton. *An Honorable Defeat: A History of German Resistance to Hitler, 1933–1945*. New York: Henry Holt and Co., 1994.

Manvell, Roger. *The Men Who Tried to Kill Hitler*. New York: Coward-McCann, Inc., 1964.

Assassins of Gandhi Trial: 1948

Defendants: Nathuram Godse, Narayan Apte, Vishnu Karkare, Madanlal Pahwa, Shankar Kistayya, Gopal Godse, Vinayak Savarkar, and Dattatraya Parchure

Crimes Charged: Conspiracy to murder Mahatma Gandhi; attempt to murder Gandhi (by Pahwa); murder of Gandhi (by N. Godse); aiding and abetting of these actions; unlawful possession of arms and ammunition (all except Savarkar and Parchure); abetting the carrying of arms and ammunition (Parchure); illegal possession of explosives (Pahwa)

Defense Lawyers: Chief Defense Counsel L. P. Bhoptkar, B. Banerji, K. L. Bhoptkar, N. D. Dange, P. L. Inamdar, P. R. Das, Hansraj Mehta, P. H. Mengale, V. V. Oke, and Ganpat Rai

Prosecutors: C. K. Daphtary, Raibahadur Jwalaprasad, J. C. Shah, and Sri Vyvaharkar

Judge: Atma Charan

Place: New Delhi, India

Dates: May 27–December 30, 1948

Verdicts: Seven found guilty; Savarkar acquitted

Sentences: N. Godse and Apte, death by hanging, along with three, five and seven years rigorous imprisonment, to run concurrently; Karkare, Kistayya, and G. Godse, transportation for life, along with three, five and seven years rigorous imprisonment, to run concurrently; Pahwa, transportation for life, with three, five, seven and ten years rigorous imprisonment, to run concurrently; Parchure, transportation for life. On appeal, Parchure and Kistayya acquitted

SIGNIFICANCE: Although the trial and appeals process apparently resulted in the correct verdicts, controversial questions of careless security and of a wider conspiracy remained unanswered.

ASSASSINATIONS

Mahatma Gandhi, who dedicated his life to non-violent action, was felled by the violence of an assassin's bullets only months after he had helped to bring about independence for India from British rule. Armed only with his moral authority and his unswerving conviction of what was right, Gandhi had tried for nearly five decades to transform India—a cauldron bubbling with religious, ethnic, caste (class), and communal discord—into a kinder, more humane society.

Independence on August 15, 1947, along with partition—which severed the Muslim nation of Pakistan from India—led to widespread riots, massacres, revenge killings, and rivers of desperate refugees streaming across the new borders. By the time it was over, some 12 million people had fled their homes and some 200,000 had died. To ease this chaotic transition, on January 13, 1948, Gandhi announced he would "fast unto the death" to force the Indian government to honor its obligation to pay to Pakistan 550 million rupees it had been withholding. At the time, Gandhi was staying at the New Delhi house of his patron and supporter, millionaire G. D. Birla. Three days later the government agreed to pay, but Gandhi vowed to continue his fast to force communal peace and a reconciliation of Hindus and Muslims. Satisfied with progress toward this goal, he ended his fast on January 18, 1948.

Meanwhile, the January 13 report of Gandhi's fast had moved the conspirators to action. According to Nathuram Godse, Gandhi's fate had

Mohandas Karamchand Gandhi, known also as the Mahatma, when he served as a barrister (lawyer) in South Africa in 1904.

been sealed as early as August 15, 1947, the day of independence as well as of partition—a geographic solution that Godse and other Hindu nationalists saw as a catastrophe. In a November 1, 1947, speech, Godse held Gandhi responsible:

> Gandhi said India would be divided over his dead body. India is divided, but Gandhi lives. Gandhi's nonviolence has left the Hindus defenseless before their enemies. Now, while Hindu refugees are starving, Gandhi defends their Muslim oppressors. Hindu women are throwing themselves into wells to save themselves from being raped, and Gandhi tells them 'Victory is in the victim.'

Godse was editor of the newspaper *Hindu Rashtra,* and his chief accomplice Narayan Apte was managing editor. Both were members of the Hindu Mahasabha ("Great Hindu Society"), a right-wing political party. They both revered Vinayak Savarkar, its former president, a one-time terrorist linked to several assassinations and founder of the Hindu Rashtra Dal, the party's militaristic arm whose members had sworn allegiance to him.

Active preparation for the assassination began in November 1947 as Godse and Apte sought arms and more participants. The original plan was the nineteenth-century Russian terrorist strategy of backing frontline units with reserves who would act if the first assassins failed: they planned an attack from all sides, using pistols and hand grenades. The plotters turned to Digambar Badge, a bookseller and dealer in contraband weapons, who along with his servant, Shankar Kistayya, assisted them by locating weapons and ammunition. Meanwhile they were joined by Vishnu Karkare, a restaurateur, former actor, and Hindu Mahasabha member and Madanlal Pahwa, Karkare's employee and a Hindu refugee who had seen his father and aunt massacred by Muslims. Godse's younger brother Gopal Godse, a storekeeper at an army depot, rounded out the group.

By January 10, 1948, Badge had found hand grenades and guncotton, but still lacked pistols. On January 14, the conspirators conferred in Bombay at the Hindu Mahasabha office, planning their trip to New Delhi. Following the meeting, Godse and Apte paid a short visit to Savarkar, their self-described "spiritual leader." By January 19, all had arrived in New Delhi. Badge had purchased a pistol and Gopal Godse brought his old service revolver. On the morning of January 20, four of them care-

ASSASSINATIONS

lessly took a taxi to Birla House and checked out the layout of the pavilion where Gandhi held his prayer meetings at the rear of the estate. That afternoon's assassination attempt, in which Badge was to do the shooting, turned out to be a fiasco. Pahwa's guncotton explosion—supposed to be a diversion—failed to panic the crowd. He was captured and four plotters fled in a taxi; the other two slipped away into the crowd.

In police hands, Pahwa soon betrayed the names of his co-conspirators. Newspaper reports of his arrest reached Bombay university professor Dr. Jagdish C. Jain, to whom he had described the plot on January 13. Jain, who initially did not believe the youth, now urgently informed officials of his knowledge. Unaccountably, the police and authorities did little to find the other plotters during the ten days before their second successful attempt on January 30.

Meanwhile the other schemers had returned to Bombay, and a disgusted Badge—together with his servant Kistayya—refused to have anything more to do with them. Undiscouraged, the Godse brothers, Apte, and Karkare planned a second try. Gopal Godse was to remain behind. Nathuram Godse, who now decided to do the deed alone, still needed a gun, as the first two they had obtained proved unreliable. On January 27, Nathuran Godse and Apte flew back to New Delhi and took a train 200 miles south to Gwalior to try to get a gun from Dattatraya Parchure, a wealthy medical practitioner and important Hindu Mahasabha figure. They bought a pistol from one of his acquaintances and promptly returned to New Delhi.

On the morning of January 30, rejoined by Karkare, they tested the pistol in some woods and in the afternoon traveled by horse cab to Birla House, where they mingled among the waiting devotees. When Gandhi arrived shortly after 5 P.M., Godse rushed up and fired off three fatal shots before being wrestled to the ground. It appeared to the world that another lone gunman had succeeded in killing a great leader; the Indian authorities would soon prove otherwise.

The Trial

The trial opened on May 27, 1948, in New Delhi's Mogul (Muslim) stronghold, the Red Fort. The court was empowered to exercise a unique right— that of giving a full pardon to an accused in a murder case. Badge, the bookseller who had dropped out from the second attempt, was granted a free pardon before the hearing of evidence started on June 22. He turned state's evidence and testified against the others.

With no jury, Judge Atma Charan presided alone. The trial dragged on for months as all questions and answers from the 149 witnesses had to be translated from English (still the common language of India) by Hindustani, Marathi, and Telugu interpreters. The press extensively reported the trial in newspapers worldwide. The sweltering courtroom was open to the public, a limited number of whom entered with one-day passes. Strict security included searching everyone at the entry gate.

Aided by Badge's damning testimony, the prosecution built up a strong case focusing on Nathuram Godse, Apte, and Savarkar. They viewed the other conspirators as playing only minor roles. Examining witnesses and recording evidence lasted until November 6, 1948, and revealed how carelessly and amateurishly the accused had carried out their plot. By January 17, it became clear that some fifty people had known of their plans.

The defendants had all entered not guilty pleas to the conspiracy charge, although Nathuram Godse confessed to the murder. The defense insisted there had been no conspiracy, claiming the attacks of January 20 and 30 were unrelated and committed by individuals acting alone. They called no witnesses, dismissing the prosecution's version that "a bad case needs no rebuttal." Apte and Karkare denied returning to New Delhi on January 30; Kistayya said that as a servant he had obeyed his master's orders; Gopal Godse denied all, even his presence in New Delhi on January 18–20; Parchure insisted Apte and Godse had approached him only for volunteers for a peaceful demonstration and that he had given no help with the pistol; and Pahwa claimed his explosion, carefully detonated far away from anyone, was an expression of resentment against the treatment of refugees.

The other two defendants were another matter. The sinister Savarkar, who had studied law in London, was well-versed in courtroom procedure and impressed the judge with his closely reasoned, legal analysis of the circumstantial evidence, read from a fifty-two-page manuscript. Despite Savarkar's denial of any complicity and his expressed admiration for Gandhi, he was seen by many as morally responsible, at least, for the assassination. He had encouraged young Hindu militants to oppose Gandhi and the Congress Party by all means possible.

Nathuram Godse took the opposite approach. He tried to assume total responsibility for Gandhi's murder by denying the existence of a conspiracy. He, too, was allowed to enter a lengthy statement into the record on November 8. Reading from a ninety-six-page manuscript in English, he explained his reasons:

> I declare here before man and God that in putting
> an end to Gandhi's life I have removed one who was

a curse to India, a force for evil, and who . . . brought nothing but misery and unhappiness, not merely to the Hindus . . . but to the Muslims.

Citing Hindu mythology, Godse predicted:

I warn my country against the pest of Gandhism. It will mean not only Muslim rule over the entire country but the extinction of Hinduism itself. There are pessimists who say that the great Hindu nation, after tens of thousands of years, is doomed to extinction.

Pronouncing sentence, the judge added that had "the slightest keen-ness been shown by [the police] in the investigation of the case at that stage [following the bomb outrage on January 20], the tragedy probably could have been averted."

The Aftermath

Before the appeals court, the defense again tried to break down the links between the plotters. Although they acquitted Parchure and Kistayya, the judges found ample evidence to uphold the verdicts and sentences against the others. Nathuram Godse and Apte were hanged on November 15, 1949. But the saga did not end there. After serving some fifteen years, Gopal Godse, Karkare, and Pahwa were released on October 12, 1964. A November 12 reception celebrated their freedom and glorified Nathuram Godse as a patriot; at this event an Indian newspaper editor spoke of his prior knowledge of the plot. Newspapers widely reported this affair, which led to heated parliamentary debates. The result was the creation on March 25, 1965, of a special Commission of Inquiry to re-investigate the assassination.

By January 24, 1969, the commission had questioned 101 witnesses and examined 407 documents. Its conclusions were clear: many people knew of the plot in advance, the police were negligent in pursuing the conspirators after January 20, security for Gandhi was woefully inade-quate, and various officials failed to respond to the developing situation with the necessary enthusiasm.

INDIA'S MAHATMA

Mohandas Karamchand Gandhi (1869–1948) was popularly known as the Mahatma, which means "great souled" in Hindi. He began his career as a lawyer in South Africa in 1893, where he fought for the rights of the Indian population. While in South Africa, Gandhi read widely and his personal philosophy underwent notable changes. In 1905 he abandoned Western ways, living in self-denial and shunning material possessions—evident in his dress of a loincloth and shawl. He returned to India in 1915, when he began to work to free India from its colonial relationship with Great Britain. He developed a tactic known as passive resistance, or *satyagraha,* in which Indians refused to cooperate with British rule but did not actively engage in violence against it. Although the British put him in jail many times, he was so enormously popular that he was usually able to obtain his release merely by threatening to fast until he died. In 1942, he was put in jail for failing to defend the British war effort of World War II, but he was released in 1944 and was able to help win Indian independence in 1947. His theories of nonviolent resistance greatly influenced U.S. civil rights leader Martin Luther King Jr. and other protest movements throughout the world.

Gandhi's assassination had another ironic twist. His influence had been fading until Godse's bullets provided him with a glorious martyr's death—what the *Hindustani Times* called "the second crucifixion"—ensuring his reputation as one of the great leaders of history.

Suggestions for Further Reading

Gandhi, Mahatma. *All Men Are Brothers: Autobiographical Reflections/Mahatma Gandhi.* New York: Continuum, 1994.

Malgonkar, Mahonar. *The Men Who Killed Gandhi.* New Delhi: Macmillan, 1981.

ASSASSINATIONS

Payne, Robert. *The Life and Death of Mahatma Gandhi.* New York: E. P. Dutton & Co., 1969.

Severance, John B. *Gandhi, Great Soul.* New York: Clarion Books, 1997.

Sherrow, Victoria. *Mohandas Gandhi: The Power of the Spirit.* Brookfield, CT: Millbrook Press, 1994.

Sirhan Bishara Sirhan Trial: 1969

Defendant: Sirhan Bishara Sirhan

Crime Charged: Murder

Chief Defense Lawyers: Grant Cooper, Russell Parsons, Emile Berman, and Michael A. McCowan

Chief Prosecutors: Lynn D. Compton, John Howard, and David Fitts

Judge: Herbert V. Walker

Place: Los Angeles, California

Dates of Trial: January 13–April 23, 1969

Verdict: Guilty

Sentence: Death, later reduced to life imprisonment

SIGNIFICANCE: The prominence of Robert Kennedy caused the trial of his killer to be of historic importance. Although the attorneys for the defense and the prosecution reached a plea bargain before the trial began, a judge decided that full disclosure of the facts was more important than simply disposing of the case.

Flushed with triumph, U.S. Senator Robert Kennedy stepped off the podium at the Ambassador Hotel in Los Angeles on June 5, 1968. He had just declared victory in the California primary election for the Democratic nomination for president. As he moved through the hotel's kitchen, on his way to meet reporters in another room, a young man emerged from the crowd and fired a gun. Three bullets struck Kennedy,

ASSASSINATIONS

one in the head. The killer continued shooting, injuring five bystanders, until people grabbed him and police took him into custody.

His name was Sirhan Bishara Sirhan, a twenty-four-year-old from Jordan who objected to Kennedy's support for Israel. The next day the senator died from his wounds.

Initial Negotiations

There was no question that Sirhan had murdered Kennedy. A roomful of witnesses saw him do it. However, many did not believe he would ever stand trial. District Attorney Evelle Younger had the results of an examination showing that Sirhan

Senator Robert F. Kennedy was shot by Sirhan Sirhan on June 5, 1968. Kennedy died from his wounds the following day.

was mentally ill. So when Sirhan admitted he was guilty of first-degree murder, she agreed to a sentence of life in prison. It was the kind of deal worked out every day in the county court system, plea bargains which go through in order to prevent a backlog of cases. But this was not an everyday case.

The memory of President John F. Kennedy's 1963 assassination was on everyone's mind. His killer, Lee Harvey Oswald, had himself been gunned down before he could stand trial. Oswald's murder left doubts about who killed the president and why. Determined to prevent this from happening again, the judge appointed to hear the Sirhan case, Herbert Walker, threw out the plea bargain. He wanted to see Sirhan tried before a jury. This ruling left the defense team one choice: to plead Sirhan not guilty and hope they could prove that he was too mentally unstable to have consciously chosen to kill Senator Kennedy.

S i r h a n
B i s h a r a
S i r h a n
T r i a l : 1 9 6 9

A Murder Plan

The prosecution's opening statement, delivered by David Fitts on February 12, 1969, contained many examples of Sirhan's devious and deliber-

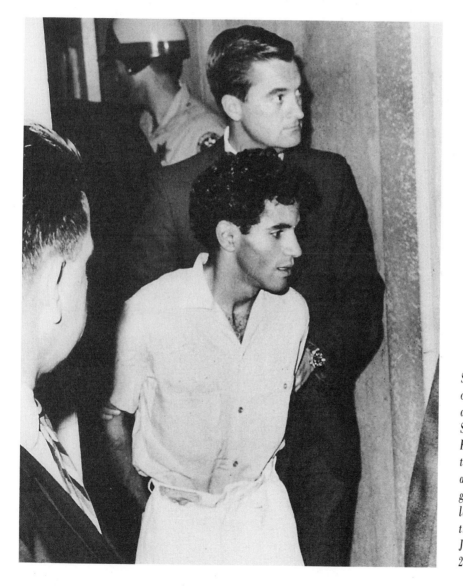

Sirhan Sirhan in custody the day after he shot Senator Robert F. Kennedy. Even though Sirhan admitted he was guilty, the trial lasted for more than three months, from January 13–April 23, 1969.

ate preparations for murder. Just two nights before the attack, someone had spotted Sirhan at the Ambassador Hotel, apparently trying to learn the layout of the hotel. He had also visited a firing range on June 4 to work on his already well-developed skill with a gun. However, the testimony of one prosecution witness, the author George Plimpton, backfired. Plimpton described Sirhan as looking ". . . enormously composed. He seemed—purged," a statement that supported the defense's position that Sirhan had shot Kennedy while in some kind of trance. More to the prosecutor's liking was the testimony of Alvin Clark, Sirhan's garbage collector, who claimed that Sirhan had told him a month before the attack of his plan to shoot Kennedy.

Mental Instability?

Defense hopes of proving that this killing was the unprepared act of a deranged man received a serious setback when Judge Walker admitted into evidence pages from Sirhan's notebooks. They revealed a mind seriously troubled, but still quite cunning and willful. One entry, written on May 18, 1968, read: "My determination to eliminate R. F. K. is becoming the more and more [sic] of an unshakable obsession. . . . Robert F. Kennedy must be assassinated before June 5, 1968."

Sirhan's behavior during the trial was strange. In the midst of some testimony about his childhood, he raged: "I . . . withdraw my original plea of not guilty and submit the plea of guilty as charged on all counts. I also request that my counsel disassociate themselves from this case completely." He then went on to say that he wanted to be executed.

Judge Walker refused to accept this new plea, and he refused to accept the resignations of Sirhan's lawyers when they volunteered to withdraw from the case. The trial continued.

Defense lawyer Grant Cooper did not mince words.

"Did you shoot Robert F. Kennedy?" he asked.

"Yes, sir."

"Did you bear any ill will towards Senator Kennedy?"

"No."

"Do you doubt you shot him?"

"No, sir, I don't."

THE SECOND KENNEDY BROTHER

Robert Francis Kennedy was born in 1925 in Brookline, Mass-achusetts, into the famous Kennedy family. Known popularly as "Bobby" Kennedy, Robert served from 1961 to 1964 as attorney general while his brother, John F. Kennedy, was president. Robert Kennedy's most famous accomplishment at this time was the prosecution of many Mafia figures. Until then the underworld fig-ures had easily evaded government monitoring. Robert Kennedy resigned from office after his brother was assassinated and went on to become a senator from New York. By the time he sought the presidential nomination in 1968, Kennedy was well-respected for his work in the civil rights movement and for aiding the Cal-ifornia migrant workers in their fight to win better pay and treat-ment through the United Farm Workers. He was also a strong op-ponent of the Vietnam War. His victory in the California primary was an upset for fellow candidate Vice President Hubert H. Humphrey, who until then had seemed a sure winner.

When asked about the reasons for his attack on Kennedy, Sirhan launched into an angry speech about the Middle East conflict between Arabs and Jews.

Cynical Performance

It took cross-examination from Chief Deputy District Attorney Lyn Comp-ton to expose Sirhan for what he was: self-absorbed and arrogant, a mas-terful manipulator.

"Do you think that the killing of Senator Kennedy helped the Arab cause?" asked Compton.

"Sir, I'm not even aware that I killed Mr. Kennedy."

"Well, you know he's dead."

". . . I've been told that."

"Are you glad he's dead?"

"No, sir, I'm not glad."

The jurors apparently saw Sirhan's answers as a cynical performance, and on April 17, 1969, they returned a guilty verdict.

During the sentencing hearing, Prosecutor John Howard demanded that Sirhan be given the death penalty. After twelve hours of deliberation, the jury decided that Sirhan would die in the gas chamber. However, because of U.S. Supreme Court decisions about other death penalty cases, Sirhan's sentence was reduced to life in prison. He remains in jail, where he regularly applies for parole. The parole board just as regularly turns him down.

Suggestions for Further Reading

Christian, John and William Turner. *The Assassination Of Robert Kennedy.* New York: Random House, 1978.

Goode, Stephen. *Assassination! Kennedy, King, Kennedy.* New York: Watts, 1979.

Kaiser, Robert Blair. *R. F. K. Must Die!* New York: Dutton & Co., 1970.

Scheim, David E. *Contract On America.* Silver Spring, MD: Argyle Press, 1983.

Indira Gandhi's Assassins Trial: 1985–1986

Defendants: Satwant Singh, Kehar Singh, and Balbir Singh

Crimes Charged: Murder (Satwant Singh), conspiracy (Kehar Singh and Balbir Singh)

Chief Defense Lawyers: Pran Nath Lekhi and P. P. Grover

Chief Prosecutor: K. L. Arora

Judge: Mahesh Chandra

Place: New Delhi, India

Dates of Trial: May 13, 1985–January 22, 1986

Verdicts: Guilty; Balbir Singh's conviction overturned by Indian Supreme Court on August 3, 1988

Sentences: Death by hanging

SIGNIFICANCE: The killing of Prime Minister Indira Gandhi and the trial of her assassins were among the most dramatic episodes in the struggle between Sikh separatists and the Indian government.

During the early 1980s, Sikh religious fundamentalists—people who strictly follow their faith and identify themselves as a separate ethnic group—began to demand autonomous control of the northern Indian state of the Punjab. Prime Minister Indira Gandhi—daughter of first Indian prime minister, Jawaharlal Nehru—viewed Sikh separatists with concern. In her eyes, allowing a religious group to separate from India would begin the unraveling of the entire nation.

By late 1983, politically motivated murders by Sikhs were so common that Mrs. Gandhi declared a state of emergency in the Punjab. As government troops poured into the region, radical Sikhs withdrew into the sanctuary of religious shrines. Sant Jarnail Singh Bhindranwhale, leader of the most violent group of Sikhs, took shelter in the city of Amritsar within the massive Golden Temple, the holiest of Sikh shrines.

For months the Indian government did not attack the temple. Meanwhile Bhindranwhale ordered more murders and built up his arsenal of weapons. Pressure from the public for government action grew.

Operation Blue Star

Indira Gandhi (second from left) as a young woman. Mrs. Gandhi was assassinated by her personal bodyguards on October 31, 1984.

On June 5, 1984, Prime Minister Gandhi ordered the Indian Army to storm the Golden Temple in a raid called "Operation Blue Star." The battle lasted for more than a day. Hundreds died, including Bhindranwhale. Many were innocent Sikh religious pilgrims who were caught in the gunfire as they worshiped in the shrine.

"What has happened is a tragedy for India," Indira Gandhi said. "It should not be celebrated as a victory."

The Indian government helped to rebuild the Golden Temple, but all of the damage caused by Operation Blue Star could not be repaired. Both militant and moderate Sikhs were outraged by the large number of deaths, as well as the desecration and occupation of the holy site. Indira Gandhi's staff cautioned her to remove Sikhs from her personal staff for security reasons. She refused, explaining that if she did so she would be unfaithful to her own government's vision of a united India.

Bodyguards Murder Prime Minister

On the morning of October 31, 1984, Indira Gandhi prepared for an interview by actor Peter Ustinov for a television program. The filming would take place on the grounds of her private residence, so Indira Gandhi felt safe in leaving her house without the bulletproof vest she usually wore beneath her *sari* (traditional Indian dress) at public appearances.

As she walked across her garden for the appointment, she encountered Beant Singh, a young Sikh policeman who had served as one of her personal guards for six years. Singh raised his revolver and shot the prime minister three times. A second guard, Satwant Singh, suddenly stepped forward and emptied his automatic rifle into her as well. Both guards dropped their weapons and raised their hands.

"We have done what we set out to do," said Beant Singh. "Now you can do whatever you want to do."

While the wounded prime minister was on her way to a hospital, her two attackers were taken to a guardhouse. Minutes later, both were shot. Satwant Singh was seriously wounded. Beant Singh died immediately. Five hours later, Indira Gandhi too was dead. Word spread quickly that Sikhs had killed her in revenge for the assault on the Golden Temple.

Mrs. Gandhi's son, Rajiv, immediately took his oath as prime minister. The government was secure, but the worst riots erupted since those that followed India's separation from Pakistan in 1947. Mobs of Hindus attacked and killed thousands of innocent Sikhs.

Conspiracy Theories Multiply

Wild rumors circulated that an army general or perhaps the U.S. Central Intelligence Agency (CIA) might be responsible for the assassination. Even the guards who had shot Indira Gandhi's killers were arrested, as some feared more individuals than the two attackers had been involved

in the plot. But the guards went free after convincing investigators that the killers had grabbed for weapons while trying to escape.

Investigators eventually concluded that the assassination was an act of revenge. They charged Satwant Singh with murder and charged both Balbir Singh—a former subinspector in the prime minister's security forces—and Kehar Singh—a government clerk and the uncle of the dead Beant Singh—with criminal conspiracy. None of the three defendants were related, even though they did share the name traditionally taken by Sikh men, *Singh,* which means lion.

The Trial Begins

The trial began on May 13, 1985, under extraordinary security. Safety concerns were so great that the trial took place in New Delhi's Tihar Central Jail, not in a court building. Judge Mahesh sat behind a bulletproof screen. The defendants sat inside a similar enclosure. Newspaper reporters sat in the hot, crowded room, but photographers, television cameras, and the public had to stay outside.

Persistent rumors of conspiracy allowed Pran Nath Lekhi, Satwant Singh's lawyer, to defend his client aggressively. Lekhi was a political enemy of Indira Gandhi and had been imprisoned during her controversial suspension of civil rights in the 1970s. Now, he angrily accused police of torturing Satwant Singh into making a false confession. Lekhi suggested that another assassin might have shot Indira Gandhi and then escaped. He noted that tests had been conducted on only two of the numerous bullets in Mrs. Gandhi's body and that no full autopsy had been performed. These failures left open the possibility that she might have been shot by unknown assailants or poisoned in the hospital. Lekhi wondered why hospital records showed her receiving a blood transfusion thirty-seven minutes after she had been officially declared dead.

Lekhi's personal hostility toward the Gandhi family erupted throughout the trial. Despite warnings to watch his language, Lekhi called Rajiv Gandhi and his wife possible suspects in the assassination. He attempted to call Rajiv Gandhi and Indian President Zail Singh as witnesses, but Judge Chandra rejected these requests.

Attorney P. P. Grover's defense of Balbir Singh and Kehar Singh was less dramatic, but no less critical of the investigators. Grover charged that incriminating documents found in his clients' homes were forgeries.

On January 22, 1986, Judge Chandra found the defendants guilty and sentenced them to death. Asked if they had anything to say, the three men maintained that they were innocent. Attorney Lekhi was more outspoken. He shouted that the trial was a farce and accused the judge of trying to advance his own career.

Appeals and Investigation Drag On

Under Indian law, the condemned men could appeal their convictions. A week after the verdict, the Delhi High Court found several technical errors in Judge Chandra's sentence, including his refusal to allow defense lawyers to argue against the verdict and his failure to specify that the condemned were to be "hanged by the neck until dead." Nevertheless, after four months of hearings, the three-judge panel reviewing the appeal declined to reverse or modify the sentence.

Next the trial came for review by the Indian Supreme Court, which overturned Balbir Singh's conviction on August 3, 1988, and set him free. The court upheld the remaining death sentences.

Satwant Singh requested a stay of execution until a suit against the guards who had shot him could be settled. Kehar Singh appealed directly to Indian President Ramaswamy Venkataraman for a pardon. The President denied his petition immediately. The swiftness of this denial earned Kehar Singh a stay of execution, when the Constitutional Bench of the Supreme Court decided that President Venkataraman's hasty decision did not provide a fair hearing. On January 5, 1989, however, five judges of the Supreme Court upheld the death sentence.

"I wish that I am born again and again and each time lay down my life," said Satwant Singh before the noose was slipped around his neck.

No End to Violence

In the years between Mrs. Gandhi's death and the execution of her accused killers, the findings of M. P. Thakkar, the Supreme Court judge who investigated the assassination and reviewed security procedures, remained secret. In March 1989, two months after Satwant Singh and Kehar Singh were hanged, the *Indian Express* newspaper published passages from Justice Thakkar's report. They revealed that Rajendra Kumar Dhawan, a prominent aide to Mrs. Gandhi, had been investigated for his role in rearranging her security on the day of her death. Pressured by political enemies who hoped to use the report against him, Prime Minister Rajiv Gandhi released the full report. The prime minister said that the report

THE SIKHS

The Sikhs are a religious community in northern India, concentrated mainly in the region known as the Punjab. Some six million Indians consider themselves to be Sikhs. The mystic and teacher Nanak (1469–1539) founded the movement. Nanak taught that all religions were fundamentally the same. He opposed the Indian "caste system," a custom by which people born into a certain social class and status remain there for life. The Sikhs gradually obtained military power, mobilizing under Govind Singh (1666–1708) to oppose Islam, the religion of the many Muslims who live in what is now Pakistan. The British conquered the Sikh state in the late nineteenth century. In 1947, after India achieved independence and was divided into (Hindu) India and (Muslim) Pakistan, the Sikhs fought the Muslims of the Punjab. When this religious war was ended, approximately 2.5 million Sikhs moved from West Punjab to East Punjab. West Punjab later became part of Pakistan, while East Punjab remained part of India.

had remained secret at the request of Justice Thakkar, who had wished to avoid influencing the trial of the men in custody.

Justice Thakkar's report was critical of security officials and looked on Dhawan's management of Mrs. Gandhi's schedule with extreme suspicion. By the time the report was publicly released on March 27, 1989, police had cleared Dhawan, and he was serving as an adviser to Rajiv Gandhi.

Within days, those who assumed that the assassination case was over got another shock when four Sikhs were arrested as part of the plot. Little came of these charges. One of the accused, Simranjit Singh Mann, had already been held without trial for four years for his alleged involvement. Mann was released in late 1989 after winning a seat in the Indian Parliament while he was still in prison.

Although thousands of Indians continued to die as a result of violence between religious and ethnic groups, these clashes were seldom as dramatic as Indira Gandhi's murder—with one exception. On May 21,

1991, Rajiv Gandhi and sixteen others died when a Tamil woman approached him at a campaign rally and set off a bomb hidden in her belt.

Suggestions for Further Reading

Ali, Tariq. *An Indian Dynasty: The Story of the Nehru-Gandhi Family.* New York: G. P. Putnam's Sons, 1985.

Gupte, Pranay. *Mother India: A Political Biography of Indira Gandhi.* New York: Charles Scribner's Sons, 1992.

Gupte, Pranay. *Vengeance: India After the Assassination of Indira Gandhi.* New York: W. W. Norton & Co., 1985.

Hazarika, Sanjoy. "New Delhi Trial Starts For 3 In Gandhi Assassination Case." *The New York Times* (May 18, 1985): 5.

Hazarika, Sanjoy. "Protests Follow Hanging of 2 Sikhs." *The New York Times* (January 7, 1989): 3.

Nyrop, Richard F., ed. *India: A Country Study.* Washington, D.C.: U.S. Government Printing Office, 1989.

Indira Gandhi's Assassins Trial: 1985–1986

ESPIONAGE

Edith Cavell Trial: 1915

Defendant: Edith Cavell
Crime Charged: Aiding enemy forces
Chief Defense Lawyer: Maitre Sadi Kirschen
Chief Prosecutor: Dr. Eduard Stoeber
Judges: Five-member German military tribunal (names not recorded)
Place: Brussels, Belgium
Dates of Trial: October 7–8, 1915
Verdict: Guilty
Sentence: Death

SIGNIFICANCE: Few incidents have so excited a nation as the execution of Nurse Edith Cavell during World War I; but was the wave of moral disapproval that swept across Britain really justified?

On August 4, 1914, German army divisions invaded Belgium in the first major military attack of World War I. British soldiers were cut off behind enemy lines. Their only hope of making it back home rested with the Belgian resistance fighters (members of an organization that secretly worked against the occupying enemy) who had recently organized to combat the Germans. But the resistance worker who is best remembered was not a Belgian, but a forty-eight-year-old Englishwoman named Edith Cavell. She spent much of her adult life in Belgium, where she worked first as a governess, then as a nurse at the Berkendael Institute, a clinic in Brussels. During the war the institute became a Red Cross outpost that also provided a means of escape for English soldiers. Over 200 of them, all seeking a way back across the channel to England, passed through the clinic doors. Cavell first took care of their wounds, then arranged with the Belgian resistance for safe passage to the coast, in opposition to the German occupying forces.

Little Regard for Security

In this building on the rue de la Culture, Edith Cavell helped allied soldiers escape to the Dutch frontier. The men entered the premises by the door closest to her office, at the far left in this picture.

Cavell organized these escapes with little regard for her own security—or that of the soldiers. She even kept a photograph album of many of them. In March 1915, she wrote her sister, "Do you think you could find out news of the soldiers on the enclosed list? They are relations of some of the girls here." In truth, the list contained names of dozens of men she had helped to escape.

Chances were good that Cavell's escape plans would be discovered at some point. One day police visited the clinic. British soldiers, still wearing boots and uniforms, hurriedly jumped into the hospital beds and pretended to be patients. The searchers left empty-handed, but they were suspicious.

Spies in the Institute

Soon mysterious men began arriving at the clinic and requesting assistance in escaping. Workers at the institute begged Cavell to be careful. Then, on June 30, 1915, a Frenchman named George Gaston Quien arrived, insisting that he be allowed to work for the resistance. By this time, even Cavell was aware of the potential for danger, and she turned Quien away. She was sure the clinic was being watched twenty-four hours a day by the enemy.

All through July, German spies put together a list of the most important resistance members. High on that list was Phillipe Baucq, an architect who published a secret newspaper. On July 31, Baucq was arrested at his house, along with an acquaintance of Cavell, Louise Thuliez. Just days before, Quien had been seen lingering outside the house. Within days, most of the resistance members were behind bars.

Edith Louisa Cavell in her early twenties, circa 1890.

Solitary Confinement

Cavell herself was arrested on August 5 and taken to Saint Gilles Prison. She spent nine weeks in solitary confinement there. She was a deeply religious woman who disapproved of lying, and she honestly admitted that she had worked secretly for the resistance movement. Although interviews with her were conducted in French, the statements she signed admitting her guilt were written in German, a language she did not understand. The

Germans falsely accused Cavell of betraying the other resistance fighters, hoping this would lessen the anger over her arrest.

Despite protests from the Belgian nurses, the German military commanders were firm in their decision to put Cavell on trial for helping the enemy. During the period before her trial, the chief prosecutor, Dr. Eduard Stoeber, refused to allow defense lawyers to see or talk to the defendants. The lawyers were not even told which charges would be brought against their clients.

On October 7, 1915, Cavell was one of thirty-five defendants to go before the tribunal of the Imperial German Council of War. Some were guides who had organized escape routes. Others had used their skills as chemists to develop passport photographs for the resistance and the escaping soldiers. A few had managed safe houses (places used to hide escaping soldiers) along the underground escape routes.

After the charges were read, guards removed the other prisoners from the court. The prosecutor questioned Cavell alone. Her cross-examination could not have been shorter:

Stoeber: "From November 14 to July 15 you lodged French and English soldiers including a colonel, all in civilian clothes. You . . . helped Belgian, French and English of military age, furnishing them the means of going to the front, notably in receiving them at your nursing home and giving them money."

Cavell: "Yes."

Stoeber: "With whom were you concerned . . . in committing these acts?"

Cavell: "With Monsieur Capiau, Mademoiselle Martin . . . [and others]."

Stoeber: "Who was the head, the originator of the organization?"

Cavell: "There wasn't a head."

Stoeber: "Wasn't it the Prince de Croy?"

Cavell: "No, the Prince de Croy confined himself to sending men to whom he had given a little money."

Stoeber: "Why have you committed these acts?"

Cavell: "I was sent to begin with, two Englishmen who were in danger of death, one was wounded."

Stoeber: "Do you realize that in thus recruiting men it would be to the disadvantage of Germany and to the advantage of the enemy?"

Cavell: "My preoccupation has not been to aid the enemy but to help the men who applied to me to reach the front. Once across the frontier they were free."

Stoeber: "How many people have you sent to the frontier?"

Cavell: "About two hundred."

Four more questions were asked and then it was over. Cross-examination of the other prisoners followed. All of them were quiet, but defiant. That afternoon, the prosecution called its only important witness. Fourteen-year-old Philippe Bodart was the son of one of the accused and had been threatened with ten years' hard labor unless he told the truth. The evidence he gave was especially harmful to Baucq.

Sentences Delivered

The next day, Stoeber gave a speech that lasted several hours. He demanded that nine of the prisoners be sentenced to death. When he was finished, the defendants were led away. They would learn of their punishments later. After a brief conference, the five men sitting in judgment recorded guilty verdicts. Then the sentences were read. Five prisoners, including Cavell, would die. The others would serve long periods at hard labor.

The weekend passed. On Monday, Cavell received the news. A fellow prisoner urged her to appeal for mercy.

"It is useless," she replied. "I am English and they want my life."

Sensitive to public opinion, the military court tried to keep the sentences secret. But soon people in Brussels knew about them, and representatives of various nations not involved in the war petitioned the German political minister, Baron Oskar von der Lancken, on Cavell's behalf. Cleverer than most of his fellow politicians, von der Lancken realized that Germany's reputation abroad would suffer, and he promised to do his best for Cavell.

But the matter was out of his hands. Cavell and Baucq would die at dawn the next day. The Belgian prison chaplain told Cavell that afternoon, yet she remained perfectly calm. She was asked if she would like the Reverend H. Sterling Gahan, the British chaplain in Brussels, to go with her to her execution. Cavell replied, "Oh, no. Mr. Gahan isn't used to things like that." She did agree to see him that evening.

The next morning at seven o'clock, Cavell and Baucq faced the firing squad together. It has been said that Cavell's last words were: "I re-

THE RED CROSS

Edith Cavell's clinic had Red Cross status. This meant that it was connected with the Red Cross organization. The Red Cross is an international association formed in 1863 to prevent suffering and promote public health. The Geneva Convention—an international treaty establishing the humane treatment of prisoners and civilians during wartime—adopted the image of the red cross in 1864. According to the Geneva Convention, the red cross was an international symbol of neutral aid. This meant that if Cavell's clinic had Red Cross status, it was supposed to be able to aid even enemy soldiers without interference. Aiding patients was supposed to be limited to caring for their wounds. The Geneva Convention might have protected Cavell for treating soldiers, but not for helping them to escape.

alize that patriotism [love for one's country] is not enough; I must have no hatred or bitterness towards anyone."

News of Nurse Cavell's execution aroused anger everywhere. The United States—still outraged by the sinking of the civilian liner *Lusitania* by a German submarine—reacted especially strongly. Germany responded by reducing the remaining death sentences to prison time. For the British government, Edith Cavell proved a valuable source of wartime propaganda. Overnight, the number of men joining the army almost doubled. In the words of Prime Minister Herbert Asquith: "She has taught the bravest man among us the supreme lesson of courage." After the war, Cavell's body was carried back to England on May 14, 1919, and reburied at Norwich, in her home county.

Suggestions for Further Reading

Richardson, N. *Edith Cavell.* London: Hamish Hamilton, 1985.

Ryder, Rowland. *Edith Cavell.* New York: Stein and Day, 1975.

Alger Hiss Trials:
1949–1950

Defendant: Alger Hiss

Crime Charged: Perjury

Chief Defense Lawyers: Robert M. Benjamin, Claude B. Cross, Chester T. Lane, Edward C. McLean, Robert von Mehren, Victor Rabinowitz, Harold Rosenwald, Harol Shapero, and Lloyd Paul Stryker

Chief Prosecutors: Thomas J. Donegan, Myles J. Lane, Thomas F. Murphy, and Clarke S. Ryan

Judges: First trial: Samuel J. Kaufman; second trial: Henry W. Goddard

Place: New York, New York

Dates of Trials: First trial: May 31–July 8, 1949; second trial: November 17, 1949–January 21, 1950

Verdicts: First trial: jury deadlocked; second trial: guilty

SIGNIFICANCE: For three years, Alger Hiss was the central figure in a great human drama that made headlines across America. The case divided the country between 1948 and 1950, becoming a symbol of American policies at the beginning of the cold war (the term used to define the struggle for power and prestige between the Western powers and the Communist bloc from 1945—the end of World War II—to 1989). Future president Richard M. Nixon's involvement in the case made him more prominent. The public debate about Hiss's guilt remains endless. Either he was a traitor or he was the victim of a framing for political advantage at the highest levels of justice.

On August 3, 1948, reporters approached Alger Hiss with shocking news. They said that Whittaker Chambers, a senior editor at *Time* magazine, had accused him of being a Communist. At this time Hiss was president of the Carnegie Endowment for International Peace.

Chambers had just appeared before the Committee for the Investigation of Un-American Activities of the House of Representatives (HUAC). There he described his fifteen years as a Soviet spy. In 1939, Chambers said, two years after he had stopped believing in Communism, he had told Assistant Secretary of State Adolph A. Berle Jr. that there were Communists in the U.S. government. One was Hiss, who had been a State Depart-

Alger Hiss arrives in the United States with the United Nations charter for delivery to President Truman.

ment official and who later organized several high-level diplomatic meetings that led to the creation of the United Nations. Hiss responded to the news by telegraphing HUAC, asking to appear before the committee and testify under oath that he did not know Chambers.

Hiss Denies Communist Link

In Washington, Hiss told the committee that the accusation was a total lie. His government service would speak for itself. However, said Karl Mundt, acting chairman of the committee, Chambers had testified that when he was trying to break with the Communists, he tried to persuade

Hiss to do the same. Hiss, said Chambers, had "absolutely refused to break." Hiss denied any such incident, repeatedly saying that the name Chambers meant nothing to him. Hiss said he would like to see the man, in fact. So an executive session of a subcommittee led by then U.S. representative Richard M. Nixon of California called Chambers to appear before them. Chambers described intimate details of the Hiss households in Baltimore, Maryland, and Washington, D.C., from ten years earlier.

Nixon then called Hiss back. Nixon showed him pictures of Chambers. Hiss said they showed a man who looked like someone he knew as George Crosley, a writer who had interviewed him when he served as legal counsel to a Senate committee. In June 1935, said Hiss, he and his wife Priscilla bought a house and rented their apartment to Crosley and his family. However, he would not say that Crosley and Chambers were the same person.

In New York the next day, Congressman Nixon and John McDowell, functioning together as a subcommittee, brought Chambers and Hiss together. Hiss noted that Chambers's teeth were in better condition than Crosley's had been and that he looked "very different in girth and in other appearances—hair, forehead, particularly the jowls [side of the face]." Hiss nevertheless identified Chambers as George Crosley.

Chambers denied ever having used the name Crosley. He said that Hiss was the man "who was a member of the Communist Party" at whose house he and his wife and child had stayed. Angrily, Hiss invited Chambers "to make those same statements out of the presence of this Committee" so that the charges would not be protected by legal privilege. Hiss implied that he would then sue Chambers for libel (a method of defamation expressed by false and malicious publication in print for the purpose of damaging the reputation of another). Soon after that incident, Chambers did so, leveling the same charges at Hiss on the "Meet the Press" radio program. Hiss then filed a $75,000 libel suit.

At a hearing before the actual trial opened, Hiss's attorney, William Marbury, asked Chambers if he could produce proof of his claims. Chambers went to his nephew's home in Brooklyn, New York. There, from a hiding place, he retrieved a large, stained envelope. In the envelope were forty-three typed copies of State Department reports, five rolls of microfilm, and four memos in Hiss's handwriting. Chambers handed the documents—but not the films—over to Marbury. He claimed that Hiss had given them to him in 1937. Hiss, said Chambers, regularly took such secret documents home for his wife to copy, using a typewriter. Hiss would then return the original documents to the State Department files the next day, while Chambers turned the copies over to a Soviet agent.

A "Bombshell," a Seaplane, a Pumpkin

Hiss told his lawyer to give the papers to the Department of Justice. The next day, Representative Nixon, who had just left on a vacation cruise to Panama, received a cable saying that a "bombshell" had exploded. He ordered a HUAC investigator to visit Chambers at his Maryland farm. Meanwhile, a Coast Guard seaplane picked up Nixon.

By the time Nixon got back to Washington, Chambers had led investigator Robert E. Stripling to his farm field. There Chambers opened a hollowed-out pumpkin and pulled out the five rolls of microfilm that had earlier been hidden in Brooklyn. Three rolls, still in their aluminum containers, were undeveloped; two, which had been developed, were in protective bags. Even though there were no paper documents in the pumpkin, the microfilms, which contained pictures of documents, became known as "the Pumpkin Papers."

By a one-vote majority, a New York federal grand jury accused Alger Hiss of two counts of perjury (lying under oath). One count was for denying that he had turned State Department documents over to Chambers. The second was for saying that he had not seen Chambers since January 1, 1937 (the jury found that he had delivered the reports to Chambers in February and March 1938).

When the trial opened on May 31, 1949, prosecutor Thomas F. Murphy told the jury, "If you don't believe Mr. Chambers's story, we have no case under the federal perjury rule." Chambers then repeated the same testimony he had given before HUAC and the grand jury. During cross-examination, Hiss's defense counsel, Lloyd Paul Stryker, quickly undercut Chambers's credibility. Chambers admitted to a number of questionable activities. He committed perjury in 1937 and 1948. He used at least seven aliases (fake names). He lied to a dean of Columbia University while he was a student. He stole books from several libraries and lived with several women (one of whom was a prostitute). Eventually Columbia expelled him for his suggestive writings.

A Typewriter Proves Elusive

For three weeks, the prosecution presented evidence. State Department witnesses identified the typewritten papers Chambers had turned over as cables from American diplomats stationed around the world. They also said that the four memos were in Hiss's handwriting. A typewriter expert from the Federal Bureau of Investigation (FBI) testified that letters the

Hisses wrote and all but one of the Chambers documents had been typed on the same machine.

The typewriter became a famous piece of evidence. The Hisses said that when they moved in December 1937 (before the documents were typed up in January and April 1938), they had given the machine to their maid's sons. One of the sons, Perry Catlett, testified that he had received the typewriter in December 1936, when he took it to a repair shop on K Street in Washington, D.C. The shopkeeper told him it was not worth repairing. Prosecutor Murphy then demonstrated, however, that the K Street repair shop had not opened until September 1938.

The FBI was not able to find the typewriter, which had been built by the Woodstock Company twenty years earlier. Believing that it would prove their client's innocence, Hiss's lawyers managed to track the machine down. Back in court, their efforts enabled a prosecution witness to demonstrate that the typewriter was in working order.

Before Alger Hiss took the stand, a number of witnesses, including a former district court judge, testified to his good character. On direct examination, Hiss denied Chambers's charges. He claimed he was not and never had been a member of the Communist Party.

Stryker's last witness was Dr. Carl Binger, a psychiatrist who had observed Chambers's testimony. Now Stryker asked Binger, "Have you an opinion within the bounds of reasonable certainty as to the mental condition of Whittaker Chambers?" Murphy objected that Chambers's mental state was for the jury to decide and the judge agreed.

In his closing statements, Murphy noted that the outcome of the trial must rest not on Chambers's charges, but on the documents and the typewriter. Stryker, for his part, concluded by saying, "The case comes down to this—who is telling the truth?"

The jurors met for fourteen hours and forty-five minutes without reaching a verdict. They were dismissed, and the judge declared a mistrial (a trial terminated and declared void before the return of a verdict).

Second Jury Reaches Guilty Verdict

Because of the mistrial, a second trial was begun on November 17, 1949. Most of the witnesses from the first trial repeated their earlier testimony. Defense attorney Claude B. Cross, who had replaced Stryker, called Dr. Binger to the witness stand. Judge Henry W. Goddard permitted Binger to testify that "Mr. Chambers is suffering from a condition known as a psychopathic personality." One important symptom of the disorder was

ALGER HISS AND THE YALTA CONFERENCE

Alger Hiss helped to organize the Yalta Conference in February 1945. Yalta was the largest resort on the Crimea, then part of the the former Soviet Union. Located on the Black Sea, it offered hotels, health spas, and tourist rest homes, many built by the nobility before the Russian Revolution in 1917. U.S. president Franklin D. Roosevelt, British prime minister Winston Churchhill, and Soviet premier Josef Stalin met in Yalta in February 1945 to discuss their plans for ending World War II. At Yalta, an ailing Roosevelt allowed the Soviet Union to control Eastern Europe. Conservative Americans later claimed that Roosevelt had "given away" Eastern Europe to the Communists. Supporters of Roosevelt pointed out that the Soviet Army and Communist partisans (supporters) already dominated the territory that Roosevelt conceded. Hiss had also helped to organize the conferences that launched the United Nations, which some Americans then viewed as another Communist tool.

"chronic, persistent, and repetitive lying and a tendency to make false accusations."

But on January 20, 1950, the jury found Hiss guilty on both perjury charges. He was sentenced to five years' imprisonment for each of the counts, with the sentences to run at the same time. Hiss denied any guilt, promising that "in the future the full facts of how Whittaker Chambers was able to carry out forgery by typewriter will be disclosed."

Hiss remained free on bail for more than a year. After his conviction was upheld in federal circuit court and the U.S. Supreme Court declined to consider it, he entered the federal penitentiary in Danbury, Connecticut, on March 22, 1951.

Appeal Efforts Fail

While Hiss was in prison, his attorney for the appeals process, Chester T. Lane, asked experts to examine the documentary evidence and the typewriter. A noted typewriter engineer, working only from samples of typing from the machine exhibited at trial, built another machine. It produced examples that could not be distinguished from documents typed on Priscilla Hiss's Woodstock machine. Lane also produced evidence that Priscilla Hiss's typewriter had been used in her father's real estate office in 1929—before the Woodstock typewriter shown at the trial had even been built.

Nevertheless, these attempts to gain a new trial failed. Hiss served three years and eight months of his sentence. After he was released, he wrote a book about the trial, worked as a stationery salesman, and, after five years, separated from his wife (although the couple never divorced). In 1976, the Massachusetts Bar Association, which had stopped Hiss from practicing law, accepted him again. Hiss began work as a legal consultant.

In 1992, at the age of eighty-seven, Hiss asked General Dmitri A. Volkogonov, chairman of the Russian government's military intelligence library, to inspect Soviet files that might concern him or Whittaker Chambers. Volkogonov eventually reported that "not a single document, and a great amount of materials have been studied, substantiates the allegation that Mr. A. Hiss collaborated with the intelligence services of the Soviet Union." Alger Hiss died in 1996, still declaring he was innocent.

Suggestions for Further Reading

Brodie, Fawn M. "I Think Hiss Is Lying." *American Heritage* (August 1981): 4–21.

Buckley, William F. "Well, What Do You Know?" *National Review* (November 19, 1990): 60.

Cooke, Alistair. *A Generation on Trial: U.S.A. vs. Alger Hiss.* Westport, CT: Greenwood Press, 1982.

Hiss, Alger. *Recollections of a Life.* New York: Seaver Books/Henry Holt, 1988.

Hiss, Tony. "My Father's Honor." *The New Yorker* (November 16, 1992): 100–106.

Tanenhaus, Sam. "The Hiss Case Isn't Over Yet." *The New York Times* (October 31, 1992): 21.

Tanenhaus, Sam. *Whittaker Chambers: A Biography.* New York: Random House, 1997.

Tyrell, R. E. "You Must Remember Hiss." *The American Spectator* (January 1991): 10.

Ward, G. C. "Unregretfully, Alger Hiss." *American Heritage* (November 1988): 18.

Trial of Julius and Ethel Rosenberg and Morton Sobell: 1951

Defendants: Julius and Ethel Rosenberg and Morton Sobell

Crime Charged: Conspiracy to commit wartime espionage

Chief Defense Lawyers: Alexander Bloch, Emanuel H. Bloch, Fyke Farmer, John Finerty and Daniel Marshall for the Rosenbergs; Edward Kuntz and Harold Phillips for Sobell

Chief Prosecutors: Roy M. Cohn, John Foley, James Kilsheimer III, Myles Lane, and Irving H. Saypol

Judge: Irving R. Kaufman

Place: New York, New York

Dates of Trial: March 6–29, 1951

Verdicts: Guilty

Sentences: Death by electrocution for the Rosenbergs; thirty years' imprisonment for Sobell

SIGNIFICANCE: The Rosenberg case, coming at the height of the anti-Communist hysteria in America, produced the harshest result possible: the deaths of two defendants who, as U.S. Supreme Court Justice Felix Frankfurter put it, "were tried for conspiracy and sentenced for treason."

The age of the atomic bomb began in 1945. That year America dropped two of the bombs on Japan, ending World War II. Four years later, on September 23, 1949, President Harry S Truman announced that another atomic explosion had occurred in the Soviet Union. The Soviet Union had been America's ally (partner) in World War II. Since then it had become an opponent in the cold war (the term used to define the struggle for power and prestige between the Western powers and the Communist bloc from 1945—the end of World War II—to 1989). Now, with the discovery that the Soviets had the ability to create an atomic bomb, panic began. Americans began digging bomb shelters in their back yards and teaching school-children to duck under their classroom desks during emergency drills.

A Web of Spies

In February 1950, police arrested Dr. Klaus Fuchs in England. He was a German-born nuclear physicist. Fuchs had worked for the American government to develope the first atomic bomb in Los Alamos, New Mexico. The code name for this secret project was the "Manhattan Project." After his arrest, Fuchs confessed that he had given atomic information to the Soviet Union. He was tried and sentenced to fourteen years in prison.

In America, former Communist spy Elizabeth Bentley faced a federal grand jury. She said that a man named Harry Gold had taken her place as a Soviet agent. Police arrested Gold on May 24. He confessed that he had carried information between Klaus Fuchs and Anatoli Yakovlev, a Soviet diplomat stationed in New York.

Invited to Spy

Gold also accused David Greenglass of spying. Greenglass lived in New York City, where he operated a machine shop with his brother-in-law, Julius Rosenberg. While he was in the army, Greenglass had worked on the Manhattan Project. After his arrest, he confessed that Rosenberg and his wife, Ethel, had asked him to become a spy. The Rosenbergs used Greenglass's wife, Ruth, to contact him in 1944. She was visiting in New Mexico while he was working on the Manhattan Project.

The Federal Bureau of Investigation (FBI) then made a new discovery. Agents figured out that two of Julius Rosenberg's college classmates, Max Elitcher and Morton Sobell, had been part of the spy ring. Elitcher confessed. He accused Rosenberg and Sobell of spying too. The FBI also learned that Rosenberg had belonged to the Communist Party. However, they thought he had dropped out in 1944.

Agents arrested Julius Rosenberg first, then Ethel. The Mexican secret police arrested Sobell while he was on vacation there. They then sent him back across the border where U.S. agents were waiting.

ESPIONAGE

The Rosenbergs and Sobell were not charged with spying. They were charged with conspiracy to commit wartime espionage. The difference between the two was important. Proving conspiracy to commit espionage was easier. Each conspirator could be held accountable for the acts of all the others. The government did not have to prove any one conspirator had knowledge of the acts of his or her co-conspirators. It was necessary only to prove that the accused planned to achieve an illegal goal, not that they had succeeded.

Prosecution Witnesses Provide Details

The trial of Julius and Ethel Rosenberg and Morton Sobell opened on March 6, 1951. Sobell, however, never took the witness stand. The first witness for the government was Max Elitcher, who connected Sobell with the Rosenbergs. Another witness testified that Sobell's trip to Mexico was actually a flight from the United States during which he and his family used aliases (fake names).

At the beginning of the trial, prosecutor Irving H. Saypol sent a warning to defense attorney Emanuel H. Bloch, saying, "If your clients don't confess, they are doomed." Saypol's assistant, Roy Cohn, questioned David Greenglass, the first witness against the Rosenbergs. Greenglass testified that while working on the Manhattan Project, he gave Julius Rosenberg rough sketches of two items used to make the atomic bomb. He said he had given his brother-in-law a "pretty good description" of the bomb America had dropped on Nagasaki, Japan, at the end of the war. Altogether, he had written a dozen pages of description and drawn several sketches. Julius paid him $200 for these items, Greenglass said.

Ruth Greenglass testified that Ethel Rosenberg told her in January 1945 that she was tired from typing up David's notes for Julius. Ruth also said that Ethel had promised to give the Greenglasses $6,000 (only $5,000 was actually paid) for travel. Judge Irving R. Kaufman asked from whom they had received the money. Ruth responded that it had come from the Russians, and it was intended to help the Greenglasses escape the United States.

Witness Harry Gold had already been convicted of espionage and sentenced to thirty years in prison. He testified that Soviet Vice Consul Yakovlev had ordered him to go to Albuquerque, New Mexico, where he would meet a new contact named Greenglass. Yakovlev had handed Greenglass a piece of paper on which was written: "Recognition signal. I come from Julius." Gold said he had picked up an envelope from Greenglass and taken it back to Yakovlev in Brooklyn, New York. In addition, he revealed that Greenglass had given him a telephone number, that of his "brother-in-law Julius," where Greenglass could be reached during his next trip to New York.

Ex-Communist Elizabeth Bentley had been an assistant to Jacob Golos. He was the chief of Soviet spying in the United States. She testified that, starting in 1943, during the time she served in that position, she had received several telephone calls from a man who said, "This is Julius." The caller had wanted Golos to get in touch with him.

A Jell-O Box Cut in Two

Taking the stand in his own defense, Julius Rosenberg denied the charges. David Greenglass and Ruth Greenglass had described a table he owned. They claimed it was specially made for taking small pictures of secret documents, and had been given to him by the Soviets. Rosenberg now claimed that the table had been purchased at Macy's department store for "about $21." He testified that he had not given Ruth $150 for a New Mexico trip in 1944 and he claimed that he had not received information about the atomic bomb from David. He also denied that he had introduced Greenglass to a man in New York who wanted details about the atomic bomb and denied introducing a neighbor to Greenglass as a spy.

Rosenberg said he had not cut a Jell-O box into two uneven pieces and given one to Ruth to be used as a signal if another courier took her place. He denied having said, "The simplest things are the cleverest," when David admired this trick. However, Judge Kaufman asked if he had even belonged to "any group" that had discussed the Soviet system of government. Rosenberg said, "Well, your Honor . . . I refuse to answer a question that might tend to incriminate me." (This is called "taking the Fifth Amendment"—the right not to say anything that could make one look guilty.)

On cross-examination, Rosenberg defended his previous testimony. In response to a question from prosecutor Saypol about conversations with David Greenglass, Rosenberg used the word "blackmail." Judge Kaufman asked Rosenberg to explain.

Rosenberg: "He threatened me to get money. I considered it blackmailing."

Kaufman: "Did he say he would go to the authorities and tell them you were in a conspiracy to steal the atomic bomb secret?"

Rosenberg: "No."

Afterward, jury members said that Rosenberg's choice of words seemed like an admission of guilt.

Ethel Rosenberg Takes the Stand

Ethel Rosenberg denied all charges. Like her husband, she took the Fifth Amendment when asked about the Communist Party. After she had been cross-examined, defense attorney Bloch said he would call no more witnesses.

Then it was the prosecution's turn to answer the case for the defense. Saypol called a surprise witness, photographer Ben Schneider. The FBI had located him only a day earlier. He testified that in June 1950 the Rosenberg family asked him to shoot a large number of passport photos, saying they were going to France. Another witness then testified that the Rosenbergs had told her the suspicious table was "a gift from a friend." Although it was their finest piece of furniture, the witness added, the Rosenbergs had kept it in a closet. (The table was not introduced in court as evidence because the Rosenbergs claimed not to know where it was at the time.)

The jury met to deliberate the verdict from late afternoon until nearly midnight, and for nearly an hour the next morning. They then declared that they found both Rosenbergs and Sobell guilty as charged. A week later, on April 15, 1951, Judge Kaufman sentenced Sobell to thirty years in prison and the Rosenbergs to the electric chair.

Appeals Last Two Years

The executions were postponed while the Rosenbergs' appealed (used a legal method to ask for a new trial or reversal of conviction). In February 1952, the U.S. Circuit Court of Appeals upheld the convictions. In October, the U.S. Supreme Court refused to review the case. In December, the defense tried to obtain a new trial for the Rosenbergs, claiming that photographer Schneider had lied under oath and Saypol had conducted an unfair trial. The motion for a new trial was denied. A motion was then made in court to reduce the Rosenbergs' "cruel and excessive" punishment on grounds that they had not been charged with treason. That motion, too, was denied.

In January 1953, the executions were again delayed while President Truman considered an appeal for clemency (mercy). After Truman left office that month, the new president, Dwight D. Eisenhower, refused to grant

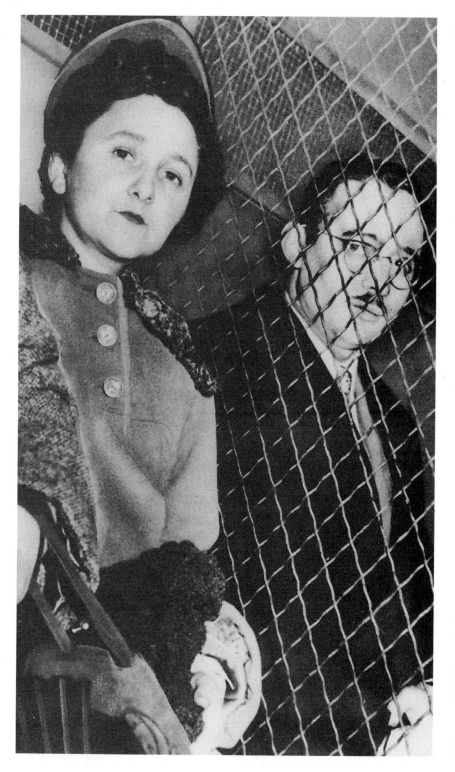

**Trial of
Julius and
Ethel
Rosenberg
and Morton
Sobell: 1951**

*As they are
transported to jail,
a wire fence
separates Ethel
Rosenberg from her
husband, Julius.
The couple was
convicted of spying
in March 1951.*

LEGACIES OF THE ROSENBERGS

The Rosenberg case continues to inspire deep feelings. The novelist E. L. Doctorow wrote a fictional version of the story. In the story, he tries to imagine what happened to the two Rosenberg children, who were adopted, changed their names, and disappeared from public view after their parents were executed. His novel, *The Book of Daniel,* was later made into a film. In 1975, the Rosenberg children, Robert Meeropol and Michael Meeropol, told their story in the nonfiction book, *We Are Your Sons: The Legacy of Ethel and Julius Rosenberg.* The Meeropols became spokespeople for the Committee to Reopen the Rosenberg Case, an organization that claimed that the Rosenberg trial had been unfair. They sought to use the new Freedom of Information Act to obtain previously classified government documents relating to the trial. In 1983, Ronald Radosh and Joyce Milton published *The Rosenberg File: A Search for the Truth.* This controversial book alleged that the Rosenbergs were in fact guilty, despite the claims of their supporters. After the fall of the Soviet Union, when new documents became available, the debate continued. To this day, scholars still argue over whether the Rosenbergs were guilty or innocent.

the Rosenbergs a pardon. Meanwhile, a committee had begun a worldwide attempt to save the Rosenbergs. An eight-car train filled with protesters rode from New York City to Ossining, New York, where the Rosenbergs sat in Sing Sing prison on death row. Three million letters and telegrams flooded the White House. Pope Pius XII twice asked for clemency. Physicist Albert Einstein and atomic scientist Harold C. Urey also appealed.

A third execution date was postponed, but the Supreme Court, for the second time, declined to review the Rosenbergs' case. The discovery of the suspicious table in the apartment of Julius Rosenberg's mother failed to justify a new trial or another stay of execution.

The Supreme Court refused a third appeal to review the case or grant a stay (postponement) of execution. Then, on June 17, Justice William O. Douglas finally granted a stay on grounds that the Rosenbergs might not have been correctly tried under the Espionage Act of 1917. The next day, President Eisenhower received clemency appeals from hundreds of organizations representing millions of people in Europe, where crowds had to be held back from U.S. embassies. The members of the Supreme Court were called back from vacation for a special session to consider the Rosenbergs' fates. Although three of the nine justices disagreed with this decision, the court removed the stay of execution. Eisenhower rejected another clemency plea.

The Rosenbergs were executed precisely at sundown on June 19, 1953. That night, New York City's Union Square filled with 10,000 protesters, while crowds gathered in capitals around the world expressed their shock.

Trial of Julius and Ethel Rosenberg and Morton Sobell: 1951

Suggestions for Further Reading

De Toledano, Ralph. *The Greatest Plot In History.* New York: Duell, Sloan and Pearce, 1963.

Goldstein, Alvin H. *The Unquiet Death of Julius & Ethel Rosenberg.* New York: Lawrence Hill, 1975.

Hyde, H. Montgomery. *The Atom Bomb Spies.* New York: Atheneum, 1980.

Meeropol, Robert and Michael Meeropol. *We Are Your Sons: The Legacy of Ethel and Julius Rosenberg.* New York: Houghton Mifflin, 1975.

Nizer, Louis. *The Implosion Conspiracy.* New York: Doubleday & Co., 1973.

Radosh, Ronald and Joyce Milton. *The Rosenberg File: A Search for the Truth.* New York: Holt, Rinehart and Winston, 1983.

Sharlit, Joseph H. *Fatal Error.* New York: Charles Scribner's Sons, 1989.

Sobell, Morton. *On Doing Time.* New York: Charles Scribner's Sons, 1974.

Wexley, John. *The Judgment of Julius and Ethel Rosenberg.* New York: Ballantine, 1977.

Markus Wolf Trials: 1993 and 1997

Defendant: Markus Wolf

Crimes Charged: First trial: treason; second trial: kidnapping, wounding, incitement

Chief Defense Lawyer: Johann Schwenn

Chief Prosecutor: Joachim Lampe

Judges: First trial: Klaus Wagner; second trial: Ina Obst-Oellers

Place: Düsseldorf, Germany

Dates of Trials: First trial: May 4–December 5, 1993; second trial: January 7–May 27, 1997

Verdicts: First trial: guilty; second trial: guilty

Sentences: First trial: six years' imprisonment; second trial: two years' imprisonment (suspended) plus $30,000 fine

SIGNIFICANCE: Justice or revenge? The trials of Markus Wolf caused arguments on both sides.

For nearly three decades Markus Wolf was "the man without a face." He was an almost imaginary figure in the murky world of cold war (the term used to define the struggle for power and prestige between the Western powers and the Communist bloc from 1945—the end of World War II—to 1989) spying. Try as they might, Western intelligence agencies were unable to obtain a photograph of the man who ran East Germany's powerful foreign intelligence agency (called Hauptverwaltung für Aufklärung—HVA). The nearest they got to this legendary figure was through the spy novels of John Le Carre. Many said the novelist had modeled his spy chief "Karla" on the shadowy Markus Wolf. However, nothing in the world of fiction could compare with the real thing.

Wolf joined the forerunner of the HVA in 1951. It was the first step on a career path that would make him the most devious spymaster of his generation. His particular talent was in placing moles (secret agents) close to the center of power in foreign governments. His most spectacular success came in the early 1970s. West German head of state Willy Brandt felt he had to resign after the public learned that his secretary, Gunter Guillaume, was one of Wolf's deep-cover spies.

Wolf left the HVA in 1986, after thirty-three years in charge. Two years later he joined the rest of world in watching with amazement as the Berlin Wall—which separated East and West Berlin in Germany—collapsed due to the fall of Communism. With East and West Germany on the verge of uniting, demands grew for former Communist leaders to face trial for their perceived sins while in office. Secret police chiefs, border guards, politicians, and espionage officers were all accused of illegal acts. With such an angry cry for justice, Wolf's arrest was inevitable.

Wolf Avoids Arrest

That was the intent on reunification day (when East and West Germany united)—October 3, 1990—when agents raided the HVA's former headquarters. However, Wolf had already fled to the Soviet Union, seeking asylum (a place of refuge). But the political confusion Wolf found there drove him back to Germany. On September 24, 1991, he surrendered to police.

Wolf's trial began at the High Court in Düsseldorf on May 4, 1993. The charges, as stated by federal attorney Joachim Lampe, were that Wolf's spying had seriously endangered West German security.

Throughout the proceedings Wolf maintained an attitude of disinterest. He spoke only once during the entire seven-month trial, an opening statement that was both arrogant and charming. First came a reminder to the court that the Nazis had once placed his family on the wanted list. "I was fourteen years old. My brother was eleven," he said. "Had the 'sound instincts of the people' borne fruit, our names would have ended up on some tombstone, perhaps in Yad Vashem Memorial in Jerusalem." Normally, appeals from Jewish victims of Nazi cruelty are well-received in German courtrooms. Here Wolf's plea drew only embarrassed silence. Somehow, few could picture this vicious cold war spy as a victim of anti-Semitism (hatred directed toward Jewish persons).

Markus Wolf and his wife on their way to court in Düsseldorf, Germany. On May 5, 1993, Wolf went on trial for alleged treason and bribery.

For the rest of his speech, Wolf's arrogance resurfaced. Dismissing the charges against him as "absurd and legally unsupportable," he demanded to know "which country exactly am I supposed to have betrayed? I would accept the most severe punishment for betraying my country. But I will not accept that I can be guilty of betraying someone else's."

After that, Wolf remained silent, occasionally smiling, always able to convey the impression that he was above such banal proceedings.

The state produced a long list of moles to testify. Gunter Guillaume, despite being seriously ill (he died in April 1995), angrily defended his actions and proved disastrous for the prosecution. He described his spying of Brandt's office as "my masterpiece as a spy." Then he boasted proudly, "I always tried to serve two men honestly—Willy Brandt and Markus Wolf." He also injected a suitably conspiratorial tone by declaring that he "was only the stick with which certain circles wanted to drive [Brandt] from office." (This was a reference to the fact that West German counterintelligence was aware of Guillaume's true allegiance for twelve months before arresting him.) At the end of his testimony, Guillaume strode across the court, grabbed hold of Wolf's hand, and shook it vigorously. Wolf smiled his appreciation.

Other agents passed through the court to tell their tales. Klaus Kuron, already serving a jail sentence, portrayed himself as the best counterintelligence officer working for the ultimate spymaster—Markus Wolf.

Markus Wolf Trials: 1993 and 1997

Bitter Betrayal

It was noticeable that almost every witness either shook hands with Wolf or else acknowledged him warmly. The lone exception was Gabrielle Gast. At her own recent espionage trial, this reluctant agent was horrified to learn that a man she had loved and trusted for years was working for Wolf as a spy. The crafty spymaster had planted him to report on her every move. More than anyone else, Gast was living proof of the harsh realities of international spying. She now knew why people called spying the "wilderness of mirrors," where nothing and no one are what they seem.

In his closing remarks to the jury, Johann Schwenn, Wolf's counsel, returned to the curious delay in arresting Guillaume. He said, "Either the secret service was incompetent, or there was the intention to harm the chancellor." If the latter was the case, said Schwenn, then Wolf was standing trial "for an offence actually committed by the accusing state authorities."

On December 5, 1993, Wolf showed no expression when Judge Klaus Wagner sentenced him to six years in jail for treason. Struggling to make

THE SECRETS OF A SPY

The memoirs (a record of events that happened to the writer) of Markus Wolf were published in fourteen countries including the United States on June 1, 1997. In them Wolf asserts that in 1990 two Central Intelligence Agency (CIA) spies visited him at his country home just outside Berlin, Germany. Supposedly, the CIA was so anxious to learn the names of the agents working for Wolf that they offered him a new identity, a "seven-figure sum," and a home in California for the information.

himself heard above the shouts of insults from the public gallery, Wagner conceded that the sentence was "mild compared with other espionage trials." However, he felt that as Wolf was spying for a legitimate government at the time—East Germany—his actions were not as bad as if he had betrayed his own country.

Free on bail during his appeal, Wolf became a TV talk show regular and even published a cookbook of his favorite recipes. Much to the embarrassment of senior German politicians, the charming former spymaster was in danger of becoming a national hero. Federal anger grew even greater on May 23, 1995, when Germany's Constitutional Court ruled it illegal to prosecute East Germans who spied against West Germany from East German soil. However, they did not apply the same standards to West Germans working against the East.

Wolf was delighted. "I hope I can recognize in the court's ruling a sign that the consequences of the Cold War are finally being done away with," he said. He added that the decision was encouraging for all those "such as myself who had doubts about the rule of law [in united Germany.]"

Despite this reversal, the government refused to back down. On January 7, 1997, Wolf again faced a Düsseldorf court. This time he fought three charges of kidnapping. Because most felt that the feud against the seventy-four-year-old ex-spymaster had lasted long enough, this second trial sparked little interest. Once again the government failed to imprison Markus Wolf. On May 27, 1997, Ina Obst-Oellers, senior judge of the sitting panel, delivered the court's verdict—a two-year suspended sentence and a $30,000 fine.

—*Colin Evans*

Suggestions for Further Reading

Colitt, Leslie. *Spymaster.* London: Robson Books, 1996.

Electronic Telegraph. [Online] Available
  http:\\www.telegraph.co.uk, January 8, 1997.

Wolf, Markus. *The Man without a Face.* London: Jonathan Cape,
  1997.

**Markus Wolf
Trials: 1993
and 1997**

MURDER

Boston Massacre Trials: 1770

Defendants: Captain Thomas Preston; Corporal William Wemms; Privates Hugh White, John Carroll, William Warren, Matthew Killroy, William McCauley, James Hartegan, and Hugh Montgomery

Crimes Charged: Murder and accessories to murder

Chief Defense Lawyers: Both trials: John Adams and Josiah Quincy Jr.; first trial: Robert Auchmuty; second trial: Sampson Salter Blowers

Chief Prosecutors (Attorneys for the Crown): Samuel Quincy and Robert Treat Paine

Judges: John Cushing, Peter Oliver, Benjamin Lynd, and Edmund Trowbridge

Place: Boston, Massachusetts Bay Colony

Dates of Trials: *Rex v. Preston:* October 24–30, 1770; *Rex v. Wemms et al.:* November 27–December 5, 1770

Verdicts: First trial: Captain Preston, not guilty; second trial: Corporal Wemms, Privates White, Carroll, Warren, McCauley, and Hartegan, not guilty; Privates Killroy and Montgomery, not guilty of murder but guilty of manslaughter

Sentences: Branding on the thumbs for Killroy and Montgomery

SIGNIFICANCE: This case was a landmark on the road to the American Revolution. Despite a politically hostile atmosphere, two reasonably fair trials were conducted and the right of self-defense was upheld.

On the night of March 5, 1770, three men lay dead and two more were dying, following shots fired by British troops into an angry crowd outside of the Custom House in Boston, Massachusetts. This scene, known as the Boston Massacre, came after months of conflict between Bostonians and the British soldiers sent to the city to protect newly appointed British Customs commissioners. The English king and his advisors viewed Boston as a birthplace of disagreement in the colonies, where hostility increased in the years following the French and Indian War. Quarrels arose over Indian and frontier affairs, import rules, and taxes—especially the

An engraving of the Boston Massacre by Paul Revere, 1770.

British Parliament's tax on the American colonies. Boston, with its unusually stormy Stamp Act riots, seemed to be the center of American political unrest.

Although some British troops had remained in the colonies after the Revolutionary War (1775–1783), the placement of a large number of troops in a colonial city was a new and unwelcome development. In the eighteenth century, British citizens and colonists viewed the existence of a war-ready army during peace time as trouble. The British troops in Boston seemed proof that colonists' civil rights and the powers of their political organizations were being ignored.

In such an atmosphere, trouble was certain. Rude behavior, shoving matches, loud arguments, and occasional fistfights occurred between Boston residents and the British soldiers almost from the first day troops arrived in the fall of 1768.

Snowballs, then Musket Balls, Fly

The series of events that led to the clash on March 5, 1770, apparently began with a nasty exchange between Private Patrick Walker of the Twenty-Ninth Regiment and William Green, a local rope-maker.

Soldiers of low rank, who were paid very little, often made additional money with odd jobs. As Walker passed Green on March 2, the rope-maker asked the soldier if he wanted work. When Walker said yes, Green told him to clean his outhouse (outdoor bathroom). Insulted, Walker swore revenge. He walked away and, in a few minutes, returned with several other soldiers.

A fight broke out between soldiers and rope-makers, who had rallied in support of Green. Clubs and sticks were used, as well as fists. The rope-makers won out over the soldiers.

However, the calm after that incident was brief. Fights popped up over the next two days. Rumors flew and tensions mounted. The commander of the Twenty-Ninth Regiment, Lieutenant Colonel Maurice Carr, wrote to Acting Governor Thomas Hutchinson to complain of the abuse his men were forced to take from the citizens of Boston. On March 5, Hutchinson put the letter before his council. Council members all agreed that the people of the town would not be satisfied until the troops were removed.

The evening of March 5 was cold, and a foot of snow lay on the ground. A wig-maker's helper named Edward Garrick insulted Private Hugh White, who was on guard at a watchman's box near the Main Guard, the army's headquarters. White struck Garrick on the head with a musket. Neverthe-less, other helpers continued to taunt White and throw snowballs at him.

Cries of "fire" could be heard in the streets, although no buildings were burning that night. Soldiers on Brattle Street carried clubs, bayo-nets, and other weapons. In Boylston's Alley, a volley of snowballs and insults was halted by a passing officer, who led the British troops to nearby Murray's barracks, where he told their junior officers to keep them inside. Outside the barracks, more angry words were exchanged before Richard Palmes, a Boston merchant, persuaded many members of the crowd to go home. Still, some of the crowd shouted that they should go "away to the Main Guard."

The Crowd Gathers

At about the same time, 200 people gathered in an area called Dock Square. More people joined them as groups flowed in from Boston's North End. Some came carrying clubs. Others picked up whatever weapons they could find in the square. The crowd eventually gathered around a tall man who urged the crowd to storm the Main Guard.

Meanwhile, White retreated from his guard's box near the Main Guard to the steps of the Custom House. From there, he threatened to fire on the approaching crowd and called for the assistance of other soldiers.

When news of the watchman's situation reached Captain Thomas Preston, he led a small group from the Twenty-Eighth Regiment to White's rescue. With bayonets ready, two groups of soldiers managed to reach Pri-vate White. When the troops prepared to leave, however, the chances of retreating through the angry crowd appeared more difficult. The soldiers positioned themselves in a semicircle, facing the crowd, with their cap-tain in front of them. Their muskets were loaded. Some in the crowd dared them to fire. Finally, someone hurled a club, knocking down soldier Hugh Montgomery. As he got to his feet, someone ordered the men to fire. Mont-gomery fired one shot. No one seemed to be hit, and the crowd pulled away from the troops. There was a pause during which Captain Preston might have given an order to cease firing. The pause between the first shot and those that followed could have been as little as six seconds or as long as two minutes, according to witnesses' accounts.

The Massacre Begins

However long the pause, the troops began firing. In the confusion that fol-lowed, most people in the crowd believed the soldiers were firing only powder, not bullets. However, two men were hit almost immediately. Samuel Gray fell, shot in the head. A sailor known as Michael Johnson (real name Crispus Attucks) took two bullets in the chest. As some members of the crowd surged forward to prevent further firing, another sailor, James Caldwell, was hit.

A bullet struck seventeen-year-old Samuel Maverick as he ran toward the Town House. He died several hours later at his mother's boarding house. The fifth death was Patrick Carr. Struck in the hip he died nine days later. His dying testimony later helped strengthen the defense attorneys' claim that the soldiers fired in self-defense.

Captain Preston yelled at his men, demanding to know why they had fired. The reply was they thought he had ordered them to shoot when they heard the word "fire." As the crowd, which had fallen back, began to help those who had fallen, the troops again raised their muskets. Preston commanded them to cease fire and went down the line pushing up their musket barrels. The crowd dispersed, carrying the wounded, the dying, and the dead. Captain Preston and his men marched back to the Main Guard. The Boston Massacre was over.

Following a brief interview with Captain Preston, Royal Governor Hutchinson promised a full investigation. He said "The law shall have its course; I will live and die by the law." Thus, the Crown began an investigation into the Boston Massacre.

The Redcoats Are Indicted

That very night, two justices of the peace went to the council chamber, where they spent the next several hours calling up witnesses. By morning, Captain Preston and his eight men had been locked up. A week later, a grand jury was sworn in, and, at the request of Attorney General Jonathan Sewall, Preston and his men were officially charged.

Sewall, a loyalist committed to Britain, busied himself with legal affairs out of town, leaving the prosecution of the soldiers to whomever the royal court appointed. The disappointing choice was another loyalist, Samuel Quincy, the colony's solicitor general. To strengthen the prosecution, radicals led by Samuel Adams persuaded Bostonians at a town meeting to pay the prosecution's expenses, thus making it possible to bring in the successful lawyer Robert Treat Paine.

The choice of loyalist Robert Auchmuty to serve as the senior counsel for Captain Preston was no surprise, but the other two attorneys who agreed to act for the defense were Josiah Quincy Jr. (brother of the prosecutor Samuel Quincy), a fiery radical, and John Adams, who was just as offended as his cousin Samuel Adams by the presence of the king's troops in Boston. For the trial of the soldiers, Auchmuty dropped out, and Adams became senior counsel, with Sampson Salter Blowers as junior counsel.

The decision on whether to hold one trial or two was not announced until the last minute. The troops wanted to be tried with Captain Preston. They believed separate trials would lessen their chances of being found not guilty. If Preston were tried first and found not guilty, the result would indicate that his men were responsible for firing without orders. Additionally, if the Captain and his men were tried together, the prosecution would have a difficult time proving that a bullet from one specific gun, fired by one specific soldier, had hit one specific victim. In the end, though, it was decided there would be two separate trials: the first for Captain Preston, the second for the troops.

Captain Preston's Trial

The captain's trial began October 24, 1770, and was over by October 30, 1770. Even so, it was the first criminal trial in Massachusetts to last longer than a day. Samuel Quincy opened for the prosecution and called as his first witness Edward Garrick, the wig-maker whose taunts had ended with his being struck by Private Hugh White. After describing this incident, Garrick testified that he had seen soldiers in the streets carrying swords before Preston had led his men to the Custom House. The next witness, Thomas Marshall, supported that statement, adding that Preston most certainly did have time to order his men to cease fire after the first shot was fired.

Witnesses who followed also gave damaging testimony. Peter Cunningham said that Preston had ordered his men to load their muskets. Later, he changed his statement slightly, saying that the man who had ordered the troops to fire was definitely an officer because of the way he was dressed. Witnesses William Wyatt and John Cox both insisted that Preston had given the order to fire.

On the following day, the prosecution had a setback. Witness Theodore Bliss said Preston had been standing in front of the guns. Bliss heard someone shouting "Fire," but he did not think it was the captain. Henry Knox testified that the crowd was shouting, "Fire, damn your blood, fire." Meanwhile, Benjamin Burdick said he heard the word "fire" come from behind the men.

The prosecution regained some ground with witness Daniel Calef, who stated that he had "looked the officer in the face when he gave the word" to fire. The next witness, Robert Goddard, also stated firmly that Preston, standing behind his men, had given the order to fire.

The first three witnesses for the defense testified to the threats uttered against the soldiers by those in the street. According to one witness, Edward Hill, after the firing, he saw Preston push up a musket and say, "Fire no more. You have done mischief enough."

On the following day, a string of witnesses clearly described the confusion and anger that dominated the scene on March 5. The first witness for the defense, John Edwards, stated firmly that it was the corporal, William Wemms, who had given the men the order to load their muskets. Another, Joseph Hilyer, said, "The soldiers seemed to act from pure nature . . . I mean they acted and fired by themselves."

Chief defense lawyer John Adams.

Reasonable Doubt

Richard Palmes testified that he had placed his hand on Preston's shoulder just as the order to fire was given. At the time, the two men were in front of the troops. Even though he was standing right next to Preston, Palmes could not be sure whether Preston or someone else had given the order. Palmes' testimony threw a strong reasonable doubt on the Crown's case.

Another major witness for the defense was a slave named Andrew. In great detail, Andrew described the explosive scene on March 5 and testified that the voice that gave the order to fire was different from the other voices calling out at the time. He was sure the voice had come from beyond Preston.

When John Gillespie took the stand, he testified about an event that occurred at least two hours before the massacre. He spoke of seeing a group of townspeople carrying swords, sticks, and clubs, coming from the South End area. The tone of Gillespie's testimony implied a "plot" to expel the troops from Boston.

In presenting closing arguments, defense attorney Adams spoke first. He said, "Self-defence is the primary canon [rule] of the law of nature," and he explained how a homicide was justifiable when an assaulted man had nowhere to retreat. Carefully reviewing the evidence, Adams demolished the Crown's weakly presented case.

In his closing argument for the prosecution, Paine, in an effort to dismiss the idea of self-defense, pointed out that defense witness Palmes had been standing in front of the soldiers' muskets. "Would he place himself before a party of soldiers and risque his life at the muzzles of their guns," Paine reasoned, "when he thought them under a necessity of firing to defend their life?"

The court adjourned at 5:00 P.M. on Monday. By 8:00 A.M. on Tuesday, the jury had reached a verdict. Preston was found not guilty.

The Soldiers' Trial

One month later at the soldiers' trial, the Crown's first witnesses testified about the behavior of troops—who may or may not have been among those on trial—in the hours before the massacre. Prosecution witnesses spoke of off-duty officers, armed with swords, running through the streets and assaulting citizens without reason.

The prosecution seemed to be widening the focus of the trial by describing criminal acts by soldiers unconnected with the massacre itself. This was a questionable move since testimony about other soldiers was not important for the case being tried. Of the Crown's first witnesses, only one made a major point. The town watchman, Edward Langford, described the death of a citizen, John Gray. According to Langford, Gray had definitely been shot by Private Matthew Killroy.

The following day the Crown's witnesses faltered. James Brewer, who denied that the crowd had uttered any threats against the soldiers, admitted that people all around were calling "fire." Asked if he had thought the cry referred to a fire or if it was an order for soldiers to fire, Brewer answered that he could not "tell now what I thought then."

Another witness, James Bailey, stated clearly that boys in the street had pelted the soldiers with pieces of ice large enough to hurt them. Bailey also stated that Private Montgomery had been knocked down and that he had seen Crispus Attucks carrying "a large cord-wood stick."

Like the prosecution's witnesses, the first defense witnesses spoke of extreme behavior throughout the town. A picture emerged of a possible riot in the making. The testimony of William Hunter, an auctioneer who had seen the tall man speaking to the crowd in Dock Square, suggested that some of the crowd's activities may have been organized rather than unprepared. For two days, the defense presented solid evidence that the soldiers at the Custom House had been threatened by a dangerous crowd.

In his closing remarks, Quincy pointed out that even a "moderate" person might seek revenge on the soldiers at the Custom House for the actions of soldiers elsewhere in the town that night. Still, the law did not permit this. The evidence demonstrated that the troops had acted in self-defense.

In his closing summary, which was a brilliant blend of law and politics, John Adams placed much of the blame on "Mother England." He pointed out, "At certain critical seasons, even in the mildest government, the people are liable to run into riots and tumults [disorder]." The possibility of such events "is in direct proportion to the [absolute rule] of the government." Adams turned his attention to a description of the crowd. "And why we should [hesitate] to call such a set of people a mob? . . . Soldiers quartered in a populous town, will always [cause] two mobs, where they prevent one. They are wretched conservators of the peace."

After over two hours of deliberation, the jury found Corporal William Wemms and Privates White, Warren, Carroll, McCauley, and Hartegan not guilty of all charges. Privates Killroy and Montgomery were found not guilty of murder but guilty of manslaughter. The evidence had shown that these two men had definitely shot their weapons. There was not enough evidence to prove which of the other soldiers had fired.

On December 14, 1770, Killroy and Montgomery returned to court for sentencing. They cited "benefit of clergy," a plea for pity originally created for members of religious orders, but later extended to those who could read and write. The court granted the request, and Killroy and Montgomery were branded on the thumbs and released from custody.

CRISPUS ATTUCKS

Crispus Attucks, the first American to die in the Boston Massacre, was born in Framingham, Massachusetts, around 1723. He was enslaved to Deacon William Brown. Although not much is known about Attucks' early life, he apparently escaped from slavery at age twenty-seven, going to work on the whale ships docked along Massachusetts' east coast. He seemed to be a leader who could quickly inspire large numbers of people to action. When the crowd of Americans—both black and white—gathered around the British barracks on March 5, Attucks was in the lead, urging the others forward. When the soldiers ordered the crowd to leave, Attucks convinced them to remain. Then the crowd heard from a man who claimed that a British guard had hit him with a musket. Furious, the crowd surged forward, Attucks in the lead. According to one witness, he actually hit one of the armed British soldiers.

In the fighting that followed, Attucks was shot and killed instantly. Attucks' fame lasted long after his death. Before the Civil War, African American military companies took the name of the "Attucks Guards." From 1858 to 1870, African Americans living in Boston held a Crispus Attucks Day. A Crispus Attucks statue was erected on the Boston Common by the black Boston community in 1888.

The mystery of who actually gave the order to fire was solved after the trials. Shortly before he left Boston, Private Montgomery admitted to his lawyers that it was he who cried "fire" after he had been knocked down by a stick.

The massacre and the following trials persuaded the British that the presence of their troops in Boston was more likely to cause a rebellion than prevent it. Although British troops were soon withdrawn from the city, American patriots continued to refer to the massacre as evidence that the British could not be trusted and to urge their fellow colonists toward rebellion.

Suggestions for Further Reading

Hansen, Harry. *The Boston Massacre: An Episode of Dissent and Violence.* New York: Hastings House, 1970.

Middlekauff, Robert. *The Glorious Cause, The American Revolution, 1763–1789.* New York: Oxford University Press, 1982.

Millender, Dharathula H. *Crispus Attucks, Black Leader of Colonial Patriots.* New York: Aladdin Books, 1986.

Zobel, Hiller B. *The Boston Massacre.* New York: W. W. Norton & Company, 1970.

Boston
Massacre
Trials: 1770

Charlotte Corday Trial: 1793

Defendant: Charlotte Corday d'Armont
Crime Charged: Murder
Chief Defense Lawyer: Chauveau de la Garde
Chief Prosecutor: Antoine Fouquier-Tinville
Judge: Jacques Montané
Place: Paris, France
Dates of Trial: July 13–17, 1793
Verdict: Guilty
Sentence: Death by guillotine

SIGNIFICANCE: Charlotte Corday's killing of the political leader Jean-Paul Marat began a new and more destructive phase of the Reign of Terror in revolutionary France. To supporters of the king and moderate opponents of the radical Jacobin Party, she became a heroine and a martyr (one who chooses suffering or death instead of giving up their religion or principles).

People fleeing for safety poured into the town of Caen in the Normandy region of France in the late spring of 1793. Members of the violently revolutionary Jacobin party had driven their political opponents out of Paris. These Girondins, members of a moderate republican party, were filling the prisons and providing a steady stream of victims for the new government many called the Reign of Terror because of the enormous number of executions of those believed to be "enemies of the state." In Caen and other local towns, Girondin leaders hoped to regroup, rally, and recruit an army for a march on Paris.

Charlotte Corday was guillotined on July 17, 1793, for the stabbing death of Jacobin leader Jean-Paul Marat.

The Jacobins rose to power after the overthrow of King Louis XVI and his queen, Marie Antoinette. However, their Girondin rivals had reason to believe this rise would not last long. In the cities of Lyons, Marseille, and Toulon, moderate political groups were in revolt against the radicals who held power in Paris. Social and economic conditions were becoming desperate: unemployment had risen, prices were shooting upward, food and other necessities of life were in short supply. Also, the Jacobins' extreme behavior—arrests, blackmail, and an unending series of beheadings by guillotine—had turned many ordinary people away from the revolution.

The Making of an Assassin

In Caen during the summer of 1793, Charlotte Corday d'Armont read newspapers, listened to what others had to say, and decided to act. Born into a family of minor Norman nobility, she was a distant descendant of the playwright Pierre Corneille. Corday was convent-educated, and brought up on the classic works of Plutarch, Voltaire, and Rousseau. She became a champion of the Republic, which she saw as the means of changing France into a country with a better sense of right and wrong. The Jacobins, she believed, were destroying the revolution.

Horrible stories of the Reign of Terror were told in Caen, a center of Girondin strength in mid-1793. Norman leaders wrote a proclamation (public announcement) condemning the revolutionary ruling authority, the Convention, as a "conspiratorial commune engorged with blood and gold." The Girondin press in Caen identified the worst culprit as Marat, the most well-known and bloodthirsty of all the Jacobins:

> **Let Marat's head fall and the Republic is saved. Purge France of this man of blood. Marat sees the Public Safety only in a river of blood; well then his own must flow, for his head must fall to save two hundred thousand others.**

So Charlotte Corday, twenty-four years old, decided to become a patriotic avenger (one who acts in revenge), a martyr in the Republican cause. "One can die but once," she wrote a friend, "and what consoles me for the horror of our situation is that no one will lose in losing me."

She had a personal motive as well. As her mother lay dying in child-birth in 1782, the priest of the church of Saint-Gilles in Caen, the Abbé Gombault, had given her the last rites. Eleven years later, the Jacobins had forced him from his church, threatened to send him out of the country, and finally arrested him. On April 5, 1793, the Abbé Gombault became the first resident of Caen to go to the guillotine, and Corday sought to avenge his death.

The Killing

Jean-Paul Marat had risen to great power by the summer of 1793. He had been a scientist and doctor before the revolution, interested in the science of vision, flying, and electrical therapy. Europe's popular scientists had not taken his medical talents seriously. With the upheaval of 1789, Marat found his true vocation at last—as well as a means of avenging himself on an ungrateful group of people who had held power for too long. He became a revolutionary writer, the editor of *L'Ami du Peuple,* through which he expressed his anger. Marat's birdlike facial appearance led his friends to compare him to an eagle. To his enemies, he was a vulture.

In July 1793, Marat was suffering intensely from an illness that caused his skin to break out all over his body. He could find relief only in a cool bath, and so he had the tub in the bathroom of his apartment made into an office.

On July 9, Corday boarded a coach in Caen, and arrived in Paris two days later. On the morning of the 13th, a bright, hot Saturday, she set out

*Jean-Paul Marat, who was stabbed to death by
Charlotte Corday on July 13, 1793.*

for the Palais-Royal, stopping at a shop to buy a hat, a dark hat with green ribbons. At another shop she bought a wooden-handled kitchen knife with a five-inch blade.

She had hoped to kill Marat in front of his accomplices. Instead, she had to settle for a visit to his apartment. She took a carriage there, arriving around 11:30 A.M. A woman turned her away at the door, saying Marat was too ill to receive callers. Corday wrote him a brief and interesting note, saying she brought evidence of plans to overthrow the escaped Girondins.

Corday returned at 7:00 P.M. with another note requesting to see Marat. This time, in the confusion of deliveries of newspapers and bread, she managed to reach the head of the stairs before anyone stopped her. She began to speak in a loud voice about treason in Caen, hoping Marat would overhear.

"Let her in," he called out from the bath.

She pulled a chair up next to the tub. For a quarter of an hour they discussed plots to remove the Jacobins from authority, and Corday supplied Marat with a list of the Caen residents who plotted against them. "Good," he told her. "In a few days I will have them all guillotined."

At these words, Corday drew the knife from the top of her dress and plunged the blade into Marat's chest. He sank into the water, now red from the blood pouring from his wound. When he called out, an aide rushed in and threw a chair at the assassin. A neighbor who had heard the cry rushed in from across the street and tried to stop the bleeding. However, within a few minutes Marat was dead.

MURDER

Trial and Execution

Revolutionary justice was swift. Six policemen questioned Corday in Marat's apartment immediately after the killing. She made no attempt to deny her responsibility. She had come from Caen for the sole purpose of killing Jean-Paul Marat, she said, and she had acted alone.

An angry crowd gathered to shout for Corday's death as the police led her from Marat's house to a cell in the Abbaye prison. There, and later in the Conciergerie prison, she continued to claim that she had not been part of a plot, that she had neither needed nor sought help to carry out her assassin's mission.

All the same, the judges of the court, the Revolutionary Tribunal, were certain there were other people involved. "It has been mathematically demonstrated that this monster to whom nature has given the form of a woman is an envoy of. . . all the other conspirators of Caen," the Jacobin Georges Couthon insisted. However, Corday would admit only to having read Girondin newspapers.

"Was it from those newspapers that you learned that Marat was an anarchist?" asked Jacques Montané, the tribunal president.

"Yes, I knew that he was perverting France. I have killed one man to save a hundred thousand. I was a republican well before the Revolution and I have never lacked energy," said Corday.

Montané wondered whether she had practiced before attacking Marat. At first angered by the question, she then admitted it had been a lucky blow.

"Who were the persons who counseled you to commit this murder?" he went on.

"I would never have committed such an attack on the advice of others," she repeated. "I alone conceived the plan and executed it."

Finally, Montané asked Corday what she thought she had achieved: "Do you think you have killed all the Marats?"

"With this one dead, the others, perhaps, will be afraid."

The court moved swiftly to convict and condemn her. Dressed in the red shirt of an assassin, she wrote her last letters from her cell in the Conciergerie prison. "I beg you to forget me or rather rejoice at my fate," she wrote her father. "The cause is good." The executioner came for her in the early evening of July 17. She stood upright in the wagon that was to carry her to her death, knees braced against the tailgate, all the way to the scaffold. A man named Pierre Notelet stood among the street crowds to see her pass. Her image haunted him for a long time.

"THE FRIEND OF THE PEOPLE"

Jean-Paul Marat was known for the newspaper he founded, *L'Ami du peuple,* which is French for "the friend of the people." His publication was devoted to attacking those in power in the name of the poor and powerless. In the political fighting of the French Revolution, Marat found himself outlawed. In 1790 and 1791 he had to flee to England. He also hid in the Paris sewers, which made his skin disease worse. Even while he was in hiding, however, Marat continued to publish his revolutionary writings. Marat was later portrayed in a 1964 play by Peter Weiss, *The Persecution and Assassination of Jean-Paul Marat as Performed by the Inmates of the Asylum of Charenton Under the Direction of the Marquis de Sade,* most often known simply as *Marat/Sade.*

"Her beautiful face was so calm that one would have said she was a statue," Notelet recalled. "For eight days I was in love with Charlotte Corday."

Suggestions for Further Reading

Dobson, Austin. *Four Frenchwomen.* Freeport, NY: Books for Libraries Press, 1972.

Doyle, William. *The Oxford History of the French Revolution.* Oxford: Clarendon Press, 1989.

Schama, Simon. *Citizens: A Chronicle of the French Revolution.* New York: Alfred A. Knopf, 1989.

Wilson, Robert McNair. *Women of the French Revolution.* Port Washington, NY: Kennikat Press, 1970.

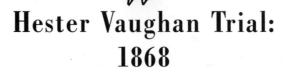

Hester Vaughan Trial: 1868

Defendant: Hester Vaughan
Crime Charged: First-degree murder
Chief Defense Lawyer: John Guforth
Chief Prosecutor: No record
Judge: James Riley Ludlow
Place: Philadelphia, Pennsylvania
Dates of Trial: June 10–July 2, 1868
Verdict: Guilty
Sentence: Death

SIGNIFICANCE: More than a century before the United States Supreme Court ruled that women's systematic exclusion from state juries was unconstitutional, women's rights leaders protested a teenage girl's murder conviction without "a trial by a jury of her peers," that is, without a woman's presence on the jury.

In the middle of the nineteenth century, Hester Vaughan left her native England for the United States to marry her American fiancé. A year and a half later, Vaughan discovered that her husband, Harris, had another wife and family. Then he left her. Too ashamed to return to England, Vaughan took back her family name and moved to Philadelphia, Pennsylvania, where she took a job as a housekeeper. A member of her employer's household raped her and she became pregnant. Shamed once more, she left the household, rented a small room, and took in sewing while she waited for her baby to be born.

What happened next is not entirely clear. However, on February 8 or 9, 1868, Hester Vaughan gave birth. At the time she was poorly nourished and living alone in an unheated room. Two days later, she asked another resident of the building for a box in which to place her dead baby. Vaughan asked the other woman not to tell anyone about her secret. However, Vaughan's neighbor informed the police. Lawmen immediately arrested Vaughan, charging her with murder.

Elizabeth Cady Stanton, first president of the National Woman Suffrage Association, helped raise funds for Hester Vaughan when the teen was convicted of murder in 1868.

Tried for Murder

Hester Vaughan's murder trial began on June 30, 1868. The prosecution called several witnesses to the stand to present the case against her. The *Philadelphia Inquirer* summarized their testimony:

> [Vaughan] explained [to the resident from whom she requested a box] that she had been frightened by a lady going into the room with a cup of coffee, and fallen back upon her child, thus killing it. . . . Dr. Shapleigh [of the Coroner's office, charged with investigating the baby's death], who examined the body, found several fractures of the skull, made apparently with some blunt instrument, and also clots

of blood between the brain and skull. The lady who took the coffee to the prisoner heard the child give one or two faint cries.

The state of Pennsylvania then rested its case against Vaughan. Judge James Riley Ludlow ordered Vaughan's lawyer, John Guforth, to present the defense witnesses the next morning. However, although Vaughan had given Guforth her last few dollars for his fee, he did not even bother to interview her before the trial. All Guforth presented the next day were a few witnesses who testified as to Vaughan's good character. Guforth added little in summing up Vaughan's case for the jury. He said only that, "the prisoner should not be convicted of murder in the first degree, because in the agony and pain she must have suffered, she may have been bereft of all reason." Thus providing an explanation for his failure to call Vaughan herself as a witness, he added only that the baby's death might have been accidental. Not surprisingly, Vaughan was convicted of first-degree murder and sentenced to death.

Women to the Rescue

Two of America's first female doctors took an immediate interest in Vaughan's case. Dr. Susan A. Smith visited Vaughan in Moyamensing prison in Philadelphia. After interviewing the prisoner several times and performing a medical examination, Smith wrote to Pennsylvania Governor John W. Geary. Of Vaughan's pregnancy, labor, and delivery, Smith said:

> [Hester Vaughan] rented a third story room . . .
> from a family who understood very little English.
> . . . She was taken sick in this room at midnight on
> the 6th of February and lingered until Sunday
> morning, the eighth, when her child was born, she
> told me she was nearly frozen and fainted or went
> to sleep for a long time. You will please remember,
> sir, throughout this period of agony she was alone,
> without nourishment or fire. . . . My professional
> opinion in Hester Vaughan's case is that cold and
> want of attention produced painful and protracted

labor—that the mother, in endeavoring to assist herself, injured the head of her child at birth—that she either fainted or had a convulsion, and was insensible for a long time.

Both Smith and another female physician, Clemence Lozier, doubted that anyone had heard the child cry. They believed the baby was born dead.

Governor Geary did not respond to Smith's request that Vaughan be pardoned. Then women's rights leaders Susan B. Anthony and Elizabeth Cady Stanton stepped in, along with members of the Working Women's National Association. They held a meeting at New York City's Cooper Institute to protest Vaughan's conviction. Stanton and Anthony strongly objected to Vaughan's "condemn[ation] on insufficient evidence and with inadequate defense." They also voiced their objections to the nineteenth-century ban on women serving on juries and voting. The crowd in attendance voted unanimously to appeal to Governor Geary for either a pardon or a new trial for Vaughan.

Hester Vaughan Trial: 1868

Women's rights advocate Susan B. Anthony.

WOMEN'S LEGAL RIGHTS

Eight years before Hester Vaughan's trial, one of her supporters, Elizabeth Cady Stanton, had addressed the New York State legislature, urging equal legal rights for women:

> Just imagine an inhabitant of another planet entertaining himself some pleasant evening in searching over our great national compact, our Declaration of Independence, our Constitutions, or some of our statute-books; what would he think of those 'women and Negroes' that must be so fenced in, so guarded against? Why, he would certainly suppose we were monsters, like those fabulous giants or Brobdingnagians of olden times, so dangerous to civilized man, from our size, ferocity, and power. Then let him take up our poets, from Pope down to Dana; let him listen to our Fourth of July toasts, and some of the sentimental adulations of social life, and no logic could convince him that this creature of the law, and this angel of the family altar, could be one and the same being. Man is in such a labyrinth of contradictions with his marital and property rights; he is so befogged on the whole question of maidens, wives, and mothers, that from pure benevolence we should relieve him from this troublesome branch of legislation. We should vote and make laws for ourselves.

Stanton and Anthony continued to broadcast their case to the public, in their travels across the country and in their own newspaper, the *Revolution.* They condemned the male-dominated American society that resulted in a death sentence for a "young, artless, and inexperienced girl." Women responded. They continued to petition the governor to release Vaughan. They even wrote poems about her case.

Finally Governor Geary did pardon Vaughan in the summer of 1869. The one condition of her release was that she return to England, and that her passage be paid with private, rather than state, funds. Stanton and Anthony raised the money. Vaughan's thank-you letter was published in the *Revolution* on August 19, 1869.

Hester Vaughan Trial: 1868

Suggestions for Further Reading

Barry, Kathleen. *Susan B. Anthony.* New York: New York University Press, 1988.

Doten, Lizzie. "Hester Vaughan." *Revolution* (March 25, 1969).

Harper, Ida Husted. *Life and Work of Susan B. Anthony,* Vol. 1, 1898. Reprint. Salem, NH: Ayer Co., Publishers, 1983.

Haymarket Trial: 1886

Defendants: George Engel, Samuel Fielden, Adolph Fischer, Louis Lingg, Oscar Neebe, Albert Parsons, Michael Schwab, and August Spies

Crime Charged: Murder

Chief Defense Lawyers: William P. Black, William A. Foster, Moses Salomon, and Sigismund Zeisler

Chief Prosecutor: Julius S. Grinnell

Judge: Joseph E. Gary

Place: Chicago, Illinois

Dates of Trial: June 21–August 20, 1886

Verdicts: Guilty

Sentences: Death by hanging for all but Neebe, who was sentenced to prison for fifteen years

SIGNIFICANCE: The Haymarket Riot was one of the most famous battles between the growing labor movement and industry and government. It was a serious setback for the unions and their efforts to improve industrial working conditions.

After the Civil War, the number of factories in the United States grew. People became famous for building new industries and businesses. Among them was John D. Rockefeller's Standard Oil, the largest company in the new petroleum industry. Another was Andrew Carnegie's Carnegie Steel (later renamed U.S. Steel). Finally there was Marshall Field, named for its founder, which changed the face of the clothing business. However, most wealthy owners did not want to share the wealth with the workers who made this success possible.

The Relationship between Workers and Employers

In the 1880s, every worker was free to bargain individually with his or her employer over wages, working hours, and conditions. In reality, however, the worker's "right to bargain" was meaningless. New workers from Europe and those just off American farms swelled the labor force. Any worker who complained about wages, hours, or sick leave was easily replaced.

The only way for workers to improve their lives was to band together, to "unionize," so that one group representing the whole workforce could push management to change its positions. Naturally, companies resisted. The relations between the union movement and management became strained and often violent. Because union members saw the government as a friend of big business, many were attracted to a political idea called "anarchism," which wanted to do away with government altogether.

Chicago: Hotbed of Radicalism

By the 1880s, Chicago was one of American's factory centers. Workers, many newly arrived from Europe, were unhappy with their jobs. They joined the labor movement and became anarchists. One of the most outspoken members of the movement was August Spies, the editor of a German-language newspaper.

In 1886, most businesses insisted on a ten-hour workday. Even longer shifts were common. Labor demanded that management reduce the workday to eight hours, while keeping the daily wage the same. On May 1, the great labor holiday, unions staged nationwide protests in favor of the eight-hour workday. Two days later, on May 3, Spies spoke before the striking workers at the McCormick farm machinery works. Fights broke out between the strikers and "scab" workers hired to replace them. The police broke up the fights by firing into the crowd and killing two and wounding many others.

Spies told of this incident in his newspaper, calling for a rally the next day in Chicago's Haymarket Square to protest police brutality. At first the meeting was peaceful. Chicago's Mayor, Carter Harrison, showed up briefly to stand before the working-class voters. The situation became violent after Spies spoke to the crowd and Harrison left. Two of Spies's fellow anarchists, Samuel Fielden and Albert Parsons, gave speeches, blasting business, government, and the Chicago police.

Chicago police captain John Bonfield ordered the 200 officers to advance towards the crowd. Suddenly, someone in the crowd threw a bomb made of dynamite at the police. The explosion killed eight officers and wounded sixty-seven others. Furious, the police struck back, firing into the crowd and killing or wounding dozens of people.

Police Arrest Eight Anarchists

The fighting between the police and labor caused the loss of life following the May Day rallies. After the Haymarket bomb explosion, however, the public blamed labor. A major Chicago newspaper ran the headline "NOW IT IS BLOOD!" Other papers copied it, fanning public fears.

Despite widespread searches and raids on working-class neighborhoods, the police never found the bomber. Prosecutor Julius S. Grinnell, charged with finding those responsible for the Haymarket disaster, needed

Police, U.S. military soldiers, and firefighters try to control the turmoil brought on by the Haymarket riots.

people to charge. The police began arresting anarchists and labor leaders. Among them were Samuel Fielden, Michael Schwab, and August Spies. Grinnell supported the arrests. Encouraged, the police arrested five more labor anarchists: George Engel, Adolph Fischer, Louis Lingg, Oscar Neebe, and Albert Parsons. On May 27, 1886, all eight faced murder charges.

The Trial

Because of the public outcry, at first the defendants had trouble finding lawyers who were willing to represent them. Eventually, however, experienced lawyers joined the defense team, and the trial began on June 21, 1886.

Jury selection took three weeks. A total of 981 potential jurors were questioned until twelve were finally selected. There have been accusations that Judge Joseph E. Gary attempted to make sure that the jury favored the prosecution. In any event, none of the twelve finally chosen worked in a factory; they were not expected to sympathize with the union movement, which was the real subject of the trial.

Poster asking for workers to attend a meeting following the previous day's violence at the Haymarket riots.

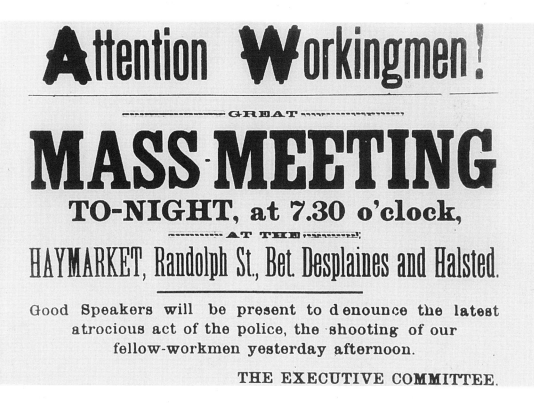

MURDER

"I WENT TO WORK TO ORGANIZE THEM . . . "

The defendant Oscar Neebe was the first to address the court after the verdict was handed down. He spoke passionately of the "crime" he had committed: "I saw that the bakers in this city were treated like dogs. . . . I helped organize them. That is a great crime. The men are now working ten hours a day instead of fourteen and sixteen hours. . . . That is another crime. And I committed a greater crime than that. I saw in the morning when I drove away with my team that the beer brewers of the city of Chicago went to work at four o'clock in the morning. They came at home at seven or eight o'clock at night. They never saw their families or their children by daylight. . . . I went to work to organize them. . . . And, your Honor, I committed another crime. I saw the grocery clerks and other clerks of this city worked until ten and eleven o'clock in the evening. I issued a call . . . and today they are only working until seven o'clock in the evening and no Sunday work. That is a great crime . . . ."

Prosecutor Grinnell tried to prove that the defendants had conspired to attack the police during the Haymarket rally and to overthrow all government authority. He called several witnesses, but all of them gave poor testimony. They were only able to testify that the defendants had at different times made pro-anarchist and pro-union statements. Such statements did not prove conspiracy or murder. Judge Gary ruled, however, that if the jury believed the defendants were guilty beyond a reasonable doubt of conspiring to attack the police or overthrow the government, they could also find the defendants guilty of murder. Also, the jury merely had to find beyond a reasonable doubt that the defendants had arranged for someone to throw the bomb. According to his instructions to the jury, it did not matter that no one had found the bomb-thrower.

Judge Gary's explanation of the law resulted, on August 20, 1886, in a guilty verdict for all eight defendants. All but Neebe, who received fifteen years in jail, were sentenced to death. The public and press applauded, and most newspapers carried glowing accounts of Grinnell. Despite the efforts of various groups—who were assisted by a young but soon-to-be-famous lawyer named Clarence Darrow—the Illinois Supreme Court upheld the death sentence. A final appeal to the U.S. Supreme Court was also unsuccessful.

Suicide, Hanging, and Pardons

Lingg committed suicide before his scheduled execution. On November 11, 1887, Engel, Fischer, Parsons, and Spies were hanged. Fielden, Neebe, and Schwab sat in jail, Neebe serving out his sentence and the others awaiting execution. Their stay in prison lasted for years. On June 26, 1893, John Peter Altgeld became governor of Illinois. He pardoned the remaining Haymarket defendants. The three left prison as free men.

The Haymarket Riot began with one political conflict and ended with another. Altgeld's pardon harmed his reputation, and he lost the next election for governor. Nevertheless, his pardon strengthened labor's claim that the trial had been unfair from start to finish and that Judge Gary had been biased.

Suggestions for Further Reading

Avrich, Paul. *The Haymarket Tragedy.* Princeton, NJ: Princeton University Press, 1984.

Foner, Philip S. *The Autobiography of the Haymarket Martyrs.* New York: Anchor Foundation, 1978.

Haymarket Remembered Project Staff. *Mob Action Against the State: The Haymarket Remembered. . . . An Anarchist Convention.* Seattle: Left Bank Books, 1987.

Roediger, David and Franklin Rosemont, eds. *Haymarket Scrapbook: A Centennial Anthology.* Chicago: C. H. Kerr, 1986.

Harry Thaw Trials: 1907–1908

Defendant: Harry Kendall Thaw

Crime Charged: Murder

Chief Defense Lawyers: First trial: Delphin M. Delmas, John B. Gleason, Clifford Hartridge, Hugh McPike, and George Peabody; second trial: Martin W. Littleton, Daniel O'Reilly, and Russell Peabody

Chief Prosecutor: William Travers Jerome

Judge: First trial: James Fitzgerald; second trial: Victor J. Dowling

Place: New York, New York

Dates of Trials: First trial: January 23–April 12, 1907; second trial: January 6–February 1, 1908

Verdict: First trial: none, jury deadlocked; second trial: not guilty by reason of insanity

SIGNIFICANCE: Harry Thaw married the glamorous performer Evelyn Nesbit, who had previously been the mistress of the famous architect Stanford White. Thaw shot White during a public performance in Madison Square Garden and later stood trial for murder. Thaw's attorneys took the insanity defense to murder to new extremes. They successfully argued that Thaw suffered from a condition supposedly unique to American men that caused Thaw to develop an uncontrollable desire to kill White after he learned of White's earlier relationship with Nesbit.

Harry Thaw was born in 1872 into a family of wealthy Pennsylvania industrialists. His father made a fortune estimated at $40 million in the Pittsburgh steel business and had also invested heavily in the Pennsylvania Railroad. Thaw's mother spoiled him when he was young and pampered him throughout his life—with tragic consequences.

As a young man, Thaw went to Harvard University, but the school expelled him for playing poker. Thaw's mother provided him with a large allowance and paid off the large gambling debts that he acquired after moving to New York City. Thaw also had a taste for activities even more damaging than gambling. In New York, he developed the habit of physically abusing prostitutes. Although Thaw had several run-ins with the police, his family's money always bought his release.

Evelyn Nesbit

Evelyn Nesbit's background in Pittsburgh was far more modest than Thaw's. Nesbit's parents were poor and could never provide for their daughter's education. Nesbit was beautiful, however, and from an early age she also showed some skill as a singer and dancer. Her family came to rely on the money she earned in New York City as a model and in the theater. Within a short time, Nesbit's career soared, and she became a "Floradora girl," joining the famous all-woman Floradora chorus.

During a performance of the chorus, Nesbit attracted the attention of architect Stanford White. White had made a fortune designing homes for wealthy New Yorkers and had also designed several famous buildings, including Madison Square Garden. White kept private rooms for himself in the Garden's tower. Evelyn Nesbit began to visit White at his apartment and became his mistress; their affair lasted for three years. Nesbit later testified at trial that at one point in their relationship, White got her drunk and assaulted her after she passed out.

Nesbit Marries Thaw

Nesbit left White early in 1905 for Thaw, who, like White, began pursuing Nesbit after he saw her on stage. Whether out of love or a desire for another wealthy supporter, Nesbit married Thaw on April 4, 1905. Thaw took Nesbit to Europe for their honeymoon and reportedly began to abuse her. He became obsessed with Nesbit's earlier relationship with White. Thaw became convinced that he had to avenge Nesbit's humiliation and rid the world of a human monster, Stanford White.

Courtroom Drama

On June 25, 1906, Thaw acted on his obsessions. At Madison Square Garden, where the Thaws were attending the performance of a new musical, Thaw spotted White. Thaw charged up to White's table and pulled out a pistol, then shot White several times while hundreds of people watched in horror. Thaw made no attempt to resist arrest by police officers who rushed to the Garden.

Thaw Is Tried for Murder

Upon learning of his arrest, Thaw's mother rushed to his defense. Declaring that she would spend the family's $40-million fortune to set Thaw free, she paid to have her son represented by one of the most famous lawyers of the age, Delphin Delmas. He brought four other attorneys with him to assist in Thaw's defense. When the trial opened January 23, 1907, however, Delmas played the main role in defending Thaw.

The prosecutor was William Travers Jerome, New York's district attorney, who had once served as a judge and was said to want to become governor. Jerome knew that the press would closely follow Thaw's trial. As *The New York Times* reported, "The Thaw trial is being reported to the ends of the civilized globe."

Thaw wanted to save himself from the electric chair, which was the penalty for murder. He also wanted to avoid spending the rest of his life in an insane asylum—the other penalty he might receive if found guilty. Therefore, Delmas conducted the defense with the aim of proving that Thaw was and always had been sane except for one day: June 25, 1906. On that day, Delmas claimed Thaw temporarily went insane and shot White. Delmas used Nesbit's beauty to appeal to the jury's emotions. He also called Nesbit to the stand and asked her to describe the events of the night on which White assaulted her.

Prosecutor Jerome, who had produced many eyewitnesses testifying that Thaw shot White at point-blank range, watched in frustration while Delmas put White's treatment of Nesbit on trial. Delmas then introduced the defense's argument of temporary insanity by asking Nesbit about Thaw's reaction upon learning about the assault incident. Delmas and Nesbit both carefully avoided the subject of Thaw's own tendency towards physical violence. Nesbit's acting experience combined with Delmas's legal ability to present a picture of a young, pretty, and innocent girl telling the story of her disgrace to her husband, who then flew into a murderous fury: "He would get up and walk up and down the room a minute and then come and sit down and say, 'Oh, God! Oh, God!' and bite his nails like that and keep sobbing."

Harry Thaw Trials: 1907–1908

OPPOSITE PAGE

Brought to trial for the murder of architect Stanford White, Harry Thaw was found not guilty by reason of insanity at his second trial.

In his closing argument, Delmas hammered the argument home to the jury:

> And if Thaw is insane, it is with a species of insanity known from the Canadian border to the Gulf. If you expert gentlemen ask me to give it a name, I suggest that you label it Dementia Americana. It is that species of insanity that inspires of every American to believe his home is sacred. It is that species of insanity that persuades an American that whoever violates the sanctity of his home or the purity of his wife or daughter has forfeited the protection of the laws of this state or any other state.

Judge James Fitzgerald reminded the jury that they could only find Thaw not guilty by reason of insanity if Thaw could not understand at the time of the murder that his actions were wrong. On April 12, 1907, the jury reported that it could not reach a verdict. Judge Fitzgerald adjourned the court until Thaw could be retried.

Thaw Is Found Insane

Thaw's second trial began January 6, 1908. Although Jerome was still the prosecutor, Thaw had a new team of defense lawyers: Martin W. Littleton, Daniel O'Reilly, and Russell Peabody. Further, Judge Victor J. Dowling had replaced Judge Fitzgerald. The same witnesses, including Nesbit, testified as in the first trial. Neither Jerome nor the defense team, however, fought as hard over the issue of temporary insanity as they had during the first trial. Perhaps both sides had decided that they would be content with a verdict of not guilty by reason of insanity, which would put Thaw in a mental institution but prevent his execution. On February 1, 1908, after a trial that lasted less than four weeks, the jury found Thaw not guilty by reason of insanity.

After the jury handed down its verdict, Judge Dowling sent Thaw to the Asylum for the Criminally Insane at Matteawan, New York. Thaw's trials had taken the insanity defense to a murder charge to new heights. The publicity surrounding Nesbit and her testimony eventually led to the making of a movie.

Thaw divorced Nesbit in 1915 and spent the rest of his life in and out of insane asylums and the courts. He escaped from Matteawan and

RENAISSANCE ORNAMENT AND INTERIOR DESIGN

Stanford White, whom Harry Thaw killed, was one of the most influential American architects of his time. In 1879, he began a partnership with Charles Follen McKim and William R. Mead. Together they created a firm whose works changed the shape of New York City, designing many new buildings in the classical style. White's specialties were interior design, furnishing, and the decorative aspects of a building, particularly Renaissance ornament. Perhaps his best-known work is the Arch in Washington Square Park. White also designed the Century Club, while his firm was responsible for the Boston Public Library, and, in New York, the Harvard Club and the Pierpont Morgan Library.

fled to Canada, but the Canadian authorities sent him back to New York. Briefly freed from the asylums by the lawyers paid for by his mother, Thaw was arrested in 1917 for kidnapping and whipping nineteen-year-old Frederick Gump nearly to death. Mother Thaw arranged for her son to go to a Pennsylvania insane asylum, where he stayed until 1924. After 1924, he appeared from time to time in the news, in connection with his involvement in wild parties or lawsuits by performers claiming that Thaw had beaten and whipped them. Thaw died February 22, 1947, at the age of seventy-six.

Suggestions for Further Reading

Abramson, Phyllis L. *Sob Sister Journalism.* New York: Greenwood Press, 1990.

Hodge, Clifford M. "The Benefactor at Dorr's Pond." *Yankee* (December 1986): 154.

Lessard, Suzannah. *The Architect of Desire: Beauty and Danger in the Stanford White Family.* New York: Dial Press, 1996.

Nesbit, Evelyn. "Beauty as Evidence." *Life* (June 1981): 10–13.

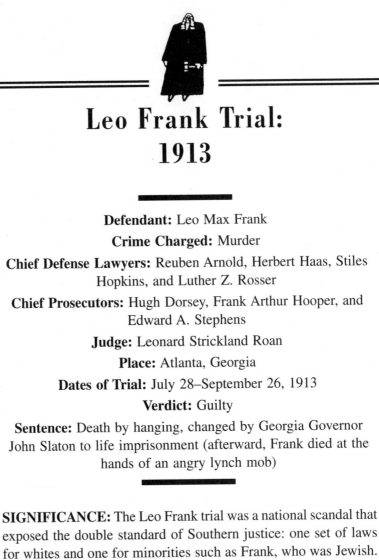

Leo Frank Trial: 1913

Defendant: Leo Max Frank

Crime Charged: Murder

Chief Defense Lawyers: Reuben Arnold, Herbert Haas, Stiles Hopkins, and Luther Z. Rosser

Chief Prosecutors: Hugh Dorsey, Frank Arthur Hooper, and Edward A. Stephens

Judge: Leonard Strickland Roan

Place: Atlanta, Georgia

Dates of Trial: July 28–September 26, 1913

Verdict: Guilty

Sentence: Death by hanging, changed by Georgia Governor John Slaton to life imprisonment (afterward, Frank died at the hands of an angry lynch mob)

SIGNIFICANCE: The Leo Frank trial was a national scandal that exposed the double standard of Southern justice: one set of laws for whites and one for minorities such as Frank, who was Jewish. Not only was Frank hung by a lynch mob, but his lynching seemed to have helped the racist organization the Ku Klux Klan, which experienced an increase in membership for years afterward.

Leo Max Frank was born in Paris, Texas, in 1884. His family moved to Brooklyn, New York, while he was still a baby. Frank's family was Jewish, and he grew up in New York City's large Jewish community. He was a quiet, shy man, but he had great mechanical ability, and he graduated from Cornell University with an engineering degree. After working for

After Leo Frank's sentence was commuted to life imprisonment, some people who disagreed hung a dummy representing Governor John Slaton as "King of the Jews."

brief periods with several companies, Frank went to work for his uncle, Moses Frank, who was the primary owner of the National Pencil Company. In 1907, when Frank became superintendent, he moved to the company's Atlanta location.

It probably never occurred to Frank that bigotry (prejudice) might be a problem in the South. Atlanta's Jewish community was small by New York standards, but it was still significant and had deep roots in the city's history. In 1911, Frank married Lucile Selig, whose family was also Jewish. Frank spent most of his time supervising the pencil factory, avoided politics and racial issues, and was honored by the Jewish community as one of Atlanta's most promising young businessmen. By 1913 Frank was one of Atlanta's leading citizens and was enjoying a successful career.

Little Mary Phagan Murdered

As was common at the time, Frank's factory employed women and children—both of whom were paid lower wages than men—to perform the light work involved in manufacturing pencils. One such worker was Mary Phagan, a thirteen-year-old girl who lived in the nearby city of Marietta. When she was laid off on April 26, 1913, she went to collect her final paycheck from Frank, who paid her and thought no more of the matter after she left. Shortly before he left for the day, he met another former employee, John Gantt, who asked if he could get some shoes he had left in his locker. Frank allowed Gantt to get his shoes.

Frank's nervous personality made him fear Gantt, who had a reputation as a drunkard and whom Frank had fired for stealing. That night, Frank called the night guard, an African American named Newt Lee, several times to ask if there was any trouble. Frank probably feared some sort of trouble from Gantt, but there was none. In the early hours of the morning, however, Lee discovered Phagan dead in the basement. Someone had raped and killed her after she collected her pay the day before. Afraid that he would be blamed for the crime, Lee went straight to the police and reported the crime. His honesty did him no good: after the police arrived at the factory and investigated the scene of the crime, they threw Lee in jail, holding him without charges for months.

The police then went to Frank's house, took him to the scene of the crime for questioning, and then to the police station for several days of further interrogation. Meanwhile, the murder became public, and the Atlanta newspapers were filled with shocking headlines describing the details of the crime and calling for justice. Hugh Mason Dorsey, the chief prosecutor for that section of Atlanta, had political ambitions that a victory in such a highly publicized case might boost. Dorsey focused on the shy Frank, who was an easy target. On April 29, 1913, police arrested Frank for the murder of Mary Phagan.

Prosecutors Emphasize Frank's Nervousness

When the trial began on July 28, 1913, Newt Lee, still in prison "under suspicion," was one of the first witnesses. Frank's telephone calls to Lee on the night of the murder came back to haunt him. The prosecutors made it look as if Frank had been checking to see if the body had been found that Saturday night. The government lawyers then turned Frank's nervous personality to their advantage. They used the testimony of the police officers who had taken Frank to the scene of the crime on Sunday, April 27, to create suspicion in the mind of the jury. They sought to reason that Frank's nervousness was the result of a guilty conscience.

Next, the lawyers tried to prove that Frank had deliberately planned to get Phagan to come to the factory that weekend. A factory employee named Helen Ferguson testified that she had been Phagan's friend and had in the past picked up her pay for her. However, on the day before the murder, Ferguson said, Frank refused to let Ferguson pick up Phagan's final check:

> [I went to] **Mr. Frank on Friday, April 25, about
> seven o'clock in the evening and asked for Mary**

Phagan's money. Mr. Frank said, 'I can't let you have it,' and before he said anything else I turned around and walked out. I had gotten Mary's money before. . . .

Prosecution Clinches Case

The government lawyers saved their best witness for last: Jim Conley, an African American who was the factory janitor. Despite some suspicion that Conley might be the actual murderer, the government put him on the stand. It has even been written that Dorsey chose to prosecute a Yankee Jew rather than an African American for purposes of sensationalism, regardless of Frank's innocence. The point of Conley's testimony was that he had been at the factory on the day of the murder and that Frank had confessed to it. The defense lawyers cross-examined Conley for several days but were unable to shake his testimony. Either Conley was a superb liar or the lawyers had coached him about what to say. The defense lawyers also had to deal with spectators in the courtroom who constantly yelled out racist comments—such as "Hang the Jew!"—while the defense attempted to make its case. Although Judge Leonard Roan had once been defense lawyer Luther Rosser's legal partner, he made no serious effort to stop these distractions.

At the conclusion of the defense's case, Frank himself took the stand. For nearly half a day he spoke, and he consistently denied murdering Phagan. He explained his nervousness as the natural result of being dragged out of his home so early on a Sunday morning to learn of the shocking crime. Further, Frank bluntly called Conley a liar. His testimony was of no avail.

Frank Convicted, Commuted, and Lynched

On September 26, 1913, after one of the longest trials in Georgia history, the jury found Leo Frank guilty of the murder of Mary Phagan. Judge Roan sentenced Frank to hang on October 10, but the defense appealed. On February 17, 1914, the Georgia Supreme Court upheld (agreed with) Frank's conviction. The defense lawyers, however, did not give up. They pursued evidence that Conley had committed the murder. Witnesses had seen Conley washing his bloody clothing at the factory after the murder. Conley's girlfriend gave evidence concerning Conley's abnormal sexual tendencies, and Conley's own lawyer told Judge Roan that Conley had confessed to the murder to him.

MURDER

THE KU KLUX KLAN

The Leo Frank case gave a new prominence to the Ku Klux Klan, which experienced a huge growth in membership in the 1910s and 1920s. The Klan had its first meeting in Nashville, Tennessee, in April 1867, in response to the growing political power of African Americans after the Civil War had ended slavery and Reconstruction (period of rebuilding following the end of the Civil War) guaranteed their voting rights. The group was organized by former military and political leaders of the Confederacy (group of Southern states during the Civil War) as well as by religious leaders. Originally, the Klansman spoke of themselves as the ghosts of dead Confederate soldiers, which led to their wearing white sheets. At a time when many former participants in the Confederacy had been stripped of their political power, the Klan attempted to regain that power through sheer terror: beatings, burnings, and lynchings. The Klan declined after 1873, when Northern troops left the South and African Americans could be suppressed through new laws, known as Jim Crow laws. However, it revived during World War I, when the poverty and anti-foreign feeling of the era made the Klan's tactics attractive to a new generation. At this point, the Klan expanded its targets to include Jews, Catholics, and the foreign-born as well as African Americans, and membership spread through the Midwest as well as the South. By 1924, the "new" Klan had from four to five million members.

Despite the evidence of Conley's guilt, Judge Roan refused to overturn the verdict against Frank, which the Georgia Supreme Court reaffirmed (let stand) on October 14, 1914. Frank's scheduled execution moved to January 22, 1915. However, his defense lawyers delayed it again by asking the U.S. Supreme Court for a writ of *habeas corpus* (release from unlawful imprisonment). On April 19, 1915, the court denied the petition.

Frank's last chance was an appeal to the governor of Georgia, John Slaton, for a reduction of his sentence. This appeal began with a hearing on May 31, 1915, before the Georgia Prison Commission. On June 9,

1915, the Commission voted 2–1 against recommending a change in sentence to the governor. Slaton, however, was an independent man and had on several occasions used his power to grant clemency, freeing prisoners when in his opinion justice demanded it, regardless of the unpopularity of his decision. On June 21, 1915, Slaton reduced Frank's sentence to life imprisonment, citing the widespread national criticism of Georgia justice and the many doubts raised about the evidence in the case.

Many in Georgia instantly condemned Slaton's decision. There were demonstrations in Atlanta and in Marietta, Phagan's home town; some people attacked Jewish homes and stores. On August 16, 1915, a vigilante group (people seeking justice on their own without legal authority) drove from Marietta to the Milledgeville Prison Farm outside Macon, Georgia. They overpowered the small crew of prison guards, and took Frank from his cell. The vigilantes then drove back to Marietta, a seven-hour trip, with Frank. In Marietta, a lynch mob of local citizens gathered and watched as Frank was hung from a tree limb on the morning of August 17, 1915.

The racist hatred stirred up by the Frank trial did not end with Frank's lynching. For decades, the Phagan case served as a rallying cry for the white supremacist Ku Klux Klan, which targeted Jews as well as blacks.

In 1982, an old man named Alonzo Mann, who had worked at Frank's pencil factory as a child, publicly declared that he had seen Conley drag Phagan's corpse to the basement. He had kept silent because Conley had threatened to kill him. On March 11, 1986, the Georgia State Board of Pardons and Paroles officially pardoned Frank. The Leo Frank trial had been a national scandal and demonstrated how Southern justice could be a double standard when applied to an unpopular minority.

Suggestions for Further Reading

Dinnerstein, Leonard. *The Leo Frank Case.* Athens: University of Georgia Press, 1987.

Liebman, James S. "Lesson Unlearned." *The Nation* (August 1991): 217.

Lindemann, Albert S. *The Jew Accused: Three Anti-Semitic Affairs (Dreyfus, Beilis, Frank), 1894–1915.* New York: Cambridge University Press, 1991.

Oney, Steve. "The Lynching of Leo Frank; Two Years Ago, and Seventy Years Too Late, a Witness Came Forward to Prove That Frank's Only Crime was Being a Stranger in the Old South." *Esquire* (September 1985): 90–98.

Phagan, Mary. *The Murder of Little Mary Phagan.* Far Hills, NJ: New Horizon Press, 1987.

Sacco-Vanzetti Trial: 1921

Defendants: Nicola Sacco and Bartolomeo Vanzetti

Crime Charged: Murder

Chief Defense Lawyers: William J. Callahan, Herbert B. Ehrmann, James M. Graham, Arthur Dehon Hill, Jeremiah J. McAnarney, Thomas F. McAnarney, Fred H. Moore, Michael Angelo Musmanno, William G. Thompson, and John P. Vahey

Chief Prosecutors: Frederick Gunn Katzmann, Donald P. Ramsey, and Harold P. Williams

Judge: Webster Thayer

Place: Dedham, Massachusetts

Dates of Trial: May 31–July 14, 1921

Verdicts: Guilty

Sentences: Death

SIGNIFICANCE: The Sacco-Vanzetti case began as a simple trial for murder. It ended as an international cause because the world believed that Massachusetts had executed two innocent men for their radical political views. A study of the trial and its consequences provides a superb lesson in how myths are made.

On the afternoon of April 15, 1920, a shoe manufacturer's paymaster (a person assigned to pay employees), Frederick Parmenter, and his guard, Alessandro Berardelli, were carrying a $15,777 cash payroll in South Braintree, Massachusetts. Two armed men shot and killed them. Seizing the money, the men jumped into a car filled with other men and sped away. Eyewitnesses thought the murderers looked Italian.

At the time, police were investigating a holdup attempted in nearby Bridgewater on the previous Christmas Eve. A group of Italians with a car seemed to be the robbers. Police Chief Michael E. Stewart suspected Mike Boda, whose car was now awaiting repairs in Simon Johnson's garage. Stewart told Johnson to call the police when anyone came to get Boda's car.

The Transportation of Red Literature

Stewart also was busy rounding up foreigners who were Communists. After raids made by the U.S. Departments of Labor and Justice, the United States deported many such individuals. In May, a prisoner holding radical political beliefs fell from the fourteenth floor of the New York City Department of Justice. He died on the pavement below. His friends, including Boda, decided they had better hide a large quantity of "Red" (Communist) literature. To move it, they needed Boda's car.

Boda and three others appeared at Johnson's garage. Mrs. Johnson called the police. Johnson refused to hand over the car because it had out-of-date license plates. Boda and another man then left on a motorcycle. The other two boarded a street car. The last two, Nicola Sacco and Bartolomeo Vanzetti, were arrested moments later. Sacco carried a .32-caliber pistol loaded with nine bullets and had twenty-three additional bullets in his pocket. Vanzetti had a fully loaded .38-caliber revolver and four twelve-gauge shotgun shells. Also found on Sacco was a notice, in Italian, of a forthcoming meeting at which Vanzetti was to speak on "the struggle for existence." The two men were active anarchists (those who believe that society can only be truly free if it does not have an organized government).

Anarchists Convicted

Questioned by district attorney Frederick Gunn Katzmann, Sacco said he had bought the gun two years earlier for $16 or $17 and had bought a new box of cartridges. Vanzetti said his gun had cost $18 or $19 four or five years earlier. Neither gun was licensed.

Vanzetti's shotgun shells made him a suspect in the failed holdup on Christmas Eve, when a twelve-gauge shotgun was fired. His alibi (excuse) was that, as a fish peddler, he had spent a busy Christmas Eve selling eels for traditional Italian dinners that night. At his trial, several witnesses identified him as the man with the shotgun at the Bridgewater holdup. He did not take the stand to answer this claim and was convicted

Bartolomeo Vanzetti (left) and Nicola Sacco on the day of their sentencing.

and sentenced to twelve to fifteen years in prison. Sacco had a solid alibi: he had been on the job in a shoe factory when the attempted robbery occurred. However, police held him for trial in the South Braintree murders, for on April 15 he had taken the day off.

Defense Committee Organized

Anarchist friends organized the Sacco-Vanzetti Defense Committee. For three months it collected money. Then the committee hired Fred H.

S a c c o -
V a n z e t t i
T r i a l : 1 9 2 1

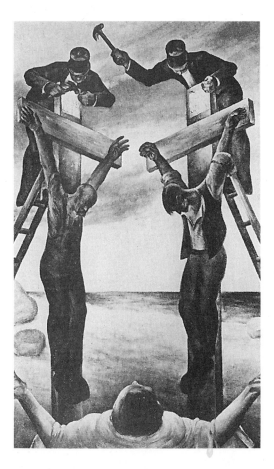

Many people felt that Sacco and Vanzetti were arrested and convicted because they were radicals. This newspaper cartoon depicts them being crucified, like Jesus. The man below represents the people, asking "Why?"

Moore, a left-wing labor lawyer from California. Moore, experienced in handling cases for unpopular political radicals, saw the Sacco-Vanzetti case as a cause. "In saving them," he said, "we strengthen our muscles, develop our forces preparatory to the day when we save ourselves."

Moore spent a busy year writing, traveling, and organizing volunteers. Labor unions such as the United Mine Workers, the Amalgamated Clothing Workers, and the American Federation of Teamsters, as well as the American Civil Liberties Union, were among the many organizations that helped him. Pamphlets protesting the innocence of Sacco and Vanzetti were printed in batches of 50,000. Publicity notices were sent every week to 500 newspapers. In all this literature, the murder charge was depicted as "a mere device to get them [Sacco and Vanzetti] out of the way."

Outdated Bullets and a Cap

Opening May 31, 1921, the trial had revealed that Sacco lied about his gun. It was several years old, and his box of "new" cartridges contained a mixture of old bullets that were all outdated. The bullet that killed Berardelli was so old that the prosecution could locate none like it with which to test Sacco's gun—except the equally outdated bullets taken from Sacco's pocket.

Vanzetti, too, had lied. Although he said he paid $18 or $19 for his gun, the jury learned that it cost $5. Vanzetti had said he bought a new box of cartridges and threw it away when only six bullets were left, which he put in the revolver. However, Vanzetti's gun held only five bullets, and the ones found in it were not all the same make. Further, Vanzetti's nickel-plated pistol was identical to the one that had belonged to the murdered guard, whose gun could not be found after the crime.

Then there was the cap found beside the dead guard. It was not his. Sacco's employer testified that it looked like a cap that Sacco regularly wore. When the government lawyer asked Sacco to put the cap on, the defendant pulled it down over his ears in an attempt to prove it was too big. He threw the courtroom into giggling hysterics. However, the state also introduced as evidence a cap of exactly the same size that had been taken from Sacco's home.

Trial for Murder, Nothing Else

Before the trial opened, Judge Webster Thayer had told the lawyers on both sides that he saw no reason to bring up the issue of anarchism. No one mentioned it during the prosecution's entire presentation to the jury. On the twenty-ninth day, however, Vanzetti himself brought up the question of the defendants' politics. Under direct examination by his attorney, Jeremiah J. McAnarney, Vanzetti explained why the four men sought Boda's car: "We were going to take the automobile for to carry books and newspapers," he said. Why hadn't he told the police that when he was arrested? "Because there was the deportation and the reaction was more vivid than now and more mad than now." In other words, his defense was that he lied out of fear of being expelled from the country because of his radicalism.

Under Massachusetts law, since the defense had brought up the issue, the door was now open for prosecutor Katzmann to cross-examine Vanzetti about all his radical activities. But the jury heard no such questions. "Neither is Radicalism being tried here," the prosecutor told them. "This is a charge of murder and it is nothing else."

Next, Sacco explained that he, too, lied when he was arrested because he feared deportation on a radical charge. And he explained another lie. Upon his arrest, he had said that he was at work all day April 15. Now his boss testified that Sacco had taken that day off to see the Italian consul in Boston about a passport for a trip to Italy. The clerk in the counsel's office testified that Sacco was there at about 2:00 P.M. on April 15, but the alibi was weak: Sacco had been turned down immediately because the passport photo he offered was too large. The jury was told that Sacco had spent an entire day in Boston. (Several witnesses for the defense testified to having seen him there in the morning, at lunch, and in the afternoon.) However, his business at the consulate had taken only ten minutes. Then Sacco noticed a spectator in the courtroom whom he had seen on the late afternoon train home. Sworn as a witness, the man could not remember seeing Sacco but was certain he had been on the train Sacco described.

As with Vanzetti, prosecutor Katzmann refrained from asking any questions that might have led the jury to consider Sacco a dangerous radical.

Bullets Convince Jury

At 3:00 P.M. on July 14, the jury retired. It immediately voted 10–2 to convict both defendants. "Then," said one juror afterward, "[w]e started discussing things, reviewed the very important evidence about the bullets, and everybody had a chance to speak his piece. There was never any argument, though. We just were convinced Sacco and Vanzetti had done what the prosecution had charged them with."

Asked later what evidence impressed him most, another juror said, "The bullets, of course. That testimony and evidence on it sticks in your mind. You can't depend on the witnesses. But the bullets, there was no getting around that evidence."

The guilty verdict brought fierce reactions around the world. American consulates and embassies in Europe and South America were flooded with letters of protest. The *Communist International* newspaper urged all Communists, Socialists, anarchists, and trade union supporters to join together to rescue Sacco and Vanzetti. Demonstrations took place in France, Italy, Switzerland, Belgium, Spain, Portugal, and Scandinavia. It took 10,000 police and 18,000 troops to hold back the crowd surrounding the American embassy in Paris. Bombs exploded in that embassy and in other areas around the world. One destroyed the home of one of the jurors. Judge Thayer's house was put under guard.

Vehement Appeals Follow

Over the next six years, people debated over the convicted men's guilt or innocence. Repeated requests for a new trial were rejected. So-called experts examined the pistols, took them apart, and put them back together incorrectly. Radical leader Elizabeth Gurley Flynn raised $25,000 in two days to pay the legal fee of Harvard Law School lecturer and political insider William G. Thompson, who replaced Moore, the radical outsider, as defense lawyer. Imprisoned criminals volunteered confessions.

In 1926, with "Sacco-Vanzetti" a worldwide battle cry, the Massachusetts Supreme Judicial Court, the state's highest tribunal, rejected an appeal. The International Labor Defense (ILD), set up by the Communists, received only some $6,000 of the millions raised in the names of Sacco and Vanzetti. Harvard law professor Felix Frankfurter (later to serve as a justice on the U.S. Supreme Court), in a magazine article, attacked the jury, witnesses, verdict, and judiciary. The state's supreme court, having already rejected Thompson's appeal, now upheld the judge. He had committed no errors of law or abuses of power.

Lowell Committee Reviews Case

In June 1927, on Thompson's urging, Massachusetts Governor Alvan T. Fuller, who was considering an appeal for mercy, appointed an advisory committee headed by Harvard president Abbott Lawrence Lowell to review the entire case. After two months, and after himself interviewing 102 witnesses in addition to those who testified at the trial, he agreed with the Lowell Committee's conclusion: Sacco and Vanzetti had received a fair trial and were guilty.

Worldwide protests grew more violent. A London demonstration injured forty people. Paris, Berlin, Warsaw, Buenos Aires, and countless other cities experienced riots. Picketers before the State House in Boston, including novelists John Dos Passos and Katherine Anne Porter, humorist Dorothy Parker, and poet Edna St. Vincent Millay, were arrested. All Boston buildings that were open to the public were heavily policed, and for the first time in memory no meetings were permitted to take place on Boston Common. Newspaper columnist Heywood Broun found his column removed from the New York *World* because of his violent comments about Lowell.

By now, Judge Thayer had denied a half-dozen requests for a new trial, the state superior trial court had denied another, and the state supreme judicial court had turned down four appeals. Several petitions requesting the prisoners' release, extensions of time, and delays of execution were denied by the Circuit Court of Appeals for the First Circuit of the United States and by U.S. Supreme Court justices Oliver Wendell Holmes and Harlan F. Stone.

DISSENT OVER THE SACCO-VANZETTI CASE

After the Sacco-Vanzetti trial was over, new information came to light about the government's role in it. Felix Frankfurter cited two affidavits (sworn legal statements), by Lawrence Letherman, head of the Justice Department's Boston office, and Fred J. Weyand, special department agent, both claiming that the Justice Department did not believe in Sacco and Vanzetti's guilt, but rather was trying to deport them for radical activities. Letherman said under oath that "The Department . . . was anxious to get sufficient evidence against Sacco and Vanzetti to deport them but never succeeded. . . . It was the opinion of the Department agents here that a conviction . . . for murder would be one way of disposing of these men. It was also the general opinion of such agents in Boston as had any knowledge of the . . . case, that Sacco and Vanzetti had nothing to do with the South Braintree crime. My opinion, and the opinion of most of the older men in Government service, has always been that the South Braintree crime was the work of professionals." This opinion was corroborated (confirmed by another person) in 1925, when Celestino F. Madeiros, under death sentence for killing a cashier in a bank robbery, sent Sacco a note confessing to the South Braintree crime. Madeiros's confession ended his own chances for appeal, but, he explained, "I seen Sacco's wife come here with the kids, and I felt sorry for the kids."

Sacco and Vanzetti were executed August 23, 1927. In 1977, their names were officially "cleared" when Massachusetts governor Michael Dukakis signed a special decree.

Suggestions for Further Reading

Montgomery, Robert H. *Sacco-Vanzetti: The Murder and the Myth.* New York: Devin-Adair, 1960.

Porter, Katherine Anne. *The Never-Ending Wrong.* Boston: Little, Brown, & Co., 1977.

MURDER

Rappaport, Doreen. *The Sacco-Vanzetti Trial.* New York: Harper-Collins Publishers, 1992.

Russell, Francis. *Sacco & Vanzetti: The Case Resolved.* New York: Harper & Row, 1986.

Russell, Francis. "Why I Changed My Mind about the Sacco-Vanzetti Case." *American Heritage* (June–July 1986): 106–108.

Sifakis, Carl. *The Encyclopedia of American Crime.* New York: Facts On File, 1972.

Sinclair, Upton. *Boston: A Documentary Novel.* Cambridge, MA: Robert Bentley, 1978.

Bruno Richard Hauptmann Trial: 1935

Defendant: Bruno Richard Hauptmann

Crime Charged: Murder

Chief Defense Lawyer: Edward J. Reilly

Chief Prosecutor: David T. Wilentz

Judge: Thomas W. Trenchard

Place: Flemington, New Jersey

Dates of Trial: January 2–February 13, 1935

Verdict: Guilty

Sentence: Death by electrocution

SIGNIFICANCE: The use of scientific crime methods and the circus-like atmosphere of the trial made the Lindbergh baby kidnapping trial a landmark in American history. Because of the popularity of the father of the murder victim, probably no case has ever attracted greater worldwide attention.

Charles A. Lindbergh became the greatest hero of modern times in May 1927, when he made the first solo trans-Atlantic airplane flight. After Lindbergh's twenty-month-old son was kidnapped and murdered in 1932, the 1935 trial of Bruno Richard Hauptmann became, as the important social critic H. L. Mencken said, "the biggest story since the Resurrection."

In 1929, Lindbergh married Anne Morrow, daughter of the U.S. ambassador to Mexico. Their son, Charles Jr., was born June 22, 1930. Hoping to escape from the crowds that followed them everywhere, the Lindberghs moved into a new home in remote Hopewell, New Jersey. There,

Courtroom Drama

on the evening of March 1, 1932, Charles Jr. was kidnapped from his nursery. His body was found May 12 in the woods, two miles from the Lindbergh home.

Discovered through Ransom Money

More than two years later, in September 1934, a man named Bruno Hauptmann used a $10 gold certificate to buy gasoline. By this time, gold certificates (bills backed by government-owned gold) were rare. The station attendant was suspicious of Hauptmann, and he took down Hauptmann's license number. The attendant then took the $10 gold certificate to the bank, where it was identified as part of the $50,000 ransom Lindbergh had paid his baby's kidnapper. Hauptmann was arrested.

Hauptmann was a German immigrant who had a record of petty (minor) crimes in his native land. He lived in the Bronx, a borough of New York City, with his wife and son (who in 1934 was the same age as the Lindbergh baby). The family occupied the rented second story of a house, where they also had the use of a garage. Behind the boards of this garage police found $14,590 in bills that had been part of the ransom payment. Written on the inside of Hauptmann's bedroom closet was the address and telephone number of Dr. John F. Condon. Condon was a seventy-one-year-old retired schoolteacher who also lived in the Bronx. He had earlier volunteered to be a go-between for Lindbergh when the aviator, unaware that his son was dead, was negotiating with the kidnapper about the ransom money. Condon had met the supposed kidnapper while Lindbergh was still within earshot. Later, at Hauptmann's trial, Lindbergh would identify Hauptmann as the kidnapper by testifying, "[Hauptmann's] is the voice I heard that night."

The Trial As Public Spectacle

The trial became one of the great news stories of the century. To cope with the demands of the press, the telephone company put together the largest telephone system ever created for a single event. It was large enough to serve a city of one million. Thousands of sightseers, 700 reporters, and hundreds of radio and telephone technicians came to Flemington, New Jersey, where the trial was held. Peddlers sold models of the ladder the kidnapper used to climb into the Lindbergh baby's nursery, fake locks of "the baby's hair," and photographs of the Lindberghs—supposedly autographed by them.

OPPOSITE PAGE

Crowds line the streets trying to gain entrance to the trial of Bruno Richard Hauptmann.

MURDER

On Sundays, tourists walked through the courtroom, posed for photographs in the judge's chair, carved initials in his bench, and tried to steal the witness chair. On Sunday, January 6, 1935, the crowd of curious sightseers numbered 60,000. The next weekend, the local Rotary Club, a group dedicated to public service, took charge of protecting the courthouse before souvenir hunters dismantled it.

Everything Matches

The thirty-eight-year-old New Jersey attorney general, David T. Wilentz, vowed that the state would prove that Hauptmann received the ransom money. He also would show that Hauptmann had kidnapped and murdered the Lindbergh baby and written the ransom notes. Wilentz produced forty examples of Hauptmann's handwriting and fifteen ransom notes that Lindbergh had received. The head of the New Jersey State Police was Colonel H. Norman Schwarzkopf (whose son would later act as commanding general of U.S. troops in the 1991 Persian Gulf War.) He testified that Hauptmann had willingly supplied samples of his handwriting. Schwarzkopf also testified that the unusual Germanic spellings found in the ransom notes and in the writing samples were Hauptmann's own, not a reflection of police dictation.

Eight handwriting experts took the stand. Two had testified at more than fifty trials. Another had helped to convict the infamous mobster Al Capone. Still another had been a key witness in a suit challenging the validity of the will of movie star Rudolph Valentino. Using enlargements, these experts pointed out similarities between words and letters in the ransom notes and in Hauptmann's handwriting. When their testimony ended after five days, Wilentz gloated about the victory he had gained for the state thanks to scientific investigation.

Even more damaging to Hauptmann was evidence concerning the ladder found alongside the Lindbergh driveway. Arthur Koehler, a wood technologist at the U.S. Department of Agriculture, told the jury how he had examined the ladder with a microscope. He determined that it was made of North Carolina pine. Using the marks made in the wood as it was finished, he traced the ladder to mills in South Carolina. The mills had sold their wood to a Bronx lumber company where Hauptmann had purchased some in December 1931. One of the suspect ladder's rails was unique: it had nail holes that matched four holes in the beams of Hauptmann's attic.

Shoebox On the Shelf

Hauptmann's defense attorney, Edward J. Reilly, had tried hundreds of murder cases. He was one of New York's most famous trial lawyers. *The*

New York Journal had hired him. It had also made a deal with Anna Hauptmann. If she would give the paper the exclusive right to publish her story, the paper would pay for her husband's lawyer.

To explain how he came to have the ransom money, Hauptmann testified that he had invested in a business with Isidor Fisch. In December 1933, Fisch had gone home to Germany, where he had died of tuberculosis in March 1934. Hauptmann said that Fisch had left behind a number of belongings, including a shoebox that Hauptmann had stored on the top shelf of a kitchen broom closet.

After rain leaked into the closet, Hauptmann found the shoebox. Inside it were $40,000 in gold certificates. In his garage, Hauptmann divided the money into piles, wrapped it up, and hid it. Because Fisch had owed him $7,500, he began spending some of the gold certificates.

Reilly called Mrs. Hauptmann to the witness stand to verify her husband's story. Under cross-examination, she revealed that although she hung her apron in the broom closet every day and kept her grocery coupons in a tin box on the shelf, she had never seen the shoebox there. Later, other witnesses testified that Fisch could not have been at the scene of the crime. Further, he did not even have money for his medical treatment when he was dying in Germany.

Reilly had boasted that he would call eight handwriting experts. But he came up with only one, who was discredited during cross-examination. Then Reilly brought in a witness who claimed to have seen Fisch in New York City on the night of the crime. The witness said that Fisch was with a woman who carried a two-year-old blond child. The woman was supposedly Violet Sharpe, a maid in the Morrow home. Like all servants in the Morrow and Lindbergh households, Sharpe had been questioned closely after the kidnapping. She committed suicide after her interrogation. Unfortunately for Reilly, this testimony was undermined by the fact that the person who gave it was a professional witness who had been paid to testify in dozens of trials.

Another defense witness claimed to have seen Fisch coming out of the cemetery where the ransom money was left. Prosecutor Wilentz made this witness admit that he had been previously convicted of a crime. Still another witness, who testified that he had seen Fisch with a shoebox, admitted under cross-examination that he had been in and out of mental institutions five times. To counter the evidence about the ladder, Reilly called on a general contractor who was an expert on wood. After the prosecutor attacked this witness's expertise, the judge allowed him to testify only as a "practical lumberman."

Bruno Richard Hauptmann Trial: 1935

MURDER

When the trial ended, no reliable witness had placed Hauptmann at the scene of the crime. His fingerprints were not found on the ladder, or in the nursery, or on the ransom notes. Still, the circumstantial evidence connecting Hauptmann to the crime was strong. He had the ransom money, experts said that he had made the ladder, and still other experts said that he had written the ransom notes.

Governor Gets Into the Act

When the jury found Hauptmann guilty of murder in the first degree, the crowds inside and outside the courtroom cheered. Hauptmann was given the death sentence. Execution was set for the week of March 18. Over the next year, however, Hauptmann's attorneys managed to postpone his execution by filing appeals.

New Jersey's governor, Harold G. Hoffman, secretly visited Hauptmann in jail and told the prisoner he was not convinced that he was guilty. Hoffman went on to say that he did not believe Hauptmann could have committed the crime by himself. In mid-January 1936, New Jersey's Court of Pardons turned down Hauptmann's request for a pardon. The governor, however, gave him thirty additional days to appeal this decision. The Court of Pardons once again rejected Hauptmann's request. By law, the governor could not grant a condemned prisoner a second stay of execution. On April 3, 1936, at 8:44 P.M., Hauptmann was electrocuted.

The Aftermath

The evidence and the testimony that led to Hauptmann's execution has been constantly re-examined. More than one examiner has criticized the investigation of the kidnapping and murder and declared that Hauptmann was an innocent man who had been framed.

In 1982, then eighty-two-year-old Anna Hauptmann sued the State of New Jersey, various former police officials, the owner of the *New York Journal,* and David T. Wilentz for wrongfully killing her husband. She claimed that newly found documents proved that government agents had manufactured some of the evidence used to convict Bruno Hauptmann. In 1983, the U.S. Supreme Court refused her request that the federal judge considering her case be disqualified. The next year, the judge dismissed her claim.

In 1985, 23,000 pages of police documents concerning the case were found in a garage that had been owned by former governor Hoffman, who

LUCKY LINDY

Charles Lindbergh was one of the great heroes of the era between World War I and World War II. Ironically, he was not actually the first to fly across the Atlantic. In 1919, two Englishmen had flown from Newfoundland to Ireland. However, their route was far shorter than Lindbergh's. Also, Lindbergh was the first to make a solo trans-Atlantic flight. His plane, *The Spirit of St. Louis,* had been specially designed to carry enough gas to allow him to make the 3,600-mile flight, which began on May 20, 1927, in Long Island. On this famous trip, Lindbergh carried only a few sandwiches and a quart of water. When he arrived in Paris thirty-three hours after takeoff, he was an international hero. His nickname became "Lucky Lindy." Partly because of Lindbergh's celebrity, the kidnapping case led to Congress passing a law that made kidnapping across state lines a federal crime. Later, Lindbergh became a supporter of German dictator Adolf Hitler and joined the "America First" movement to keep the United States out of World War II. He made many anti-Jewish remarks, and in 1938, he received a medal from Hermann Goering, Hitler's air minister. Nevertheless, during World War II, Lindbergh flew combat missions in the Pacific and after the war, he became a consultant to the Defense Department.

had died. Anna Hauptmann claimed that these documents, along with 30,000 pages of FBI files not used in the trial, proved the government had acted in bad faith. Again she appealed to the Supreme Court. The court let its previous ruling against her stand. In 1990, New Jersey Governor Jim Florio refused her appeal for a meeting intended to clear Bruno Hauptmann's name.

In October 1991, Mrs. Hauptmann, then ninety-two years old, called a news conference to plead for the case to be reopened. "From the day he was arrested, he was framed, always framed," she said. By that time, interest in the case had faded. Bruno Hauptmann's case seemed, to most of the public, to have been settled at last.

MURDER

Suggestions for Further Reading

Behn, Noel. *Lindberg: The Crime.* New York: Onyx, 1995.

Fisher, Jim. *The Lindbergh Case.* New Brunswick, NJ: Rutgers University Press, 1987.

Kennedy, Ludovic. *The Airman and the Carpenter.* New York: Viking, 1985.

Kennedy, Lodovic. *Crime of the Century: The Lindbergh Kidnapping and the Framing of Richard Hauptmann.* New York: Penguin Books, 1996.

King, Wayne. "Defiant Widow Seeks to Reopen Lindbergh Case." *The New York Times* (October 5, 1991): 24.

"Lindbergh Kidnapping's Final Victim." *U.S. News & World Report* (November 4, 1985): 11.

Rein, Richard K. "Anna Hauptmann Sues a State to Absolve Her Husband of 'The Crime of the Century.'" *People* (September 6, 1982): 34–35.

Scaduto, Anthony. *Scapegoat: The Lonesome Death of Bruno Richard Hauptmann.* New York: G. P. Putnam's Sons, 1976.

Samuel Sheppard Trials: 1954 and 1966

Defendant: Samuel Sheppard

Crime Charged: Murder

Chief Defense Lawyers: First trial: William J. Corrigan, William Corrigan Jr., Fred Garmone, and Arthur E. Petersilge; second trial: F. Lee Bailey

Chief Prosecutors: First trial: Saul S. Danaceau, John J. Mahon, and Thomas J. Parrino; second trial: John Corrigan

Judges: First trial: Edward C. Blythin; second trial: Francis J. Talty

Place: Cleveland, Ohio

Dates of Trials: October 18–December 21, 1954; October 24–November 16, 1966

Verdict: First trial: guilty, second-degree murder; second trial: not guilty

Sentence: First trial: life imprisonment

SIGNIFICANCE: In this, the most sensational American murder case of the 1950s, bias (unfair influence) connected with harmful media publicity deprived the defendant of his constitutional rights—including the right to a fair trial.

Balancing the news media's First Amendment right to free speech against a defendant's right to a fair trial has never been easy. In covering the Sam Sheppard trial, Cleveland's major newspapers ignored the defendant's rights altogether. The offenses they committed at a local level, popular radio columnist Walter Winchell committed nationally. Nearly everyone in

GOSSIP COLUMNISTS

The journalists who helped to make the Sheppard trial "a Roman circus"—Walter Winchell and Dorothy Kilgallen—were part of the new breed of "gossip columnists" that flourished in the 1920s. Gossip columnists were just what the name suggests: journalists who reported on gossip about famous personalities, as well as covering sensational trials like the Sheppard case. In Hollywood, Hedda Hopper and Louella Parsons were the most famous gossip columnists. Nationwide, however, Walter Winchell was one of the most influential journalists in America from the 1920s through the 1950s. Millions used to listen to his radio show, which began "Good evening, Mr. and Mrs. America," and which always ended, "This is Mrs. Winchell's little boy, Walter."

America believed Sheppard was guilty before even a word of testimony was heard. Certainly, his story sounded unlikely, but that alone did not prove Sheppard was guilty.

Sheppard's Wife Brutally Slain

This amazing story began on July 3, 1954. Samuel Sheppard, a well-to-do thirty-year-old doctor, and his pregnant wife, Marilyn, invited their neighbors, the Ahearns, over for drinks at the Sheppard home on the shores of Lake Erie. While the others watched TV, Sheppard dozed on the couch. Just after midnight the Ahearns left. Sam Sheppard remained sleeping on the couch while Marilyn Sheppard went to bed.

Sometime later, according to his version of events, Sheppard heard a loud moan or scream. He rushed upstairs to the bedroom and saw "a white form" standing beside the bed. Then, he said, everything went black. When he came to, Sheppard realized he had been clubbed on the neck. He stumbled across to the bed where his wife lay motionless. A sudden noise sent him racing downstairs. By the rear door he spotted "a man with bushy hair." He chased the intruder onto the beach and tackled him from behind. During the struggle Sheppard blacked out again. This time when he came to, he was partially immersed in the waters of Lake Erie. Groggily, he staggered back to the house and phoned for help.

OPPOSITE PAGE

Sam Sheppard at his trial on October 18, 1954. He was charged with the murder of his wife, Marilyn, on July 4th of that same year.

Police found Marilyn Sheppard's half-nude body lying in a pool of blood. Downstairs, a writing desk had been looted and the contents of Sheppard's medical bag lay spread across the floor. It appeared that someone had come to rob the house and ended up killing Marilyn Sheppard.

Meanwhile, Sam Sheppard's two brothers whisked him away to the hospital they owned. It was this departure, more than anything else, that caused the press to treat Sheppard so harshly. Newspaper editors, eager to increase the number of their readers, claimed that the wealthy "Sheppard Boys" had drawn together to protect a member of their family.

The discovery at the house of a canvas bag, containing Sheppard's wristwatch, key chain and key, and a fraternity ring, caused some to speculate that he had faked a robbery to conceal the murder. When it was revealed that he was involved with another woman, official suspicion about Sheppard's innocence increased. Urged on by an increasingly hostile Cleveland press, police arrested Sheppard and charged him with murder.

The Carnival Begins

The state of Ohio opened its case against Sheppard on Monday, October 18. Judge Edward Blythin set the tone for the trial early. He would be up for reelection the following November. In order to increase his popularity with the press, he gave handwritten passes to the trial to such notable reporters as Dorothy Kilgallen and Bob Considine. He even provided them with their own special table at which to sit. Blythin presided over a court that was in an uproar, what *The New York Times* would later describe as "a Roman circus."

Prosecutor John Mahon made the most of what was a very weak case. Without any direct evidence against the defendant, other than that he was in the house when Marilyn Sheppard was killed, Mahon emphasized the possible flaws in Sam Sheppard's story. Why was there no sand in his hair when he claimed to have been stretched out on the beach? Where was the T-shirt that he had been wearing? Had bloodstains received during the attack forced him to destroy it? Also, why would a burglar first take the belongings found in the canvas bag and then throw them away? Besides which, said Mahon, "Police . . . could find no evidence that anyone had broken in." For a motive, Mahon pointed to Sheppard's affair with Susan Hayes, a lab technician at the family hospital, as reason enough for Sheppard to want to be rid of his wife.

Initially, the lack of a murder weapon posed problems for the prosecution. However, Cuyahoga County coroner Samuel R. Gerber got around this difficulty by telling the court that a bloody imprint found on the pillow beneath Marilyn Sheppard's head was made by a "two-blade surgical instrument with teeth on the end of each blade." He said it was probably the missing weapon. For some reason, the defense attorneys did not question this vague statement, a failure that would ruin their client's chances of acquittal.

Morals, not Murder

Hayes testified about her romantic relationship with Sheppard: "He said he loved his wife very much but not as a wife. He was thinking of divorce." Other than showing that Sheppard was unfaithful, Hayes' testimony proved nothing. Still, the damage had been done. Sheppard wound up being tried more for his morals (sense of right and wrong) than for any crime.

Probably the most effective prosecution witness was Judge Blythin. His dislike of the defendant was plain. Early in the trial he had remarked to Kilgallen: "Sheppard is as guilty as hell," and throughout the proceedings he made things as difficult as possible for the defense. Such an attitude on the bench ensured that Sheppard had no chance of receiving a fair trial. His own appearance on the witness stand made little difference. He performed well, but not well enough to overcome the hostile atmosphere in court.

Jury discussions lasted four days and resulted in a guilty verdict for second-degree murder. (A rumor that some jurors were unwilling to commit Sheppard to the electric chair and might therefore acquit him had forced Judge Blythin to offer them the possibility of a second-degree murder conviction.) Blythin pronounced sentence: "It is now the judgment of this court that you be taken to the Ohio Penitentiary, there to remain for the rest of your natural life."

A Second Chance

In November 1961, twenty-nine-year-old attorney F. Lee Bailey took up Sheppard's cause. He filed a stream of legal papers on Sheppard's behalf, every one of which was rejected. In March 1964, however, by chance Bailey attended a dinner party. Among the guests was Kilgallen, and she happened to repeat the off-the-record remark Judge Blythin made to her during Sheppard's trial. Bailey listened intently. If he could show that the judge had been biased, this would be grounds for a new trial.

Four months later a judge ordered Sheppard freed on bail, saying that the carnival conditions surrounding his trial "fell far below the minimum requirements for due process."

SAM REESE SHEPPARD

Sam Reese Sheppard, son of accused murderer Sam Sheppard and murder victim Marilyn Sheppard, has continued to investigate his mother's murder, believing that justice was not served by his father's conviction. In 1995, nearly forty years after his mother's death, he co-authored *Mockery of Justice: The True Story of the Sheppard Murder Case,* with attorney and investigative reporter Cynthia L. Cooper. In 1997, in response to his efforts, the process of exhuming Sheppard's body to compare DNA samples to blood left at the crime scene got underway. Reese Sheppard still campaigns against the death penalty and works with groups such as Murder Victim Families for Reconciliation, Amnesty International, and the National Coalition to Abolish the Death Penalty.

The following year Bailey argued Sheppard's case before the U.S. Supreme Court. He claimed that Blythin had displayed prejudice and that the trial had been conducted in such a way that Sheppard's right to a fair trial had been violated. The court agreed. On June 6, 1965, the justices handed down their decision setting aside Sheppard's 1954 conviction because Judge Blythin "did not fulfill his duty to protect Sheppard from inherently prejudicial publicity which saturated the county."

Ohio tried Sheppard again. Media interest remained high, but this time it was kept in check when the trial opened October 24, 1966, before Judge Francis J. Talty. Prosecutor John Corrigan led witnesses through essentially the same stories that they had told over a decade earlier, but they now faced a defense attorney who was working at the peak of his powers. Bailey managed to overcome all their testimony, particularly that of coroner Samuel Gerber. Referring to the "surgical instrument" that might have served as a murder weapon, Gerber announced that he had spent the last twelve years looking for just such an item "all over the United States."

"Please tell us what you found?" asked Bailey.

Sadly, Gerber shook his head: "I didn't find one."

On December 16, 1966, the jury took less than twelve hours to return a verdict of not guilty: Sam Sheppard's ordeal was over. However, Sheppard had only a few years of freedom; he died in 1970.

Suggestions for Further Reading

Bailey, F. Lee with Harvey Aronson. *The Defense Never Rests.* New York: Stein and Day, 1971.

Cooper, Cynthia L. with Sam Reese Sheppard. *Mockery of Justice: The True Story of the Sheppard Murder Case.* Boston: Northeastern University Press, 1995.

Gaute, J. H. H. and Robin Odell. *The Murderers' Who's Who.* London: W. H. Allen, 1989.

Pollack, Jack Harrison. *Dr. Sam—An American Tragedy.* Chicago: Regnery, 1972.

Sheppard, Sam. *Endure And Conquer.* Cleveland: World, 1966.

Sheppard, Stephen with Paul Holmes. *My Brother's Keeper.* New York: David McKay, 1964.

Samuel Sheppard Trials: 1954 and 1966

Angela Davis Trial: 1972

Defendant: Angela Y. Davis

Crimes Charged: Murder, kidnapping, conspiracy

Chief Defense Lawyers: Leo Branton Jr., Margaret Burnham, Howard Moore Jr., Sheldon Otis, and Dorris Brin Walker

Chief Prosecutor: Albert Harris

Judge: Richard E. Arnason

Place: San Jose, California

Dates of Trial: February 28–June 4, 1972

Verdict: Not guilty

SIGNIFICANCE: An unusual mix of murder, race, and politics made this trial memorable.

At 10:45 A.M. on August 7, 1970, a gunman interrupted the Marin County trial of San Quentin inmate James McClain, who was facing a charge of attempted murder. The gunman, Jonathan Jackson, one of the so-called "Soledad Brothers," handed weapons to McClain and two other men in the courtroom, Ruchell Magee and William Christmas. Together, they took Judge Harold Haley, prosecutor Gary Thomas, and three women jurors hostage, then tried to escape in a van. When guards opened fire, Haley, Jackson, McClain, and Christmas were killed. Thomas and Magee were seriously injured.

Suspicion that the plot was connected to the Soledad Brothers—three radical black Soledad Prison inmates—increased when Angela Davis suddenly disappeared. Davis, a supporter of the Soledad Brothers, had recently been fired from her job as a professor at the University of California at Los Angeles because of her Communist sympathies. She was finally found in New York on October 13. After she was sent back to California, she was formally charged with murder, conspiracy, and kidnapping. The prosecutors wanted to prove that Davis had arranged the escape attempt in order to exchange hostages for the freedom of her boyfriend, George Jackson, the older brother of Jonathan Jackson.

Trial Opens

The task of selecting a jury began before Judge Richard E. Arnason on February 28, 1972. The racial and political aspects of the case made jury selection an especially difficult task, but eventually an all-white jury was chosen, and prosecutor Albert Harris was able to make his opening address. He outlined four elements necessary to establish guilt using circumstantial evidence (when there is nothing directly connecting the accused with the crime). The elements were motive, means, opportunity, and consciousness of guilt. "The evidence will show," he said, "that her [Davis's] basic motive was not to free political prisoners, but to free the one prisoner that she loved." The means came on August 5, 1970, when, in the company of Jonathan Jackson, "she purchased the shotgun that was used in the commission of the crime." Harris believed that the days leading up to the crime, many of which Davis spent with Jonathan Jackson, provided an opportunity to commit the crime. Finally, Davis's consciousness of guilt was proven by the fact that just hours after the shooting, she boarded a flight and went into hiding.

Davis Ridicules Case

Although she had an impressive team of attorneys, Davis chose to make the opening remarks to the jury herself. Wisely, she said little about her political beliefs. She focused instead on the flaws in the prosecution's case. These were that she had bought the shotgun openly, using her own name, and, more importantly, that the Marin shooting seemed to have had nothing to do with George Jackson. "The evidence will show that there's absolutely no credible proof of what the precise purpose of [the events of] August 7 was," she said.

This argument was answered by a prosecution witness, news photographer James Kean. He had taken several photographs of the shooting incident and now testified to hearing McClain say at the time, "Tell them we want the Soledad Brothers released by twelve o'clock."

Courtroom Drama

Chief defense attorney Leo Branton cross-examined Kean: "This remark that was made about freeing the Soledad Brothers—it was the last thing that was said just as the group got on the elevator . . . is that a fact?"

"Yes. That's right."

"You never heard Jonathan Jackson say anything about free the Soledad Brothers, did you?"

"No, I did not."

"You didn't hear anybody say it other than McClain and it was the last thing he said as he headed down the elevator; is that right?"

"Yes."

"As though it were a parting gesture, is that correct?"

"That's right."

Branton must have been satisfied with this testimony. His satisfaction must have increased when Deputy Sheriff Theodore Hughes testified that he had heard some of the escaped convicts shout clearly, "Free our brothers at Folsom, free all our brothers."Again, there was no mention of Soledad Prison.

The testimony of Gary Thomas, the prosecution's star witness, was more difficult to dismiss. Permanently paralyzed by his bullet wound, he was brought into court in a wheelchair. The key part of his testimony was his statement that he had seen up close Magee shoot Judge Haley with the shotgun.

Branton had the difficult task of attempting to prove that Thomas's memory might have been clouded by the trauma he had suffered. "Isn't it a fact, sir, that the first fusillade [rapid fire] of shots that came into the van killed both Jonathan Jackson and McClain, and that you thereupon grabbed the gun that McClain was holding . . . and that you turned around and began firing into the back of the van . . . and that you hit Christmas and you hit Magee, and you possibly even hit Judge Haley?"

Thomas angrily denied this assertion, and Branton had to back down. He made little headway with Thomas, except getting the witness to agree that at no time did he hear anyone mention the Soledad Brothers.

Mysterious Telephone Number Surfaces

Prosecutor Harris next turned his attention to a piece of paper found on the body of Jonathan Jackson. On it was written a number that was assigned to a public telephone at San Francisco International Airport. Har-

OPPOSITE PAGE

Angela Davis is escorted by two FBI agents after her arrest in October 1970.

THE FIRST AFRICAN AMERICAN WOMAN JUDGE IN MASSACHUSETTS

Angela Davis's lawyer, Margaret Burnham, went on to have a distinguished legal career. Davis was actually Burnham's first client after she had graduated from the University of Pennsylvania Law School. She later defended a prisoner charged with assault in the 1971 riots at Attica Prison in New York State. When the Communist Party tried to get on the ballot for the 1976 presidential elections, Burnham represented it. Then, on August 12, 1977, she was sworn in as an associate justice of the Boston Municipal Court, the first African American woman judge ever to serve in Massachusetts. Burnham was appointed by then-Governor Michael Dukakis. She chose a symbolic site for her swearing-in ceremony: the Harriet Tubman Community Center in the heart of Roxbury, a poor African American community. About her appointment, Burnham said, "I don't have any illusions that I can make *tremendous* changes in the character of justice by taking this particular seat. But I see it as *one* way to extend the struggle for human rights."

ris contended that this piece of evidence clearly showed that Jonathan Jackson intended to telephone Angela Davis at the airport. Further, when Davis did not receive the call she panicked and took the next flight to Los Angeles.

All of this sounded fine but did not hold up. First of all, Branton pointed out that the telephone was in the airport's South Terminal, near the Western Airlines counter. Why, he asked, had nobody seen Davis waiting by the phone? And why had she left the counter for Western Airlines—which offered flights every hour to Los Angeles—and walked over to the Central Terminal to catch a flight on Pacific Southwest Airlines? It did not make sense.

In one last desperate effort to save their case, the prosecutors fought to introduce into evidence an eighteen-page "diary" that Davis had kept.

While the diary clearly showed the love that Davis felt for George Jackson, it did not provide any evidence to support the charges against her.

Such a poor prosecution hardly called for much of a response. Branton called just twelve witnesses to support his assertion that Angela Davis was entirely innocent. The case went to the jurors on June 2, 1972. They came back two days later with not-guilty verdicts on all three charges.

But for Angela Davis it was not much of a victory. Six months before she faced her accusers, George Jackson had himself been shot to death in an alleged prison break.

Before the trial many people, including some on her own defense team, doubted Davis had a good chance of receiving a fair hearing from an all-white jury. That the jurors were able to separate politics and race from the essential facts of the case said a great deal about their individual honor and helped to make this trial one of the legal system's finer moments.

Suggestions for Further Reading

Aptheker, Bettina. *The Morning Breaks.* New York: International, 1975.

Davis, Angela. *Angela Davis.* New York: International, 1988.

Major, Reginald. *Justice in the Round.* New York: Third Press, 1973.

Mitchell, Charlene. *The Fight to Free Angela Davis.* New York: Outlook, 1972.

Timothy, Mary. *Jury Woman.* San Francisco: Glide, 1975.

Guildford Four Trial: 1975

Defendants: Patrick Armstrong, Gerard Conlon, Paul Hill, and Carole Richardson

Crimes Charged: Murder and conspiracy to cause explosions

Chief Defense Lawyers: John Leonard, Q.C. (Queen's Counsel), Arthur Mildon, Q.C., Eric Myers, Q.C., Gordon Ward, and Lord Basil Wigoder, Q.C.

Chief Prosecutors: Sir Michael Havers, Q.C., and Michael Hill, Q.C.

Judge: Sir John Donaldson

Place: London, England

Dates of Trial: September 16–October 22, 1975

Verdicts: Guilty

Sentences: Life imprisonment

SIGNIFICANCE: When the Irish Republican Army bombed three pubs (bars), killing seven people, the British people were outraged. Police were determined to produce quick arrests to calm the public and press. This case is a tragic example of how the overly intense investigation of terrorist activities led to a failure of justice.

During 1974, Irish Republican Army (IRA) threats to bring terrorism to the British mainland became a reality. The bloodshed peaked on October 5, when bombs exploded at two pubs popular with soldiers in Guildford, Surrey: the Seven Stars and the Horse and Groom. Five people, including four army recruits, were killed. A month later, on November 7, a second bomb thrown through the window of the Kings Arms pub in Woolwich, South London, killed two customers. On each occasion, in addition to the deaths they caused, the bombs injured many. Before the month was over, Parliament had passed the Prevention of Terrorism Act. Its most important section gave police the power to arrest with warrants individuals they reasonably suspected of being involved in terrorism.

Arrests Made

The first person arrested under this act was Paul Hill, age twenty, who had been born in Belfast, Northern Ireland, but was living in a run-down house in Kilburn, North London. Officially Hill's name first came to police attention from an informant's tip. However, they already suspected Hill of involvement in the abduction and murder of an ex-soldier, Brian Shaw, a crime for which he was later convicted. However Hill came to be detained by police, what is certain is that, while in custody, he signed a statement admitting responsibility for the Guildford and Woolwich bombings. He also named Gerard Conlon, twenty, as a co-conspirator (someone who helps commit a crime). The next day, Conlon was arrested at his home in Belfast. Further interrogation of these two led to more arrests, among them those of Patrick Armstrong, twenty-four, and his seventeen-year-old English girlfriend, Carole Richardson.

It appeared to be an easy case. When asked to plead, each defendant answered "Not Guilty," except for Hill, who declared, "I refuse to take part in this. Your justice stinks!" Hill's refusal to plead guilty or innocent—a tactic often used by IRA prisoners—made matters worse for his co-defendants. For the men, the sole defense was that the "confessions" had been made under pressure. This meant police threatened them or their families.

Strong Defense for Richardson

Carole Richardson was on far firmer legal ground. In late December 1974, a friend, Frank Johnson, had gone to police. He told them that, on October 5, he and Richardson had been watching a band together in south London at the time of the Guildford explosion. The band checked their records and confirmed the date, and there were even photographs of Richardson taken in the band's dressing room to confirm that she was there. According to Johnson, this information did not please the police, and he was repeatedly beaten until he took his story back. However, on the witness stand he stood by what he had originally said. Eric Myers, Q.C., Richard-

After spending fifteen years in prison, a court finally found the Guildford Four innocent of terrorism. Pictured below is Gerard Conlon, clenching his fist in victory.

son's lawyer, told the jury that the police had not "breathed a word" of Johnson's statement to the defense, adding, "This was straight out of the dirty tricks department."

Chief prosecutor Sir Michael Havers, Q.C., chose to ignore the most significant part of Johnson's testimony—that he had met Richardson in London at 6:30 P.M. Instead he concentrated on showing that Richardson had time to place the bomb in Guildford at 7:00 P.M. and get to the concert fifty minutes later. A police car, he announced, had managed to make this thirty-mile trip through South London's busy streets in a remarkable forty-eight minutes.

Detective Inspector Timothy Blake then took the stand. Conlon's lawyer, Lord Basil Wigoder, Q.C., accused him of physically abusing Conlon during questioning. Blake responded that he had not even set eyes upon Conlon until after he had been interrogated. Wigoder then asked Blake to roll up his sleeves. During the course of his beating, Conlon had seen tattoos on Blake's arms and was able to describe them clearly; now the court was able to see just how correct Conlon's description had been. Asked how Conlon could have come by such personal details, Blake

weakly suggested that Conlon might have seen him in his shirt sleeves at the police station.

As one of the main interviewing officers, Detective Sergeant Anthony Jermey denied defense claims that Hill had been threatened while in custody by a police officer with a gun. He was less sure, though, when Wigoder asked about the way the various confessions had been obtained. Jermey had produced twenty pages of confessions and the record of Conlon's interrogation; all of it was incriminating (showed proof of involvement in the crime) and none of it mentioned police brutality. Wigoder asked Jermey when he wrote these notes.

"Seven hours later," said Jermey. When Wigoder remarked that he had an excellent memory, the officer explained how a good memory was a requirement for good police work. At this point Wigoder inquired: "What was the first question I put to you in the witness box?" Jermey's mind appeared to go blank. He had just claimed to be able to recall a thirteen-hour interrogation word for word seven hours after it ended, yet he could not now repeat a question put to him just minutes earlier.

When it came time to testify, Hill kept his self-assured attitude, refusing to answer questions or responding sarcastically. When Conlon's turn came, he had to deal with accusations from Havers that he had deliberately inserted mistakes into his confession in order to "pull the wool" over the jury's eyes.

"I have no need to pull the wool over the jury's eyes," Conlon protested, "I am telling the truth."

"Did you enjoy leading the gang which blew up these people in Guildford?"

"I'd never been to Guildford till the police took me there. If they'd told me to put down the Pope's name as one of the bombers, I would have done it. I'd have put down anybody's name to save my Ma!" He was referring to police threats to hurt his family.

In summing up, Justice John Donaldson boiled the trial down to a single issue, telling the jury that they had to decide whom to believe—police officers with many years of distinguished service, or the defendants.

On October 22, 1975, the jury made it clear which version of events they favored. The verdict was guilty. In passing sentences of life imprisonment on all four defendants, the judge sounded as if he were sorry that the death penalty was no longer available. However, he did recommend that Hill should only be released "on grounds of old age or infirmity." This made Hill's the longest sentence ever handed down in a British court.

Captured IRA Militants Claim Responsibility

MURDER

As the case of the Guildford Four faded from the headlines, its place was taken by yet another trial arising from recent IRA terrorism. On January 24, 1977, four Irishmen arrested after a siege (attack) on Balcombe Street in London stepped into court. All of the defendants were admitted terrorists who refused to plead innocent or guilty because their indictments (charges of illegal acts) failed to include the bombings for which the Guildford Four had been convicted. On behalf of his fellow defendants, Joseph O'Connell admitted carrying out both bombings. He proved his claim by mentioning that he had spoken to a soldier at the Guildford pub about late-night bus schedules just before the bomb had exploded. This incident, related by the soldier at the time of the investigation, had never been made public.

Because of these developments, an appeal (legal request for new trial or reversal of conviction) was filed on behalf of the Guildford Four. On October 10, 1977, their hearing for a new trial began. All of the Balcombe Street defendants—Joseph O'Connell, Harry Duggan, Eddie Butler, and Brendan Dowd—gave evidence, freely admitting their terrorist activities and claiming they did not know anything about Hill and the others. At this hearing, Havers, once again the chief prosecution lawyer, was forced to admit that O'Connell, Duggan, and Butler had indeed been responsible for the Guildford bombing, yet he insisted that Hill had helped them. Despite the fresh evidence, the court preferred to rely on the confessions the Guildford defendants had signed, probably under great stress. On October 29, Lord Justice Roskill said: "We are all of the clear opinion that there are no possible grounds for doubting the justice of any of these four convictions or for ordering new trials."

A large number of people believed that O'Connell, a hardened terrorist destined to spend the rest of his life behind bars, had nothing to lose by admitting to the Guildford and Woolwich bombings. In any event, he succeeded in causing the British government great embarrassment.

Doubts About Statements

Others preferred to debate the justness or unjustness of the Guildford Four convictions. Those voicing concern about the convictions included two men at the top of the judicial system, Lord Patrick Devlin and George Scarman. As far back as the 1950s, Devlin, a distinguished trial judge, had expressed doubts about the truth of certain confessions and statements that had allegedly been given to police officers. Years of sitting on the bench listen-

THE IRISH REPUBLICAN ARMY

The Guildford Four were convicted in part because of strong British feeling against the Irish Republican Army (IRA). Originally, the IRA was organized by Michael Collins, a young Irish leader who had participated in the 1916 Easter Rebellion in Dublin. The rebellion was the first modern military attempt by the Irish to win national independence from Great Britain. However, the British suppressed the rebellion and struck back by executing many of its leaders. Collins and his colleagues fought back by forming a military group for the defense of Ireland. The IRA became the military wing of a political party that worked for Irish independence called the Sinn Fein (shin-FAYN). In 1922, southern Ireland was granted partial independence, but Northern Ireland remained under British rule. This the IRA could not accept, and it continued to agitate against the British. In 1969, the group split: the "official" majority opposed violence, while the "provisional" (temporary) wing believed that the British could be defeated only through terrorist actions.

ing to supposedly word-for-word accounts had taught Devlin something. There were often great differences between the speech patterns in the confessions and those of the accused individuals who appeared before him.

Such support kept the Guildford Four case in the public eye, and finally led to a request for an independent panel of police officers to examine all of the evidence. Exposed at last to fair examination, the prosecution's case collapsed. Investigators found draft notes that clearly proved that police officers had lied in saying that statements made by the accused had been written down as they were spoken. Investigators also found that genuine statements had been either deliberately withheld or changed.

Convictions Overturned

On October 19, 1989, a court under Lord Chief Justice Geoffrey Lane threw out the convictions of all four defendants. All were then released from prison.

MURDER

The latest chapter in this tragedy came on April 20, 1993. Three police officers connected with the investigation, Vernon Attwell, John Donaldson, and Thomas Style, went on trial, charged with conspiring to distort the course of justice. In effect, their hearing became a retrial of the Guildford Four. Defense lawyers successfully argued, however, that although the police might not have followed proper procedures, the men who were originally convicted were still guilty. On May 19, 1993, each officer was acquitted.

Suggestions for Further Reading

Bennett, Ronan. *Double Jeopardy.* London: Penguin, 1993.

Conlon, Gerry. *Proved Innocent.* London: Penguin, 1991.

Hill, Paul and Ronan Bennett. *Stolen Years.* London: Doubleday, 1990.

Maguire, Anne. *Miscarriage of Justice.* Boulder, CO: Roberts Rinehart, 1994.

McKee, Grant and Ros Franey. *Time Bomb.* London: Bloomsbury, 1988.

Woffinden, Bob. *Miscarriages of Justice.* London: Hodder & Stoughton, 1987.

Baader-Meinhof Trial: 1975–1977

Defendants: Andreas Baader, Ulrike Meinhof, Gudrun Ensslin, and Jan-Carl Raspe

Crimes Charged: Murder, attempted murder, robbery, the forming of a criminal association

Defense Lawyers: Marie-Luise Becker, Peter Grigat, Hans Heinz Heldmann, Dieter Konig, Manfred Kunzel, Karl-Heinz Linke, Arndt Muller, Rupert von Plottnitz, Helmut Riedel, Otto Schily, Dieter Schnabel, Eberhard Schwarz, and Gerd Temming

Prosecutors: Siegfried Buback, Werner Widera, Heinrich Wunder, and Peter Zeis

Judges: Theodor Prinzing and Eberhard Foth

Place: Stammheim, West Germany

Dates: May 21, 1975–April 21, 1977

Verdicts: Guilty

Sentences: Life imprisonment

SIGNIFICANCE: The notorious Baader-Meinhof gang injured, rather than advanced, its cause. During the trial, the defendants' disorderly behavior caused a change in the Code of Criminal Procedure. Trials thereafter could go forward without the defendants present. The trial also brought about a law that gave officials the power to end communication between unruly prisoners and their lawyers, other prisoners, or the outside world. Finally, the trial led to the assassination of West Germany's federal prosecutor general.

MURDER

The German terrorist group, the Baader-Meinhof Gang, began among students in West Germany. They believed that the private property system (capitalism) was unjust. Its young people, who grew up in comfort, drew inspiration from Ulrike Meinhof, a radical writer.

In 1968, a court convicted Andreas Baader and his girlfriend, Gudrun Ensslin, of firebombing two Frankfurt department stores. However, their jailers later released them as lawyers appealed their case. When the court rejected these appeals, they went into hiding to avoid jail. In February 1970, they met Meinhof. Their mutual interests in left-wing causes and such drugs as LSD soon bound them together.

Courthouse guards stand watch outside while accused group leaders from the Baader-Meinhof gang began their first day of trial on May 21, 1975.

Guerrilla Training

Baader and Ensslin established a Berlin headquarters for their followers. The group robbed banks, stole cars, and took over the apartments of their supporters. They traveled to Jordan for intensive training in guerrilla warfare and terrorist tactics. Back in Germany, they formed an organization known as the Red Army Faction, or RAF.

Authorities soon realized that the RAF had taken the law into its own hands. It was heavily armed and did not stop at arson and bombing. After American military forces mined harbors in North Vietnam in May 1972, terrorist bombings began in Germany. At the Fifth U.S. Army Corps officer's dining room in Frankfurt, one person was killed and thirteen were injured.

The RAF declared responsibility, saying, "West Germany will no longer be a safe hinterland for the strategists of extermination in Vietnam." Also in May, a pipe bomb injured five police officers in Augsburg. Sixty cars were blown up in Munich. The wife of a federal judge was severely injured in Karlsruhe. Seventeen people were injured in Hamburg. Finally, in the dining hall of the U.S. Army in Heidelberg, five American soldiers were injured and three were killed.

Leaders Seized

On June 1, 1972, the West German Federal Border Police went to a garage in Frankfurt where they had found large amounts of explosives. Amid tear gas and gunfire they captured Baader, Jan-Carl Raspe, and Holger Meins. A police sharpshooter wounded Baader in the thigh. A week later, police arrested Ensslin in a Hamburg dress shop after a sales clerk noticed a pistol in her jacket. Next, acting on a tip, police found Meinhof in an apartment in Hanover.

Imprisoned for nearly three years awaiting trial, the group undertook a hunger strike. They insisted they would eat only if guards released them from solitary confinement (being kept alone in a prison cell). Holger Meins died of starvation.

The trial opened on May 21, 1975, in a fortress-like building constructed specifically for the event. Barbed wire covered the area around it. Mounted police patrolled nearby. Steel netting covered the roof to catch any dropped explosives, even though aircraft were banned from the airspace over the building.

"Shut Up, Linke!"

Some 200 spectators were witnesses to the confusion that surrounded the trial. The defendants protested the use of courtroom microphones, interrupted constantly, and refused to sit down. Baader repeatedly told his court-appointed lawyer, "Shut up, Linke!" Ensslin ordered defense counsel Manfred Kunzel not to speak for her. The loud chaos soon included shouts from the audience. The judges frequently ordered the four defendants removed from the courtroom. The defense lawyers argued that their clients were physically unfit to stand trial. All suffered from such low blood pressure and loss of weight that their powers of concentration diminished. The defense lawyers finally walked out in protest when the judges allowed the trial to continue.

The next day, Baader and Raspe called their attorneys an obscene name, and the four were again expelled. Brought back one by one (Meinhof was carried in, her hands and feet held by four officers), they repeated their insulting language. They yelled "Fascist," and called the presiding judge an "old swine."

At last, after twenty-six days, Federal General Prosecutor Siegfried Buback was able to present the charge against Baader, Ensslin, Meinhof, and Raspe:

> . . . that maliciously and by methods constituting danger to the public they did on two occasions murder in all four persons, and on other occasions attempted to murder at least fifty-four other persons;
>
> . . . that they did employ explosive materials . . . endangering life and limb and causing danger to other objects of particular value . . . and they did form an association with the object of committing criminal offenses.

The defendants were not present. They were in their cells, which guards described as masses of cluttered, rotting food, cigarette butts, ashes, books, files, and newspaper clippings.

In the Absence of the Defendants

On the trial's fortieth day, the Code of Criminal Procedure, which governed how criminal trials took place, was changed. A trial could now continue in the absence of defendants if the judge ruled that they were themselves responsible for their absence. Noting that the prosecution had promised to present 997 witnesses, including 80 experts on various aspects of the evidence, Judge Theodor Prinzing ordered the proceedings to continue.

The defense lawyers charged bias. Meinhof pleaded, "The prisoner kept in isolation has only one possible way of showing that his conduct has changed, and that's betrayal. When you're in isolation, either you silence a prisoner, by which I mean he dies, or you get him to talk. And that means confession and betrayal."

On January 13, 1976, the defendants acknowledged they were members of a guerrilla group and claimed "political responsibility" for the bombings, while not admitting criminal responsibility. In February, March, and April, with the defendants usually absent, witnesses presented evidence on the bombings in the cities of Heidelberg, Augsburg, Munich, and Hamburg.

Prison guards reported bitter conflicts between Meinhof and the others, especially Ensslin. Meanwhile, defense lawyers tried to call several prominent witnesses, including former U.S. President Richard M. Nixon, former U.S. Secretary of Defense Melvin Laird, and former German Chancellor Willy Brandt. The defense wanted to determine whether using force against military establishments of the United States on West German territory was justified. Their request was denied.

"The Last Act of Rebellion"

On May 9, guards found Meinhof hanging from the grating of the window of her cell. She had made a rope by tearing prison towels into strips and tying them together. She left no note. Months earlier she had written, "Suicide is the last act of rebellion." The defense team then asked that the trial be adjourned. This request, too, was denied, as spectators cried, "Prinzing, murderer!" and "The suicide's a lie!"

The defense proposed to call five American witnesses to testify that the I. G. Farben building in Frankfurt had been a center of U.S. operations during the Vietnam War. "The Vietnam war is not the subject of this trial," ruled Judge Prinzing in refusing to admit the witnesses.

Witness Klaus Junschke, another gang member, calling Judge Prinzing "you Fascist," leapt from the witness box and grappled with a jurist. Both fell to the floor as Junschke shouted, "For Ulrike, you swine!"

Raspe, ordered to leave the courtroom after continued disruptions, had to be forcibly expelled. Baader and prison guards exchanged blows. Ensslin, when not screaming at her guards, was permitted to play her violin in her cell.

On December 8, 1976, the court ordered that from then on, for reasons of security, defense lawyers had to be searched at the checkpoint set up before the courtroom. A search of the prisoners' cells had revealed the presence of drugs as well as a toaster and a camera. Three weeks later, the defense brought its eighty-fifth charge of bias against Judge Prinzing. This time it was upheld by the judge's colleagues, and he was replaced by Judge Eberhard Foth.

Prosecutor Assassinated

Three court-appointed lawyers protested that conversations with their clients were bugged (electronic devices were used to eavesdrop on conversations). When the trial continued, the lawyers walked out in protest. On the morning of April 7, 1977, Federal Prosecutor General Siegfried Buback and his driver were assassinated on their way to court. A letter to the German Press Agency said "the Ulrike Meinhof Commando" took responsibility.

The trial ended on April 21, 1977. One week later, Judge Foth handed down the verdict. Baader, Ensslin, and Raspe were each guilty of three murders connected to six attempted murders, one further murder in connection with one attempted murder, and twenty-seven other attempted murders in connection with bomb attacks. They were also guilty of having formed a criminal association. All received life imprisonment.

A high-security block was built on Stammheim Prison's seventh floor by prisoner laborers. There, ten additional gang members, awaiting trial or already convicted of RAF terrorism, joined their leaders in "the safest prison in the world."

On September 5, 1977, Hanns Martin Schleyer, president of the Employers' Association, was kidnapped. His driver and three police officers were killed. A ransom note demanded the release of Baader, Ensslin, Raspe, and other gang members, and their free passage to "a country of their choice" in exchange for Schleyer's life. A Europe-wide manhunt for the kidnappers and their victim began. Over the next forty-four days, more ransom notes arrived, along with audiotapes and letters from Schleyer that reported on his health and mental condition. German authorities considered how they could negotiate with the kidnappers. On September 20, the parliament passed a special law that permitted the justice ministers to cut off all contact among the prisoners or between the prisoners and their lawyers or with the outside world. Baader, Ensslin, and Raspe threatened suicide.

Jet Hijacked

A Lufthansa Airlines jet bound from Palma de Mallorca in Spain to Frankfurt, carrying eighty-six passengers, was hijacked and flown to

ARMY BASES AND VIETNAM

The Baader-Meinhof gang portrayed its actions as a protest against the United States' involvement in the Vietnam War. At the same time, under its right of occupation after World War II, the United States was allowed to place its military bases in Germany. One of these was the base in Frankfurt where terrorist bombings began in May 1972. During the 1970s, under its North Atlantic Treaty Organization (NATO) agreements, many European countries hosted U.S. bases. Many also faced protests against U.S. involvement in Vietnam, as well as opposition to U.S. nuclear policy.

Rome on October 13. There, the hijackers' leader announced that Schleyer's life depended upon the release of the RAF prisoners as well as the release of two Palestinians imprisoned in Turkey and $15 million in ransom. The plane's passengers were held as hostages. Refueled, the plane was flown to Bahrain in the Persian Gulf, then to Dubai in the United Arab Emirates.

Meantime, German authorities worked to arrange for the delivery of the ransom money, and Baader, Raspe, and Ensslin filled out written questionnaires on where they would like to be sent if they were freed. In a radio interview, the Dubai defense minister praised the Lufthansa captain for giving information in code on the number of hijackers aboard. The hijackers heard the broadcast, executed the pilot, and ordered the copilot to take off for Aden, Yemen, another Persian Gulf state. Refueled there, the plane was flown to the Mogadishu airport in Somalia in northern Africa. There, German commandos who had followed the hijacked plane's zigzag course stormed aboard, killing three of the four hijackers and wounding one. All of the hostages were rescued.

That night in Stammheim Prison, Baader and Raspe each committed suicide with a pistol, and Ensslin hanged herself. Searches of the cells revealed that hiding places for guns, radios, and other illegal items had been built into the walls when the prisoner laborers constructed them.

Two days later, the body of Schleyer was found with three bullets in the head. Police caught his six kidnappers, who received life sentences.

MURDER

Suggestions for Further Reading

Aust, Stefan. *The Baader-Meinhof Group: The Inside Story of a Phenomenon.* Translated by Anthea Bell. London: The Bodley Head, 1985.

Becker, Jillian. *Hitler's Children: The Story of the Baader-Meinhof Terrorist Gang.* Philadelphia and New York: Lippincott, 1977.

Carr, Gordon. *The Angry Brigade.* London: Victor Gollancz, 1975.

Wright, Joanne. *Terrorist Propaganda: The Red Army Faction and the Provisional IRA, 1968–86.* New York: St. Martin's Press, 1991.

Stephen Biko Inquest: 1977

Presiding Magistrate: Martinhus Prins
Chief Lawyers for Biko Family: Sidney Kentridge and Ernest Wentzel
Chief Lawyers for State/Police: Klaus von Lieres and Retief van Rooyen
Place: Pretoria, South Africa
Date of Inquest: November 14–30, 1977
Verdict: Accidental death

SIGNIFICANCE: All the horrors of apartheid were uncovered in this single case.

For most of the twentieth century South Africa was a divided nation. Through a brutal system of racial separation known as apartheid (a-PART-hade), the ruling Nationalist Party ran the country as two separate systems. On the one side was the privileged white minority—rich and all-powerful. On the other were the millions of deprived "non-whites" that made up the overwhelming majority of the country, who endured lives of harsh repression and economic hardship.

While countries all over the world condemned South Africa, the seeds of ultimate change were sown from within the country by a few courageous voices. One of the most forceful and well-spoken of these belonged to Stephen Biko.

Biko was born in King William's Town, a black suburb of Cape Town, and grew up with the miseries of apartheid. Highly political, in the

MURDER

The body of Stephen Biko lies in a mortuary in King Williams Town, South Africa. This picture was taken shortly after his death in September 1977.

late 1960s he founded the Black Consciousness Movement, and in so doing made himself a marked man. Three times he was taken into custody, twice briefly and once for 101 days. His fourth and final imprisonment began on August 18, 1977, when he was stopped by the Security Police in the Eastern Cape Province and charged with breaking a restriction order that confined him to his own township.

Three weeks later he was hustled into room 619 of the Sanlam Building in Port Elizabeth, handcuffed, placed in leg irons, tortured, and beaten. Eventually, he lapsed into a coma from which he never recovered. On September 13, 1977, Stephen Biko died. He was just thirty-one years old.

At first, the officials blamed his death on the after-effects of a hunger strike. They then changed their story to say he had struck his head against a wall during a struggle while being questioned. Finally, after the conflicting stories had gone to absurd lengths, the government reluctantly agreed to an inquest (legal investigation) to determine if there had been wrongdoing on the part of police.

It was held at the Old Synagogue in Pretoria, and began on November 14, 1977. Despite a large media presence representing countries from all over the world, officials decided to conduct as much of the in-

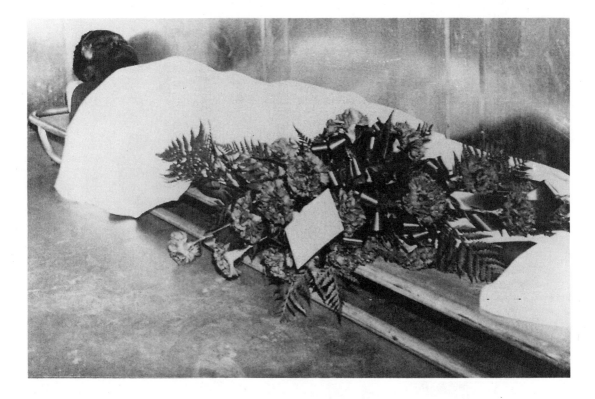

quest as possible in Afrikaans, the language of the ruling white Nationalists. This, combined with the court's poor sound level, often made it difficult to follow the testimony, which began with an autopsy report by Chief State Pathologist Dr. J. D. Loubser, who found that Biko had died of "extensive brain injury."

The Interrogation Begins

The Transvaal's Deputy Attorney General, Klaus von Lieres, led the officer in charge of Biko's interrogation, Major Harold Snyman of the Security Police, through his evidence. Snyman said the interrogation began at 10:30 A.M. and lasted until 6 P.M. During that time, he said, Biko was "extremely aggressive" and very uncooperative about answering questions concerning his political activities.

Sidney Kentridge, chief counsel for the Biko family, wanted to know "what method of persuasion did you use to make an unwilling witness talk to you?"

Snyman denied that he and other officers had beaten Biko, declaring such actions were necessary because they had unlimited time to get the information required. This explanation sounded fine until Kentridge pointed out that for Biko, a man used to prison cells, threats of incarceration would be meaningless.

Under Kentridge's persistent questioning, Snyman described how, after Biko's leg irons and handcuffs were removed, he went "berserk" and tried to attack Warrant Officer Johann Beneke. Snyman said he and Captain Daantjie Siebert went to Beneke's assistance and tried to restrain Biko, who was "clearly beside himself with fury." Several tables were knocked over in the scuffle. Snyman said the amount of violence used against Biko to get him under control was "reasonable, and only as much as was necessary to pin him down on the floor and handcuff him." Next morning Snyman visited Biko again. The shackled man, who had a "wild expression" in his eyes, and a visible swelling on his upper lip, still refused to answer questions and would not take any water. The following day Biko slipped into a coma. He was taken to hospital but failed to respond to treatment and died.

"How did you feel when you heard that Mr. Biko had died?" asked Kentridge.

"I felt bad about it," said Snyman. "He was worth more to us alive than dead."

"Were you surprised he had died?"

"I was surprised. We did not think there was so much wrong with him."

Snyman was followed to the stand by the other members of the interrogation team, all of whom repeated basically the same story as their commanding officer. None of this seemed to make sense alongside the photographs taken of Biko after his death, however, which showed vicious bruising around the wrists and ankles, where the shackles had cut into his skin.

In his final speech, after delivering a bitter attack on those doctors who had attended Biko in hospital, Kentridge asked the court to find that Biko had met his death from "a criminal assault upon him by one or more of the eight members of the Security Police in whose custody he was . . . on September 6th and 7th, 1977."

Answering for the police, Retief van Rooyen dismissed all talk of a cover-up as "sounding just like [mystery writer] Agatha Christie."

On November 30, 1977, Magistrate Martinhus Prins announced his decision. In his opinion, "on the available evidence the death cannot be attributed to any act or omission amounting to a criminal offense on the part of any person."

Mandela's Freedom

With those few words, Prins must have thought he had left the death of Stephen Biko to history. However, history never stands still, and with Nelson Mandela's release from prison in 1990 came the clearest indication yet that white-dominated South Africa was nearing its end. Mandela's election to the presidency shortly afterward raised hopes that something would be done to make up for the wrongs of the past, and ultimately led to the establishment of the Truth and Reconciliation Commission. Under the chairmanship of Archbishop Desmond Tutu, the commissions's task was to confront, expose, and, in most cases, forgive the past, in particular the worst excesses of the ruling Nationalists.

Then, on January 28, 1997, came the bombshell news that five of the officers who interviewed Biko had applied to the Truth Commission for amnesty (forgiveness for offenses). In their application, Snyman, Siebert, Beneke, and two other men—Lieutenant-Colonel Gideon Niewoudt, then a detective sergeant, and Warrant Officer Ruben Marx— all claimed that they were ordered to treat Biko "robustly" but that his death was an accident.

Their confessions sparked off demands, especially from the Black Consciousness Movement, that they should be punished. This was un-

A DISPUTE OVER LANGUAGE

One part of the Biko trial that angered many people was the government's decision to conduct most of the trial in Afrikaans, the language of the ruling Nationalists. Afrikaans came from Dutch, the language of the first permanent European settlers, who populated the Dutch East Indian Company station set up in South Africa in 1652. By 1795, the British had come to rival the Dutch as European settlers, and the two groups struggled over the right to dominate South Africa throughout the nineteenth century, ending in the British victory in the Boer War in 1902. The British established the Union of South Africa in 1910, and in 1931 the British colony achieved its independence. Throughout this time, however, Afrikaans-speaking settlers continued to live and work in South Africa. They were important figures in the Nationalist Party, which established apartheid when it came to power after World War II. The British, by contrast, were associated with more liberal ideas towards black South Africans. Moreover, English was seen as a language connecting South Africa and its people to the world, whereas Afrikaans represented the isolation of the apartheid government. Many political struggles, including riots at Soweto, concerned whether the country's schools should teach black children in Afrikaans or in English.

likely to happen. Without the protection of amnesty, which expired May 1997, the guilty would never have come forward to set the record straight. As for all those who complained that too many people were "getting away with it," President Mandela had this to say: "You can't build a united nation on the basis of revenge."

In 1987 the events surrounding the death of Stephen Biko were dramatized in the movie *Cry Freedom,* starring Denzel Washington and Kevin Kline.

—*Colin Evans*

Suggestions for Further Readings

Attenborough, Richard. *Richard Attenborough's Cry Freedom: A Pictorial Record.* New York: Random House, 1987.

MURDER

Briley, John. *Cry Freedom.* London: Penguin, 1987.

Lewis, Anthony. "Painful Truth." *The New York Times* (February 7, 1997): A33.

Woods, Donald. "Requiem for a Heavyweight." *Newsweek* (February 10, 1997): 43.

Red Brigades Trial: 1982–1983

Defendants: Mario Moretti, Prospero Gallinari, sixty-one others

Crimes Charged: The murder of Aldo Moro and his five bodyguards, eleven additional murders, related terrorist crimes

Chief Defense Lawyers: Various

Chief Prosecutor: Nicolo Amato

Judge: Severino Santiapichi

Place: Rome, Italy

Dates of Trial: April 14, 1982–January 24, 1983

Verdicts: Thirty-two: life imprisonment; twenty-seven: lesser sentences; four: acquitted.

SIGNIFICANCE: The arrest, imprisonment, trial, and conviction of sixty-three terrorists broke the power of the Red Brigades, a terrorist organization that nearly paralyzed Italian political life from 1976 to 1980.

Someone asked Red Brigade leader Mario Moretti what he expected from his trial on charges of killing the former Italian prime minister Aldo Moro. "The Moro trial has already taken place," Moretti said, turning away from the questioner. "It was held four years ago, by us."

That "trial" ended in the execution of Moro, the leader of Italy's Christian Democratic Party and the organizer of the party's historic 1978 alliance (partnership) with the Communist Party of Italy. Moro hoped to increase his party's popularity with a partnership with the Communists.

MURDER

For their part, the Communists, who had never played an important role in the Italian government, the alliance offered a chance to share power.

The alliance drew intense opposition. Rightists (those with conservative political opinions) viewed any dealings with Communists as associating with the forces of Satan. Leftists (those with liberal political opinions) accused the Communist leader, Sergio Berlinguer, of selling out to middle-class politicians to advance his own career. Nevertheless, Moro and Berlinguer forged ahead. By March 1978, the alliance seemed certain to hold.

Former Prime Minister Kidnapped

The Italian Army State Police crowd the Red Brigades into vans after the first day of their trial.

On March 16, 1978, Moro was traveling to a session of parliament in Rome to celebrate the agreement when the Red Brigades struck. A new government, one that included Communists, was to be sworn in that day. Moro never reached the palace. In a carefully planned ambush near the Christian Democratic Party's headquarters and Moro's apartment, a commando squad opened fire on Moro's car. They killed his five bodyguards,

Courtroom Drama

seized Moro—who was unharmed—and whisked him away to a terrorist hideout. There began the fifty-five-day ordeal that Moretti named the "people's court trial" of Aldo Moro.

The Red Brigades grew out of the radical student movement of the late 1960s. With Communist leaders Karl Marx, Vladimir Lenin, and Mao Zedong as revolutionary guides, the extreme tip of the left wing turned increasingly to violence. By the early 1970s, the Red Brigades had become a terrorist organization, calling for "revolutionary violence" against such officials as police officers, magistrate judges, and executives. Aldo Moro, his captors charged, had been "for twenty years the supreme manager of power in Italy."

Moro Murdered

An intense manhunt failed to uncover the Red Brigades' hideout. There the movement's political thinkers tormented the former prime minister. Moro apparently responded with dignity. Told he was being prosecuted in "the name of the people," he responded that the party he headed had received twelve million votes in the last election. He issued pleas through his captors to the Italian government and to Pope Paul VI to bargain in good faith for his release.

The government of Prime Minister Giulio Andreotti, with the support of Berlinguer's Communists, refused to consider the Red Brigades' demand of thirteen jailed terrorists for Moro. For this, Moro's wife Eleonora would later accuse the Italian government and the United States of being responsible for her husband's death. Moro's captors allowed him to write a last letter home. Then the shots rang out. On May 9, 1978, the police found Moro's bullet-riddled body in the trunk of a car parked near the Christian Democratic headquarters.

The authorities launched another manhunt. Police hauled in suspects, questioned and released them. Finally, in 1982, the kidnapping of an American general in Italy by the Red Brigades led to a big break in the case. Italian police raided the house in which General James Dozier was being held, freed him unharmed, and arrested a number of his kidnappers. Mario Moretti's plumbing sprang a leak, creating a second big break. Tenants on the floor below spotted a water stain on the ceiling and called the fire department. One thing led to another, and the police captured both evidence and the mastermind of the Moro killing.

Many Tried and Convicted

Legal action opened in mid-April 1982 to a burst of gunfire. Terrorists shot at security guards surrounding the trial location, the Olympic Sports Center in Rome. Three men were wounded; in the end, 1,500 troops and police were assigned to protect the sports center. Inside, the sixty-three defendants—twenty-three charged in connection to Moro's death, the others with various other murders, kidnappings, and lesser crimes—were held in six white cages. They were not handcuffed; they were allowed cigarettes. They could even chat with reporters and other observers (some of the defendants threatened those who had written unfavorably about them with violence).

The prosecution presented Moretti, a short, stocky twenty-six-year-old, as the leader of the Moro assassination plot. Prospero Gallinari, thirty-three years old, was Moro's jailer and executioner. The government accused Gallinari of killing his captive with a pistol shot, followed by a burst from an automatic weapon. Antonio Savasta and Patrizio Peci testified against their codefendants in exchange for lighter sentences. The judge, Severino Santiapichi, questioned Savasta closely, but Savasta resisted these attempts to make him give up his commitment to his political beliefs and manner of expressing them. "You have to respect my human dignity," Savasta shouted. "You have to understand that inside the Red Brigades there is difficult debate, much indecision. You should show there's not only scorn for us."

The trial continued well into the autumn. The presentation of dozens of witnesses and tens of thousands of pages of documents met with loud complaints from the defendants in their cages. Another five Red Brigade suspects followed the example of Savasta and Peci, rejecting terrorism, yet refusing to give evidence against any of the other defendants. Moretti stood by his beliefs. "You are trying to wipe out five years of armed struggle, but you will not succeed," he told the court. Moro's widow and children sat through many of the sessions, as did the families of the five slain bodyguards and the other victims.

Italy's top government officials testified towards the end of September. Prime Minister Andreotti said the government regarded the attack on Moro as the possible beginning of widespread revolt (uprising against the government). For that reason, the authorities decided against any form of truce (temporary pause in warfare). "In the first moments we had no idea whether the Moro kidnapping was an isolated incident or part of a nationwide armed revolution." Handing over thirteen experienced revolutionary leaders, he suggested, would have been stupid.

Bettino Craxi, the Socialist leader, took the witness stand on September 28. His party, he testified, established private links to the Red Brigades for the purpose of winning Moro's release. However, the Socialists, too, refused to go along with the terrorists' demands for the freedom of the thirteen jailed terrorists, and so the Craxi talks broke down.

The Christmas and New Year's holidays came and went. Finally, in early January, Judge Santiapichi sent the case to the jury of eleven men and one woman. After a week, the jurors announced their verdicts. Santiapichi handed down the sentences on January 24, 1983. Altogether, thirty-two Red Brigade terrorists, among them Moretti and Gallinari, received life imprisonment. (There is no death penalty in Italy.) Other defendants were given sentences ranging from four months to thirty years. Four were acquitted (found not guilty). Four other defendants, including a senior Red Brigade leader convicted in the Dozier kidnapping, remained a wanted criminal in 1983. They had been convicted despite their absence, as permitted under Italian law.

Some of the defendants looked grim, even stunned, others joked and lit up cigarettes, a few climbed the bars of the white cages to wave at friends or family members in the back of the courtroom.

Moro's Bitter Last Words Discovered

The government said that the verdicts were a substantial blow to the Red Brigades terror organization, and they were. "I remember, almost five years ago, a feeling of impotence (helplessness)," Virginio Rognoni, the interior minister, said afterward. "It seemed impossible to think that one day those responsible for the massacre would be in front of the judges."

Red Brigade attacks continued for several more years, but the organization's back had indeed been broken. The Moro case remained in the news, however. In 1990, the authorities announced that a group of workmen in a former Red Brigades apartment in Milan had found some letters Moro had written during his captivity. In them, Moro had harsh words for Andreotti and other senior government officials; Andreotti, he wrote, "moved at ease with his colleagues from the CIA." However, there were touching as well as bitter words in the doomed man's last communications. "Norina," he wrote his wife, "you can imagine the choir of angels that will conduct me from earth to heaven." And finally: "I have been killed three times—through insufficient protection, through refusal to negotiate, through inconclusive politics."

In 1996, the government finally convicted Moro's second killer, Germano Maccari. He received a life sentence for the crime.

MULTI-PARTY GOVERNMENT

Italy has a multi-party (more than one party) form of government. The Italian Communists and the Christian Democrats were the two strongest parties in Italy during the 1980s. However, the Christian Democrats worked together with other political groups to exclude the Communists. In the Italian multi-party system, it is common for different political parties to share power and divide up governmental posts between them.

Suggestions for Further Reading

Drake, Richard. *The Aldo Moro Murder Case.* Cambridge, MA: Harvard University Press, 1996.

Haberman, Clyde. "Italy Sees Hidden Hand Reviving Moro Case." *The New York Times* (October 21, 1990): A6.

Katz, Robert. *Days of Wrath: The Ordeal of Aldo Moro.* Garden City, NY: Doubleday, 1980.

O'Grady, Desmond. "The Trial of the Red Brigades." *Commonweal* (July 16, 1982): 389–91.

Argentina's "Dirty War" Trial: 1985

Defendants: Jorge Videla, Emilio Massera, Orlando Agosti, Roberto Viola, Armando Lambruschini, Leopoldo Galtieri, Jorge Anaya, Omar Graffigna, and Basilio Lami Dozo

Crimes Charged: Murder, kidnapping, illegal detention, torture, robbery, use of false identification to conduct illegal searches

Chief Defense Lawyers: Twenty-two defense attorneys

Chief Prosecutors: Julio Strassera and Luis Moreno Ocampo

Judges: Six-member Federal Court of Appeals, presiding judge León Arslanian

Place: Buenos Aires, Argentina

Dates of Trial: April 22–December 9, 1985

Verdicts: Guilty (Videla, Massera, Viola, Agosti, and Lambruschini); not guilty (Galtieri, Anaya, Graffigna, and Lami Dozo)

Sentences: Life imprisonment (Videla and Massera); seventeen years' imprisonment (Viola); eight years' imprisonment (Lambruschini); four and a half years' imprisonment (Agosti).

SIGNIFICANCE: The trial of military officers responsible for the "dirty war," in which thousands of innocent civilians died, was Argentina's first major step in restoring democracy after years of dictatorship and political violence. It was also the first public trial of military dictators in Latin American history.

MURDER

On March 24, 1976, the military overthrew (forced from power) the government of President Isabel Perón in Argentina. Many hoped that the new government would strengthen the country and end violence. Between 1976 and 1979, however, this need for order became a national nightmare.

The new government—led by Army Lieutenant General Jorge Videla, Navy Admiral Emilio Massera, and Air Force Brigadier General Orlando Agosti—dismissed the nation's congress, got rid of elected officials, and banned all political activity. The new government was secretive about its goals. The leaders and their allies within the military agreed that Argentina needed social change if "Western, Christian values" were to survive there. They decided that everyone suspected of opposing the new government would have to die. The name of this policy was "the Process of National Reorganization." It soon came to be known by a name the government gave itself—"the dirty war."

The Terror Begins

The terror began quietly. Argentines were slow to recognize an enormous increase in arrests. Security forces kidnapped blue collar workers, professionals, students, journalists, nuns, teachers, psychiatrists, union members, and thousands of others. They tortured and murdered most. Some were buried in secret mass graves. Many more were thrown out of aircraft flying over the ocean, often while they were still alive.

The terror soon became great. Many Argentines would not openly speak of friends or relatives taken away by soldiers for fear that they too might be taken away. From 1976 to 1979, between 9,000 and 30,000 men, women, and children vanished. They were known as "the disappeared."

Courts rejected legal requests from worried family members that their loved ones either be freed or formally charged with crimes. Authorities reasoned that the police had no record of those named in these requests. Therefore, no charges against them existed. This made such requests meaningless. Suddenly those who made the requests were missing. Police sped up the deaths of prisoners named in them.

News of the Argentine government's secret war on its own people continued to leak out of the country. Other countries criticized Argentina but the dirty war continued well into 1979. In 1982, Argentina lost a war to England over control of the Falkland Islands, off Argentina's Atlantic coast, and the military leaders resigned in disgrace, clearing the way for free public elections. Before giving up control, though, the military passed a law pardoning anyone who had ever been involved in the dirty war.

Military Leaders Face Prosecution

Upon taking office on December 10, 1983, President Rául Alfonsín ordered the nine military leaders who held power between March 1976 and June 1982 to face trial. Also charged was the Buenos Aires police chief, General Ramón Camps. The pardon the military leaders had given themselves was canceled.

In spite of Alfonsín's pre-election promise to investigate the dirty war, prosecution went slowly. The Supreme Council of the Armed Forces, formed at Alfonsín's request and made up of retired military officers, was originally supposed to try the accused officers. After eight months of hearings, the council announced that it was having difficulty reaching a verdict. The council stated that the defendants could only be held "indirectly responsible" for the actions of those who actually carried out the crimes.

However, Alfonsín had also asked the National Commission on Disappeared Persons (CONADEP) to investigate the "disappearances." Its report arrived in September 1984, the same month the military council declined to charge the officers. CONADEP's 50,000-page report, "Never Again," revealed the dirty war as a well-organized plan for acts of cruelty approved by the military rulers. Testimony of witnesses described hundreds of cases of kidnapping, robbery, rape, murder, and secret burial. The report documented 8,921 "disappearances," and concluded that lives of thousands more had probably been lost in this "national tragedy." The investigation also named 1,300 military and police officers who had been involved in the terror, but their names were not made public.

Authority to try the cases was taken away from the military council and given to the Federal Court of Appeals. The cases of several hundred accused junior officers remained before the military council, but the officers responsible for authorizing the terror would now face a public court.

None of the military leaders were personally charged with crimes relating to the "disappeared." However, the leaders were held responsible for the crimes committed by those who carried out their orders. Six defendants—generals Jorge Videla, Roberto Viola, and Leopoldo Galtieri; admirals Emilio Massera and Armando Lambruschini; and Brigadier General Orlando Agosti—were charged with murder, kidnapping, torture, robbery, and making illegal searches with false identification. General Omar Graffigna faced the same charges, except homicide (murder). Admirals Jorge Anaya and Basilio Lami Dozo were charged with kidnapping and using false documents.

Testimony Recounts Horrors

The trial began on April 22, 1985, with hundreds of spectators packing the courtroom of the Palace of Justice. Six public judges would decide the fate of the accused.

The CONADEP report's list of horrors was repeated in testimony that lasted for four months. Prosecutor Julio Strassera called over 1,000 witnesses. Over 700 individual cases were described. One mother who had been arrested for searching for her disappeared child spoke of hearing her daughter's screams through jail walls. Asked if she had anything more to say at the close of her testimony, her reply echoed the heartache of thousands: "I want to know if my daughter is alive or dead."

Prosecutors argued that as supreme rulers of the country, the nine commanders were not simply following orders by allowing cruel acts to take place. Evidence proved there was a pattern of crimes against humanity of which the commanders must have been aware.

The prosecution's final statement lasted for five days. When prosecutor Julio Strassera ended by crying *"Nunca mas!"*—"Never again!"—the hundreds of spectators crammed into the court began clapping.

While prosecutors called over 1,000 witnesses, the defense called fewer than 30. Defense lawyers argued that the military leaders could not be held responsible for any wrongs committed by junior officers or the police. The defense also said that the dirty war was a part of the government's earlier war with rebels.

The accused chose not to sit in court during testimony describing the crimes committed during their rule. When they appeared during the lawyers' final statements, none of them showed sorrow for their acts. They felt that they were on trial because their political enemies were out to get them.

Questions Remain

Although the law allowed prosecutors to seek the death penalty, they asked for life sentences for the military commanders. Long prison terms were requested for the other defendants.

The verdicts were announced on December 9, 1985. Videla and Massera were found guilty and sentenced to life in prison. Viola received a seven-year prison term and Lambruschini eight years. The Argentine air force was found to have been less involved in the terror than the army

REMEMBERING THE "DISAPPEARED"

Despite the brutal cover-up of the "dirty war," the Argentine people did organize protests. Women would bring pictures of "disappeared" family members to vigils, demonstrating that they remembered the loved ones they had lost, and demanding that the world remember, as well. The rock star Sting was so moved by these protests that he commemorated them in his song, *They Dance Alone.*

and navy. Instead of life imprisonment, the air force commander during the first military government, Agosti, received a sentence of four and a half years. Those who took his place in the second military government, Graffigna and Lami Dozo, were found not guilty. So were Galtieri and Anaya, who commanded the army and navy during the third military government, after the worst violence was past. All of those convicted were kicked out of the military.

Both prosecutors and defense attorneys were unhappy with the verdicts and sentences. Both sides appealed, without success. Human rights groups believed the sentences were too soft. Supporters of the military were equally angered by the verdicts. Still, many Argentines saw the guilty verdicts as a hopeful sign that the justice system might finally be free of government control.

The trial did not end questions about the dirty war. Several more high-ranking officers were convicted in later trials. President Alfonsín remained under pressure to pardon the men or, at least, to end the prosecution of hundreds of accused murderers and torturers still serving in Argentina's powerful military. Hoping to put the dirty war behind him, Alfonsín agreed to laws that stopped further prosecutions. The next president, Carlos Menem, continued to silence the right wing by granting pardons for 100 defendants still facing prosecution. On December 29, 1990, President Menem pardoned and freed Videla, Massera, and all other convicted officers still in jail.

Menem stated that five years he had spent in illegal detention during the dirty war gave him the right to "close a sad and black period of

MURDER

national history." Yet thousands of Argentines paraded to protest the unpopular pardons, proving that the dirty war was an open wound that would not soon heal.

Suggestions for Further Reading

Chavez, Lydia. "In Argentine Court, Tales of Horror and Heroism." *The New York Times* (May 28, 1985): 2.

Nunca Más: The Report of the Argentine National Commission on the Disappeared. New York: Farrar, Strauss, Giroux, 1986.

Rudolph, James D., ed. *Argentina: A Country Study.* Washington, D.C.: The American University, 1986.

Simpson, James and Jana Bennett. *The Disappeared and the Mothers of the Plaza.* New York: St. Martin's Press, 1985.

Timerman, Jacobo. *Prisoner without a Name, Cell without a Number.* New York: Alfred A. Knopf, 1981.

The Sharpeville Six Trial: 1985

Defendants: Mojalefa "Ja-Ja" Sefatsa, Reid Mokoena, Oupa Diniso, Theresa Ramashamola, Christiaan Mokubung, Gideon Mokone, Duma Khumalo, and Francis Mokhesi

Crimes Charged: Murder of Jacob Dlamini; a subversion charge of "acting with a common purpose unlawfully . . . [to influence the government . . . and/or to intimidate, demoralize, or persuade members of the public to do or not do something]"; other charges of malicious damage to property; arson

Chief Defense Lawyers: Jack Unterhalter, Ismail Hussain, and Prakash Diar

Chief Prosecutor: Eben Jordaan

Judges: Acting Justice Wessel Johannes Human, Assessors Dr. D. W. R. Herzog and I. L. Grindlay-Ferris

Place: Pretoria, South Africa

Dates of Trial: September 23–December 13, 1985

Verdicts: Guilty of murder (Sefatsa, Mokoena, Diniso, Ramashamola, Khumalo, and Mokhesi); guilty of public violence (Mokubung and Mokone); guilty of subversion (all)

Sentences: Sefatsa, Mokoena, Diniso, Ramashamola, Khumalo, Mokhesi: death by hanging on murder count (death sentences later changed to imprisonment); Mokubung, Mokone: five years' imprisonment on count of public violence; all defendants: eight years' imprisonment on count of subversion

SIGNIFICANCE: Judges and police ignored basic human rights in this case. This was common in South Africa, when the races were legally separated by the system of apartheid (a-PART-hade).

MURDER

Sharpeville is a black township of 6,000 small brick houses in the Johannesburg region of South Africa. It first came to world attention as the site of a 1960 massacre of sixty-nine blacks by white police officers. On September 3, 1984, widespread protests erupted against recent increases in public service fees. One local black leader died and police arrested eight local blacks. Police singled out people almost randomly as scapegoats for the violence committed by mobs. Courts gave them the death sentence for an act in which they played either a very minor role or possibly no role at all. The case of the Sharpeville Six (named after six of the eight defendants condemned to death) became well-known internationally.

The 1984 Incident

It started with the 1982 Black Local Authorities Act. Under this law, the white government shifted responsibility for local government to elected black councils. At the same time, they withheld proper funding for road maintenance and construction, trash removal, sewerage, electrification, and basic services. To close the financial gap, the councils raised service fees. Violence erupted, often directed at the black officials, many of whom were seen as corrupt servants of the white rulers.

In Sharpeville, Jacob Dlamini, a deputy mayor, became the focus of mob anger. On the night of September 2, stones shattered all the windows of his house. The next morning, several hundred protesters gathered to march to the township administrative offices to picket against rent increases. They carried placards (signs), sang, shouted slogans, and along the way forced onlookers to join them by threatening injury and damage to their houses. As the protesters neared Dlamini's house, they paused to throw stones. Police chased away the crowd with tear gas and rubber bullets, and asked Dlamini to leave with them because it was not safe to stay. Because of emergencies elsewhere, however, the police had to leave. A mob of some 100 shortly regrouped to stone the house some more. Dlamini shot a gun from inside and injured at least one person. Enraged, the mob tossed gasoline bombs at the house, setting it on fire. As Dlamini ran out, one or more persons struggled with him and took away his gun. They threw stones and knocked him down. Then they pushed his car into the street, overturned, and burned it. More horribly, the crowd dragged the unconscious Dlamini into the street and set him on fire. He was dead when the police returned at 9:00 that morning.

Two months passed before police took any action. They then arrested eight suspects. The police first came for Mojalefa "Ja-Ja" Sefatsa, a twenty-nine-year-old fruit seller. He insisted that at the time of the murder he had been away at his aunt's house. However, different testimony by Mrs. Dlamini and her neighbor, Jantjie Mabuti, placed him at the scene. Mabuti also placed five others at the scene. He said that Theresa Ramashamola, a twenty-four-year-old cook, had slapped a woman who had objected to the burning of Dlamini. Ramashamola said that she had been forced to join the march, had been hit in the head by a police rubber bullet, sought treatment, and then went home. Police tortured both Ramashamola and Sefatsa during interrogation.

Mabuti also testified that both Christiaan Mokubung and Gideon Mokone were in the mob tossing stones at the house. Mokone, in fact, had been injured by the bullet from Dlamini's gun, and then carried away for treatment at the hospital. Crowds had forced both to join the march. Mokubung had fled when the police broke up the crowd. Neither was present when the mob regrouped. Mabuti also placed at the scene Duma Khumalo, a twenty-six-year-old teacher-trainee. Mabuti said Khumalo had handed out gasoline bombs. Khumalo's story was that he had been forced to join the march. He admitted that he had witnessed the stoning of the house. (He was in fact related to Dlamini and said he had no anger against him.) However, he then carried a friend injured by a rubber bullet to a nearby house for treatment and later took him home. Therefore, he had not been present when the mob continued its attack.

Mabuti also accused Francis Mokhesi, a twenty-eight-year-old professional soccer player, of taking the lead in making gasoline bombs and of helping to push the car into the street. Arrested seven months after the murder, Mokhesi had as his alibi a week-long ankle injury that had sidelined him from soccer. Another witness, Joseph Manete, also accused Khumalo and Mokhesi. (In 1988, Manete would confess in a newspaper interview that he had given false testimony when pressured by police.)

Of the remaining two defendants, Reid Mokoena, a twenty-one-year-old unskilled laborer, had been arrested by the police and tortured into signing a false confession that he had thrown a stone at the house. He claimed that he had been forced to join the march, had been tear-gassed, and after washing his face at a nearby house had returned home. He had never reached Dlamini's house.

The final defendant, Oupa Diniso, a twenty-nine-year-old factory inspector, was arrested merely for possession of what the police claimed was Dlamini's gun. He had spent the day of the riot at a church and at home. The next day he came across three young boys arguing over a gun they had found. For reasons of safety, he said, he took the gun away from the boys and took it home. The state claimed that he had taken the gun from Dlamini.

The Trial

Police arrested and held the suspects under the Internal Security Act. They kept seven in solitary confinement for over nine months before the trial. In court for the first time on April 25, 1985, they finally learned the charges against them: they were responsible for the actions of the mob. The state claimed that the defendants had intended to make the government give up its plan to give local authority to black leaders. It claimed they had caused those black authorities in office to resign and to have service fee increases canceled. The attorney general prevented the court from granting the defendants bail. In effect, this had become a political trial that could become a model for future trials of rioters.

The state brought seventy-two-year-old Wessel Johannes Human out of retirement to act as judge, even though most of his experience had been as a lawyer. The prosecution presented six state eyewitnesses. Of these, three gave evidence that did not relate to any of the defendants. Mrs. Dlamini implicated Sefatsa, Manete falsely implicated Khumalo and Mokhesi, and Mabuti—the key state witness—implicated all except Mokoena and Diniso. Defense cross-examination revealed serious problems with Mabuti's detailed story. Despite defense witness testimony supporting the alibis of the accused, the judge refused to accept this testimony. Instead he chose to accept that of Mabuti. Neither did the judge accept medical testimony pointing to the use of electric shock torture to make Mokoena talk. That the judge had already made up his mind in advance was suggested by his questioning of Mokoena:

Judge: But those people who told you . . . to walk with them, we know now . . . that these people were not on the way to the municipal offices, they were on the way to Dlamini's house in order to burn it down and to burn him to death. . . . Did they not say to you, look, we have to go to Dlamini's house now, and set it on fire and kill him?

Mokoena: No.

The Verdict and Sentences

In his verdict, the judge rejected evidence raising reasonable doubt or favoring the accused. Apparently to set an example for other violent protesters, he disregarded other factors, such as the effects of mob psychology, that might help to clear the defendants. Whereas a jury might well have considered the total situation, he simply found the defendants guilty. He condemned six to death and the two others to lengthy prison terms.

FROM SOWETO TO SHARPEVILLE

The 1984 incident at Sharpeville reminded many of a previous incident at Soweto in 1976. Whereas Sharpeville was the name of a single township, Soweto was the name for a group of townships about ten miles southwest of South Africa's capital, Johannesburg. The incident at Soweto began as a black student protest against the use of the Afrikaans language in the schools. (Afrikaans is a language that developed from the Dutch, spoken by the original European settlers of the region.) The students claimed that they should learn their native languages and English instead of Afrikaans, which is a language spoken only in South Africa, and only by a portion of the whites who lived there. The student protest was met with severe racial violence, and the riots that followed spread to other black urban centers. Many people at the time saw both Soweto and Sharpeville as symbols of police violence as well as signs of black resistance.

In the end, it was international publicity and pressure that embarrassed the president of South Africa, P. W. Botha, on November 23, 1988, into commuting the death sentences of the Sharpeville Six to 18, 20, and 25 years' imprisonment. This move did not, however, wipe out the original injustice of their conviction. The trial was, according to one foreign journalist, an exercise in "judicial terrorism."

An attempt was eventually made to right this wrong when the South African government began to reform itself. Christiaan Mokubung and Gideon Mokone—who had been found guilty only of public violence—were released on December 10, 1990. Oupa Diniso and Duma Khumalo were released on July 10, 1991. Theresa Ramashamola and Reid Mokoena were released (on parole) on December 13, 1991. Mojalefa Sefatsa and Francis Mokhesi were released on September 26, 1992.

Suggestions for Further Reading

Diar, Prakash. *The Sharpeville Six*. Toronto: McClellan & Stewart, Inc., 1990.

MURDER

Phillips, Norman. *The Tragedy of Apartheid: A Journalist's Experiences in the South African Riots.* New York: David McKay, 1960.

Reeves, Ambrose. *Shooting at Sharpeville: The Agony of South Africa.* Boston: Houghton Mifflin, 1961.

Smith, William E. "Black Rage, White Fist." *Time* (August 5, 1985): 24–32.

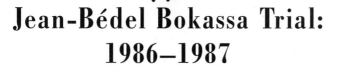

Jean-Bédel Bokassa Trial: 1986–1987

Defendant: Jean-Bédel Bokassa

Crimes Charged: Murder, cannibalism, embezzlement of state funds, illegal use of property, assault and battery

Chief Defense Lawyers: François Gibault and Francis Szpiner

Chief Prosecutor: Gabriel-Faustin M'Boudou

Judge: Presiding Judge Edouard Franck

Place: Bangui, Central African Republic

Dates of Trial: December 15, 1986–June 12, 1987

Verdict: Guilty

Sentence: Death, commuted to life imprisonment

SIGNIFICANCE: The prosecution of Bokassa for crimes committed during his notorious reign was the first fair trial by jury of a head of state in the history of post-colonial Africa.

Many dictators have been brought to justice for mistreating the people they rule. In 1986, however, Jean-Bédel Bokassa became the first tyrant to be prosecuted for eating his subjects.

Bokassa was the army chief of staff in the Central African Republic, a former French colony. In 1966, he led a successful effort to overthrow the government of his cousin, David Dacko. A decade after taking control, Bokassa imitated his hero Napoleon Bonaparte, the nineteenth-century French emperor, by declaring himself emperor of the Central African Republic. He marked the beginning of his reign with a lavish coronation that cost $25 million. This was a fantastic sum of money for his poor African country to spend.

Bokassa's Crimes

This extravagant show was soon surpassed by Bokassa's greed and cruelty. When he took for himself the choicest gems in the Central African Republic's diamond mines, he nearly drove the country into bankruptcy. He executed hundreds of politicians he imagined to be his enemies, and he had foreign journalists who criticized his actions beaten and jailed.

Bokassa's treatment of his subjects was even more vicious. He celebrated Mother's Day 1971 by hanging all those imprisoned for crimes against women. People whispered that those who crossed him were sometimes fed to the crocodiles and lions he kept in cages on the palace grounds. Some said that Bokassa himself ate the flesh of those he had killed.

Jean-Bédel Bokassa in 1979 during a trip to Paris. In 1987, a court found Bokassa guilty of murder, along with other crimes, and sentenced him to life in prison.

None of the Central African Republic's neighbors confronted Bokassa when they heard of his crimes. France, which hoped to keep its access to the country's diamond mines, also turned a blind eye. In April 1979, however, Bokassa personally participated in the slaughter of more than 100 schoolchildren. This proved too much for the rest of the world to ignore. On September 20, while Bokassa was visiting the northern African country of Libya, French paratroopers landed in the Central African Republic and restored David Dacko to power.

Bokassa went into exile (leaving one's country, not to return). First he went to Abidjan, the capital of the Ivory Coast, on the west coast of

Africa. Then he went to Paris, where he gained entry using the French passport he had earned fighting with France during World War II. Although many French citizens protested his presence, Bokassa stayed in the country for the next seven years, living off his French military pension. When that proved to be too little money, he sold the rights to his memoirs. One of the claims he made in the resulting book was that he had shared women in the Central African Republic with French President Valery Giscard d'Estaing when he visited Bokassa there. This claim resulted in French courts ordering that all 8,000 copies of Bokassa's books be destroyed. Bokassa also claimed that he had given Giscard d'Estaing $250,000 worth of diamonds in 1973. The French president's bid for reelection the next year failed, largely because of this claim.

Jean-Bédel
Bokassa
Trial:
1986–1987

The Emperor Returns to Face Trial

On October 23, 1986, Bokassa flew back to the Central African Republic. Incredibly, he expected his former subjects to welcome his return. Instead, he was arrested as soon as he stepped off the plane. Fifteen charges were filed against him, including murder, stealing state funds, and acquiring human flesh for purposes of cannibalism. In 1980, he had been convicted on these same charges in his absence and sentenced to death. However, now that he was back in the country, the law required the government to try him in person and give him a defense lawyer.

Prosecutors considered holding the trial in the capital's sports stadium, which had been the site of Bokassa's coronation. They decided against it, however, thinking that this plan might result in chaos. Instead, the trial opened on December 15, 1986, in the chambers of the Palace of Justice. Bokassa had two French lawyers. Judge Edouard Franck presided over a jury of six and a panel of three judges. This was the first time since foreign powers had left Africa that the continent saw a fair trial by jury of a head of state. For the first time the public had access to the trial.

Those who did not attend in person were able to follow the trial over the radio. All over the country, people listened to testimony about the cruelty they had experienced under Bokassa's government and the relatives they had lost. His victims ranged from political enemies to the newborn son of a palace guard who had been executed after trying to assassinate Bokassa. A nurse testified that the guard's pregnant widow told her Bokassa had threatened to kill her child if it was a boy. When the boy was born, Bokassa had the newborn killed by giving an injection of poison.

Bokassa also faced charges for the two crimes that led to his downfall. In January 1979, he had ordered all students wear expensive uniforms made in a factory owned by one of his wives. When a group of school-children protested, Bokassa ordered soldiers to fire on them. Several were killed. And when some elementary school children threw rocks at his car three months later, Bokassa ordered 180 children arrested and put in jail. That night the emperor went to the prison, where he smashed the skulls of half a dozen children with his walking stick. He ordered his soldiers to kill the others. Only 27 children survived.

Bokassa denied all the charges against him. Instead, he blamed others in his government. "I'm not a saint," he told the court. "I'm just a man like everyone else." As the evidence against him mounted, however, Bokassa lost his temper. "The aggravating thing about all this is that it's Bokassa, Bokassa, Bokassa. I have enough crimes leveled against me without you blaming me for all the murders of the last twenty-one years!"

Testimony about Cannibalism

Cannibalism was certainly the most sensational charge leveled against Bokassa, but it was not the most serious one. Laws forbidding cannibalism in the Central African Republic classified all acts connected with eating human flesh as minor crimes. When Andre Kolingba seized power from David Dacko in 1981, Kolingba pardoned all those guilty of misdemeanors that had been committed during Dacko's administration. Bokassa could not, therefore, be punished for cannibalism, even if he were found guilty.

Former president Dacko testified that he had seen photographs of cut-up bodies hanging in the cold storage room of Bokassa's palace in 1979. Bokassa's chef also testified that he had cooked human flesh and served it to Bokassa. The court did not examine rumors that Bokassa had served human flesh to President Giscard and other visiting foreign leaders.

On June 12, 1987, Bokassa was found guilty. The court found that although many murder charges had been brought against him, the evidence was strong in only about twenty cases. Regardless of the number, the result was the same. Bokassa cried quietly as he was sentenced to death. His lawyers appealed the sentence on grounds that the nation's constitution allowed only a former head of state to be charged with treason. The supreme court rejected this appeal.

On February 29, 1988, President Kolingba abolished (canceled) the death penalty in the Central African Republic. Bokassa was then ordered to spend the rest of his life in solitary confinement.

A REPUBLIC IN CENTRAL AFRICA

The Central African Republic rests on a savanna-covered plateau, with tropical forests to the south and a semidesert area to the east. Although the country has many rivers, only the Ubangi can be navigated by commercial vessels. The major economic activity of the nation is agriculture, with about 90 percent of the population engaged in subsistence farming. The country also produces cotton and coffee for export, as well as diamonds and timber. Despite the rich natural resources of the Central African Republic, the country remains extremely poor, with no railroads and few paved roads. The country is populated by the Mandjia-Baya, the Banda, the Mbaka, and the Zandhe peoples. Although French is the official national language—a legacy of colonial days—Sangho is the language most widely spoken. More than half of the people of the Central African Republic practice traditional *animist* religions (religions that believe that spirits inhabit and animate the natural world); most of the rest of the country's people follow Christianity.

Suggestions for Further Reading

Harmon, Jeff B. "His Former Majesty, Bokassa." *Harper's* (May 1980): 34–39.

Shoumatoff, Robert. *African Madness.* New York: Alfred A. Knopf, 1988.

"Trying the 'Butcher of Bangui.'" *Newsweek* (December 29, 1986): 27.

O. J. Simpson Trial: 1995

Defendant: Orenthal James Simpson
Crime Charged: Murder
Chief Defense Lawyer: Johnnie L. Cochran Jr.
Chief Prosecutor: Marcia Clark
Judge: Lance A. Ito
Place: Los Angeles, California
Dates of Trial: January 24–October 2, 1995
Verdict: Not guilty

SIGNIFICANCE: With its mixture of race and celebrity, the trial of sports hero O. J. Simpson attracted enough public attention to be called the "trial of the century." The racially divided reaction to the verdict in the case indicated how deep a gulf still separated black and white in America in the 1990s.

For many people, the murder trial of football hero and actor O. J. Simpson was "the trial of the century." The case began around midnight on June 12, 1994. Neighbors of Simpson's ex-wife, Nicole Brown Simpson, heard her dog whimpering and barking. The dog led some of these neighbors to the bodies of Nicole and Ronald L. Goldman, one of Nicole's friends. The bodies lay on the walkway outside Nicole's home in the Brentwood section of Los Angeles, California.

Police Detectives Investigate Murders

Before dawn, Detectives Philip Vannater and Tom Lange of the Los Angeles Police Department (LAPD) were investigating the crime. The de-

FOOTBALL HERO

When O. J. Simpson was first suspected of the murders of Nicole Brown Simpson and Ronald L. Goldman, the nation was shocked. Simpson had achieved widespread fame and admiration for his achievements as a football player. As a running back for the University of Southern California, he won the 1968 Heisman Trophy for the best college player of the year. From 1969 to 1977, Simpson played with the Buffalo Bills, and from 1978 to 1979 he played with the San Francisco 49ers. In his twenty-year career, his record of 11,236 yards gained rushing was second only to that of Jim Brown. Simpson ranked first in season records for most yards gained (2,003 in 1973) and for most touchdowns (twenty-three in 1975). After his football career ended, Simpson became a sportscaster, a movie actor, and a spokesperson for Hertz car rentals.

tectives were ordered to notify O. J. Simpson of his ex-wife's death and to arrange care for the Simpsons' two young children. After the children were taken from Nicole's home to police headquarters, the detectives went to Simpson's estate. They took with them Detective Mark Fuhrman. Fuhrman had been called to the estate ten years earlier to answer a distress call placed by a bruised and battered Nicole. Up until that time, most people thought that the Simpsons had the perfect interracial marriage: Simpson was African American, Nicole was white.

At Simpson's house, no one answered the bell outside the walled estate. While the detectives were waiting to get in, Fuhrman examined a Ford Bronco parked in the street near the estate's rear gate. He noticed what appeared to be bloodstains on the door of the car. Vannater then ordered Fuhrman to climb over the wall and let him and Lange inside. When no one answered the front door of the house, the detectives went to the guest house. Let in by Simpson family friend Brian "Kato" Kaelin, the detectives also found that Simpson's adult daughter, Arnelle, lived in the guest complex. She told them that her father had taken a late night flight to Chicago. Detective Ronald Phillips telephoned Simpson there to give him the news.

Kaelin told the other detectives that around 10:40 P.M. he had heard loud thumps outside the wall of his room. Fuhrman went outside to investigate a narrow passage between this wall and a chain-link fence. There he found a black leather glove that seemed to be bloody. It matched another glove the LAPD had found at the murder scene. The detectives also saw what appeared to be drops of blood on the driveway, on the path to the front door of the main house, and in the entryway of the house.

When Simpson returned the next day, Los Angeles police questioned him for three hours. They noticed that he had a cut on his left hand, which was bandaged and swollen. They also obtained a blood sample from him. When they declared Simpson their prime suspect and prepared to arrest him, however, he was gone.

The mug shot of O. J. Simpson, taken June 17, 1994, soon after he surrendered to police at his Brentwood estate in Los Angeles, California. The District Attorney charged him with two counts of murder in connection with the killings of his ex-wife, Nicole, and her friend, Ronald Goldman.

The "Chase"

That evening, networks broadcast the strange sight of police cars following a white Ford Bronco as it drove slowly along the Los Angeles freeways. Inside were O. J. Simpson's friend, Al Cowlings, and O. J. himself—reportedly holding a gun to his own head. After ninety minutes, the

Bronco returned to Simpson's estate, where Simpson was arrested. On Monday, June 20, a Los Angeles County grand jury charged him with murder. He was jailed without bail.

The news media coverage was intense. As television provided live coverage of every aspect of the case, thousands of people flocked to Simpson's estate to stare.

On July 29, Simpson appeared in court to be formally charged. He was accompanied by Robert L. Shapiro, a well-known white California lawyer, and Johnnie Cochran, who would soon become America's most famous African American trial attorney.

The state was represented by Deputy District Attorney Marcia Clark, who had not lost a murder case in ten years. She was also an expert on using circumstantial evidence and DNA (a molecule that appears in all living cells but is different in each individual) to prove guilt. She was assisted by Deputy District Attorney Christopher Darden, an African American prosecutor who had much experience trying murder cases.

O. J.
Simpson
Trial: 1995

O. J. Simpson and the "Dream Team" defense attorneys (left to right): Robert Shapiro, Johnnie Cochran, and Simpson.

The Trial Begins

Toward the end of 1994, Judge Lance A. Ito seated twelve jurors and twelve alternate jurors. The majority of these jurors were African American and female. The trial itself opened on January 24, 1995. Clark told the jury that the prosecution would present evidence of "a trail of blood where there should be no blood." It led from the path outside Nicole Brown Simpson's home to a pair of socks found in Simpson's bedroom. Darden added a description of Simpson's years of abusing his wife, both physically and mentally. Cochran opened by telling the jury that the defense would present more than a dozen witnesses that the prosecutors did not know existed. Clark responded that this tactic amounted to "trial by ambush."

Judge Lance A. Ito presided over the Simpson murder trial, which opened on January 24, 1995.

The Prosecution Presents Its Case

The prosecutors first presented evidence of Simpson's past abuse of Nicole. Then they turned to the night of the murders. They carefully laid out the details of how the bodies had been discovered. Then the defense team went on the attack, claiming that the LAPD had mismanaged the entire murder investigation. The prosecution's theory was that a jealous Simpson had set out to kill his ex-wife, but ended up murdering two people when Ron Goldman unexpectedly appeared on the scene. The defense team responded with a theory of its own: that Nicole was murdered by drug dealers. When the prosecutors put Detective Fuhrman on the witness stand, however, he gave testimony that pointed strongly at Simpson as the murderer.

Experts on gloves were called to testify that the bloody gloves found at the murder scene and at Simpson's estate belonged to the defendant. Shoe experts testified that bloody shoe prints found at the murder scene had been made by shoes that belonged to Simpson. Still other experts testified about DNA evidence that strongly indicated Simpson was the murderer. As the trial went on for months, one juror after another was excused from the case and replaced by an alternate juror. On July 6, 1995, after 24 weeks during which it had presented 58 witnesses and 488 exhibits, the prosecution rested its case.

O. J. Simpson Trial: 1995

The Defense and the "Race Card"

At this point in the trial, the defense changed tactics. The first indication of this change came on July 12. Robert Heidstra, a witness for the defense, testified that at 10:40 P.M. on the night of the murders, he had been walking his dog past Nicole's home. As he passed, he heard two people arguing. He said they sounded to him like a younger white woman and an older black man. Cochran erupted. "You can't tell by someone's voice when they're black. That's racist, and I resent it."

The defense continued to present other evidence. Witnesses testified to such things as Simpson's arthritis, which they said was so disabling as to prevent him from carrying out the murders. Others testified that there had been no blood on the Bronco. Still others testified that the blood evidence that pointed to Simpson as the murderer had been contaminated.

None of these arguments was especially convincing. Then the defense delivered a bombshell. A North Carolina screenwriter, Laura Hart McKinny, revealed that she had sixteen hours of taped interviews with Detective Fuhrman. She had made these tapes years before as part of her research for a project. On the tapes, Fuhrman admitted to having in the past done such illegal things as arresting people without just cause and destroying evidence. Most telling of all, he repeatedly referred to African Americans—whom he clearly disliked—as "niggers."

Fuhrman's use of the "N word" made him guilty of perjury (lying under oath). Earlier in the trial, he had told defense attorneys under cross examination that he never referred to blacks in such a way. Simpson's attorneys had been trying to demonstrate that their client was framed by the LAPD because he was a rich, successful black man. Now, their task was easier. It appeared to many that the blood evidence had not just been mishandled, it had been tampered with. And Fuhrman, who had found the

THE VERDICT—HOW THE PUBLIC FELT

In a *Newsweek* survey published in their February 17, 1997 issue, results showed that 82 percent of black Americans felt that O. J. Simpson should keep custody of his children. Only 44 percent of white citizens polled felt that he should keep custody. From *all* people questioned in this survey, 70 percent felt that Simpson would never be able to resume his part as a public figure, and 53 percent felt that they would refuse to buy a product he endorsed.

telltale bloody gloves, now seemed to be a lying racist who could easily have planted this crucial evidence.

By the time the attorneys delivered their closing arguments, nearly all of the original jurors had been replaced by alternates. Three-quarters of the jury was now African American. Cochran repeatedly referred to Simpson's failed attempt to try on the bloody gloves (the prosecution argued that as the blood dried, the leather gloves shrank): "If it doesn't fit, you must acquit."

After the trial was over, Shapiro, who had had a falling out with Cochran, said that the defense team had played "the race card" from the bottom of the deck. The claim of racism, Shapiro implied, was a dirty trick.

Less than four hours after the jury began its deliberations, it returned with a verdict. On October 2, 1995, the jury declared O. J. Simpson not guilty of either murder. Americans, who had followed the case for over a year, were divided into two camps, largely along racial lines. Whites for the most part believed that Simpson had gotten away with murder. Most African Americans, however, were elated that Simpson had beaten what they saw as an unfair judicial system. The split between blacks and whites over the case of O. J. Simpson was symbolic of the state of race relations in America in the 1990s.

Suggestions for Further Reading

Clark, Marcia with Theresa Carpenter. *Without a Doubt*. New York: Viking, Penguin, 1997.

Cochran, Johnnie. *Journey to Justice*. New York: Ballantine, 1996.

Timothy McVeigh Trial: 1997

Defendant: Timothy McVeigh

Crimes Charged: Murder, conspiracy to cause an explosion

Chief Defense Lawyers: Stephen Jones, Richard H. Burr III, Jeralynn Merritt, Robert Nigh Jr., and Cheryl Ramsey

Chief Prosecutors: Joseph Hartzler, Patrick Ryan, and Beth Wilkinson

Judge: Richard Matsch

Place: Denver, Colorado

Dates of Trial: March 31–June 2, 1997

Verdict: Guilty

Sentence: Death

SIGNIFICANCE: The mindless horror of the 1995 Oklahoma City bombing guaranteed that this would be one of the most important trials in American history.

At 9:02 A.M. on April 19, 1995, a rental truck packed with 4,000 pounds of explosives blew up outside the Alfred P. Murrah government building in Oklahoma City, Oklahoma. The bomb killed 168 people and injured hundreds more. This was the worst terrorist attack ever committed on U.S. soil.

Just seventy-eight minutes after the explosion investigators got a break. Some eighty miles north of Oklahoma City, State Trooper Charles Hanger stopped a car because it had no license plate. He found that the driver, a twenty-seven-year-old ex-soldier named Timothy McVeigh, had a 9-millimeter pistol. Hanger took McVeigh into custody. Forty-eight

MURDER

hours later McVeigh became a suspect in the Oklahoma City bombing. Officers matched his looks to a sketch of the man who had rented the truck used in the explosion.

That same day Terry Nichols, an old army buddy of McVeigh, surrendered to authorities near his home in Kansas. Newspapers had linked him to the bombing. A search of Nichols' house revealed enough evidence to charge both McVeigh and Nichols with the Oklahoma City bombing.

Trial judge Richard Matsch ordered that the two defendants face trial separately. He next granted a change of venue (the location of the trial)

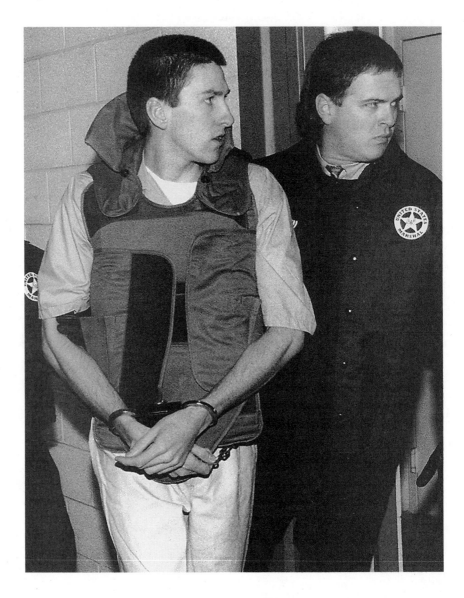

Two U.S. Marshals escort Timothy McVeigh to the Federal Courthouse in Oklahoma City on January 31, 1996, to discuss a change of venue for McVeigh's trial. The government charged him and co-defendant Terry Nichols in the April 19, 1995, bombing of the Alfred P. Murrah Federal Building that killed 168 people.

to Denver. It was here, amid scenes of high security, that McVeigh went on trial for his life on March 31, 1997. Despite the mass murder in Oklahoma City, he faced just eight federal counts of murder and three charges of criminal conspiracy.

"Hate-Filled Mastermind"

After three weeks of jury selection, Joseph Hartzler opened for the prosecution. He depicted McVeigh as the "hate-filled" mastermind of the bombing. He said he was a man consumed by hatred for the federal government. He claimed McVeigh's murderous intentions were revealed in a file found on his sister's computer. The file threatened that "blood will flow in the streets." McVeigh's rage was fueled mainly by the 1993 Waco, Texas, siege that left seventy-five members of the Branch Davidian cult dead after a standoff with agents from the Bureau of Alcohol, Tobacco, and Firearms. In McVeigh's opinion the cult members had been victims of governmental oppression. Significantly, said Hartzler, the Oklahoma City Bombing had occurred two years to the day after Waco.

Defense counsel Stephen Jones responded dramatically. In a solemn voice he intoned the names of all 168 victims of the Murrah Building attack, saying "It is to our generation what the bombing of Pearl Harbor was to our parents." While conceding that McVeigh harbored strong feelings of mistrust toward the U.S. government, Jones argued a total absence of proof to suggest that his client had acted on that rage.

An early prosecution witness, Helena Garrett, brought an intensely human dimension to the grim proceedings. She recalled dropping off her sixteen-month-old baby at a day care center in the Murrah Building that morning. Then came the explosion. "I didn't see Tevin outside . . . I was screaming 'My baby's in there'. . . . Then they started bringing out the babies."

Several days would pass before she learned for sure that her son was dead. Because of the horrible injuries she was not allowed to see the whole body. "I kissed his feet and his hands," she told a tearful courtroom. "I couldn't go any higher."

The star prosecution witnesses would be Michael Fortier and Lori Fortier, long-time friends of McVeigh, who had been the best man at their wedding. First to testify was Lori Fortier. She described regular visits from McVeigh before the explosion during which he outlined plans to blow up the Murrah Building. He once pulled soup cans from the kitchen cupboard to illustrate how he would arrange barrels of explosive material in a truck.

She also claimed to have helped fake the driver's license in the name Robert Kling that prosecutors alleged was used by McVeigh to rent the Ryder truck that carried the deadly bomb. When she heard about the bombing her immediate reaction was that McVeigh had carried out his threat.

Jones was merciless on cross-examination. "You would agree with me that if your testimony is accurate, all you had to do to prevent the death of these 168 people was to pick up the telephone?"

"Yes," Fortier replied.

"And you did not do that, did you?"

"No, I did not."

"And as a result of your failure to pick it up, 168 people died?"

"Yes."

Lori Fortier admitted that she had received protection from prosecution in exchange for the truth. Then she admitted that she and her husband had lied to friends, family and the Federal Bureau of Investigation (FBI) about their friendship with McVeigh. "At the time we were lying about everything to everyone," she said.

The first flaw in the government's case came when Eric McGown, an employee at a Kansas motel supposedly used by McVeigh, testified that he saw McVeigh with the truck on Easter Sunday, 1995. This was one day before the date the government charged he had rented it. This helped the defense claim that more than one Ryder truck—and a widespread conspiracy—was involved in the bombing.

Michael Fortier proved a key witness for the government. He said McVeigh had revealed his murderous plans in letters, phone calls, and face-to-face talks between September 1994 and early April 1995. In December 1994, he and McVeigh had visited Terry Nichols in Kansas. Driving east on I-40 through New Mexico, McVeigh had pointed to a Ryder truck. He said he planned to rent one and convert it into a deadly truck bomb. Later, in Oklahoma City, they had slowly cruised past the Murrah Building's glass-fronted north side. McVeigh had asked Fortier if he thought a Ryder truck would fit into the loading zone at the north entrance, right where the Ryder truck ultimately exploded. Fortier had agreed that it would.

According to Fortier, McVeigh vowed to stay with the bomb-laden truck until it exploded. He would even drive it through the doors of the Murrah Building if necessary. McVeigh was not worried about the inevitable loss of life, said Fortier, calling the federal employees who worked there "storm troopers" who were "guilty by association."

THE DEATH PENALTY

On June 3, 1997, the Denver jury found Timothy McVeigh guilty on all charges. However, they still had to decide whether or not he should be executed for his offenses. Within a week of the announcement of the verdict, *Time* magazine conducted a poll (survey), asking "Do you think Timothy McVeigh should receive the death penalty?" Of all people surveyed, 78 percent said that he should receive the death penalty, while 17 percent said he should not. On July 13, 1997, Denver jurors decided that Timothy McVeigh should be put to death.

Like his wife, Michael Fortier admitted doing nothing to warn of the plot, excusing his silence on grounds that he had known McVeigh for a long time.

In a blistering cross-examination, Jones made the link between Michael Fortier's testimony and any punishment he might subsequently receive to a "sword of Damocles" hanging over the former hardware clerk's head. "They [the government] haven't made that sentencing decision yet," Jones said. "You are hoping that they feel you cooperated 100 percent. . . . It would not be to your advantage to say Tim is innocent."

"No," Fortier said, "because that would be a lie." Even so, the witness admitted that he had bragged to friends about making a million dollars off the case.

Key Evidence?

Toward the end of its case, the prosecution team sprang a surprise. It introduced a key, supposedly from the Ryder rental truck and found in the alley where McVeigh parked his getaway car. However, defense attorney Cheryl Ramsey got FBI agent Louis Hupp to admit that McVeigh's fingerprints were not on it. They were not found in any of the motels where McVeigh supposedly stayed in the weeks before the bombing, or on the rental agreement for the Ryder truck.

THE GOVERNMENT'S CASE

Prosecution and defense teams both agreed that the U.S. Government's evidence against Timothy McVeigh and Terry Nichols was plentiful. Only a fraction, however, would be used at their trials. The material included 25,000 witness statements, 5,000 pieces of physical evidence, 160,000 documents containing telephone records and satellite photographs, 500 hours of videotape surveillance (teller machines and security cameras), and an overwhelming amount of audiotape.

Prints were found, however, on a receipt for 1,000 pounds of ammonium nitrate fertilizer. Lawmen discovered this in Terry Nichols' home. This fertilizer, said FBI agent Steven Burmeister, loaded into barrels of fuel oil, formed the heart of the Oklahoma City bomb. Burmeister found traces of this fertilizer embedded in a piece of the Ryder truck found at the scene. He also identified traces of a chemical used in blasting caps on the blue jeans and two T-shirts McVeigh wore that day.

The defense argued that someone else, not McVeigh, had driven the truck to the building and set off the bomb that day. Mild support for this theory came from Oklahoma state medical examiner Fred Jordan, who testified that one human limb was unmatched to any body identified in the blast. "We have one left leg which we don't know where it belongs," Jordan said, raising the possibility that the bomber had been killed in the explosion.

A big shock came with the testimony of Daina Bradley. Since the tragedy this witness, who lost three family members in the explosion and was herself grievously injured, had consistently told investigators the same story. She had seen a single, olive-skinned man get out of the truck and walk quickly away. Now, on the stand, she claimed there was a second, lighter-skinned male, although she could not be sure that this was McVeigh.

After this setback the defense regained some ground by attacking the FBI's handling of trace evidence. FBI forensic scientist Frederic Whitehurst, a highly vocal critic of his employers, said he could not be sure that ammonium nitrate was the basis of the bomb. British explosives expert Dr. John Lloyd agreed that FBI procedures for processing evidence were "not satisfactory."

To conclude what was a surprisingly brief defense, attorney Jones played a tape of Michael Fortier joking to his brother about all the media attention he had received. "Talk about a career! I can spin a fable," Fortier was heard to say. "I can talk all day!"

In his instructions to the jury, Judge Matsch cautioned them to "disregard anything you have heard, seen, or read outside this courtroom," and to return a verdict solely based on the evidence presented.

On June 2, 1997, after four days of deliberation, the jury convicted Timothy McVeigh of all charges. At the penalty phase of the trial the jury sentenced him to death. While McVeigh prepared his appeal, Nichols awaited trial for his alleged involvement in the bombing.

—Colin Evans

**T i m o t h y
M c V e i g h
T r i a l : 1 9 9 7**

Suggestions for Further Reading:

Annin, Peter. "Selling Out a Soulmate." *Newsweek* (November 25, 1996): 34.

Hackworth, David and Peter Annin. "The Suspect Speaks Out." *Newsweek* (July 3, 1995): 23.

Padilla, Lana. *By Blood Betrayed: My Life With Terry Nichols and Timothy McVeigh.* New York: Harper Paperbacks, 1995.

Ross, Ryan. "A McVeigh Acquittal?" *The National Law Journal* (March 24, 1997): 1.

Stickney, Brandon M. *"All American Monster:" The Unauthorized Biography of Timothy McVeigh.* New York: Prometheus Books, 1996.

Toobin, Jeffrey. "Victim Power." *The New Yorker* (March 24, 1997): 40–43.

POLITICAL
CORRUPTION

Samuel Chase Impeachment: 1805

Defendant: Associate Supreme Court Justice Samuel Chase

Crime Charged: "High Crimes and Misdemeanors" within the meaning of Article II, Section 4, of the Constitution

Chief Defense Lawyers: Robert Goodloe Harper, Joseph Hopkinson, and Luther Martin

Chief Prosecutor: "Trial managers" John Randolph and Caesar Rodney

Judges: The United States Senate, with Vice President Aaron Burr presiding

Place: Washington, D.C.

Dates of Trial: February 4–March 1, 1805

Verdict: Not guilty

SIGNIFICANCE: For the first and only time, Congress exercised its power under the Constitution to try a justice of the U.S. Supreme Court.

Samuel Chase was born in Somerset County, Maryland, in April 1741. Over the next seventy years, until his death in 1811, he would become one of America's most famous and controversial figures.

Chase's Early Career

Chase was active in politics from an early age. He was first elected to colonial Maryland's Assembly because of his anti-English platform. He was Maryland's delegate to the Continental Congress of 1774 in Philadelphia, Pennsylvania. In 1776 he became one of the signers of the Declaration of Independence. After fighting in the Revolutionary War, during which he became a friend to George Washington, Chase returned to Maryland. He used his influence with the Federalist Party to further his career as a judge. He quickly rose through the judicial ranks, gaining appointment as the presiding justice of the Maryland Court of Appeals. Finally, in 1796, President George Washington appointed him to the U.S. Supreme Court.

Chase On the Supreme Court Bench

In its entire history, the U.S. Congress has only impeached one Supreme Court justice, Samuel Chase.

In the Maryland courts and the on Supreme Court, Chase served openly as a member of the Federalist Party, never hiding his political loyalties. He enthusiastically enforced the Alien and Sedition Acts, that punished rebellion against the government. He supported the strict prosecution of anyone involved in antigovernment demonstrations or so-called treason. Chase presided at several trials involving supporters of Thomas Jefferson, a presidential contender. Jefferson, the Democratic-Republican candidate, won the hotly contested election of 1800.

Jefferson had a series of political struggles with the Federalists, whose supporters dominated the Supreme Court. For several years, Jefferson's energies were focused on the legal issues of *Marbury v. Madison* (1803). This ended with Chief Justice John Marshall proclaiming that the judiciary is the only branch of government that can say what the law is.

Congress Impeaches Chase

S a m u e l
C h a s e
I m p e a c h m e n t :
1 8 0 5

After *Marbury,* Jefferson adopted a different tactic in attacking the Federalist judiciary. He decided to use his party's domination of the Senate. There twenty-five of the thirty-four senators were Democratic-Republicans. Under Article II, Section 4, of the Constitution, federal judges can be impeached (charged with wrongdoing while in office) for "High Crimes and Misdemeanors." Under Article I, Section 3, the impeachment proceeding must be held before the Senate. Jefferson's allies in the House of Representatives passed articles of impeachment against Chase. These were then passed on to the Senate.

The Senate's High Court of Impeachment, presided over by Vice President Aaron Burr, opened on February 4, 1805. There were eight articles, or charges, which listed Democratic-Republican complaints against Chase. All of them concerned trials over which he had presided. The charges included giving a false definition of treason during the trial of tax rebel John Fries. It also covered making political comments to a Baltimore grand jury.

There was certainly plenty of evidence that Chase was a highly opinionated Federalist judge. He had often acted with little regard to the finer points of courtroom procedure. However, there was very little proof that his actions were serious enough to violate the Constitution. Even the Democratic-Republican senators felt uncomfortable with the impeachment. In his closing argument, trial manager Rodney begged the Senate:

> Remember, if this honorable court acquit the defendant, they declare in the most solemn manner
> . . . that he has . . . behaved himself well, in a manner becoming the character of a judge worthy of his situation.

On March 1, 1805, the Senate voted on Chase's impeachment. On each of the eight articles, enough Democratic-Republican senators joined the Federalists in voting "not guilty" to acquit Chase on all charges. Chase continued to serve on the Supreme Court until his death in June 1811.

Samuel Chase's acquittal was a defeat for Thomas Jefferson, who may have planned to impeach Chief Justice Marshall had he been successful in removing Chase. The impeachment of Samuel Chase was the

IMPEACHMENT: ANOTHER KIND OF TRIAL

Usually, a trial involves a judge and jury. In the case of public officials charged with breach of office, however, a trial is known as an *impeachment,* and it is conducted by a legislature. The charges are known as *articles of impeachment.* The U.S. process of impeachment is based on a procedure that was first developed in England in the fourteenth century. In the United States, the House of Representatives can bring articles of impeachment against any federal official. The trial is conducted by the Senate, which must convict by a two-thirds vote of the members present. The penalty for losing a regular trial is a sentence imposed by a judge. The penalty for losing an impeachment, however, is removal from office. In U.S. history, there have been only eleven federal impeachments.

first and only time Congress attempted to impeach a justice of the U.S. Supreme Court.

Suggestions for Further Reading

Elsmere, Jane Shaffer. *Justice Samuel Chase.* Muncie, IN: Janevar Publishing, 1980.

Haw, James. *Stormy Patriot: The Life of Samuel Chase.* Baltimore: Maryland Historical Society, 1980.

Rehnquist, William H. *Grand Inquests: The Historic Impeachments of Justice Samuel Chase and President Andrew Johnson.* New York: Morrow, 1992.

President Andrew Johnson Impeachment Trial: 1868

Defendant: President Andrew Johnson

Crime Charged: "High Crimes and Misdemeanors" within the meaning of Article II, Section 4, of the Constitution

Chief Defense Lawyers: William Maxwell Evarts and Benjamin R. Curtis

Chief Prosecutors: Seven "trial managers" from the House of Representatives

Judges: The United States Senate, with Chief Justice Salmon P. Chase presiding

Place: Washington, D.C.

Date of Trial: March 30–May 26, 1868

Verdict: Not guilty

SIGNIFICANCE: Under the U.S. Constitution, Congress has the power to impeach (charge with misconduct while in office) the president for certain offenses. This power was exercised for the first and only time against Andrew Johnson. Johnson survived the Senate impeachment by one vote. However, his hopes for re-election in 1868 were destroyed.

After five years of the bloody Civil War, the Union emerged victorious. To the horror of the nation, on April 14, 1865, John Wilkes Booth assassinated President Abraham Lincoln at Ford's Theatre in Washington, D.C. The next day, Vice President Andrew Johnson became president. The man who would lead the United States during Reconstruction (the period of readjustment following the Civil War, 1865–1877) was a Southerner.

Born in North Carolina and raised in Tennessee, Johnson enjoyed a successful career with the Democratic Party. He represented Tennessee in the U.S. Senate. When the Southern states left the Union to form the Confederacy, Johnson was the only Southern senator to remain loyal while his state withdrew from the Union. He was greatly admired in the North for his honor and courage.

Johnson's fame caught the attention of President Lincoln. First, Lincoln appointed Johnson as the Union's military governor of Tennessee. When Lincoln was up for re-election in 1864, he chose Johnson as his running mate. As a Southern Democrat and loyalist, Johnson would attract moderate voters to Lincoln's camp. They would join the abolitionists (those who were against slavery) and radical Republicans who already supported Lincoln.

Lincoln won the election of 1864. His assassination makes it impossible to know how his administration would have proceeded. Many historians believe that Lincoln would have taken a moderate and friendly attitude toward the former Confederacy. He had chosen Johnson as vice

The Senate impeachment trial of President Andrew Johnson.

president, afterall. He had also used the phrase "with malice towards none, with charity for all" in asking the victorious North to show tolerance toward the South.

President
Andrew
Johnson
Impeachment
Trial:
1868

An Unpopular President

Johnson lacked Lincoln's stature. He did not have the prestige necessary to convince Congress or the American people that he was up to the job of president. Union voters, having just gone through the bloodiest war in the nation's history, sent mostly Republicans to Congress, because Lincoln had been a Republican. In Congress, the Republican majority became Johnson's enemy.

The political hostility between Johnson and Congress was made worse by Johnson's opposition to the Fourteenth Amendment to the Constitution. The amendment was intended to expand civil liberties. It was also aimed at protecting such congressional programs as the Freedmen's Bureau, which helped former slaves. Johnson went on a nationwide speaking tour to promote his own views. The tour became known as the "Swing Around the Circle." During the trip he made a series of blunt speeches criticizing his enemies in Congress. The tour only served to weaken Johnson's public support.

Sensing Johnson's weakened position, Congress moved against him. It passed the Tenure of Office Act, limiting Johnson's ability to remove cabinet officers without congressional approval. Johnson fought back. He wanted to get rid of Secretary of War Edwin M. Stanton, now an ally of Johnson's opponents. Thaddeus Stevens, a representative from Pennsylvania and a radical Republican who favored harsh treatment of the South, led the fight to prevent Stanton's removal. The House of Representatives voted 126–47 in favor of a quick resolution. It read: "Resolved, that Andrew Johnson, President of the United States, be impeached of high crimes and misdemeanors in office."

Senate Tries President Johnson

The House of Representatives adopted the resolution to impeach Johnson. However, the Constitution requires the Senate to conduct an impeachment trial. Article I, Section 3, of the Constitution also states that two-thirds of the Senate must vote in favor of impeachment to in order to convict. Because a president was being brought to trial, the chief justice of the Supreme Court would preside.

The House appointed seven congressmen to serve as "trial managers," or prosecutors. One of them, Thaddeus Stevens, had been the House leader. However, illness forced him to give most of his authority to Congressman Benjamin Butler. Butler was a colorful character. He had been a Union army general during the Civil War and had served as the military governor of New Orleans after the city was taken. During his governorship, he tolerated no demonstrations of pro-Southern sentiment. One day he thought he had been insulted by a group of women from New Orleans. In response he issued an order that any woman showing "contempt for a United States officer" should be charged with prostitution. After the war, Butler returned to Massachusetts and was elected to the House. He immediately attacked Johnson. From the beginning, it was clear that the proceedings would largely be about the political struggle between the two men.

Under Butler's direction, the trial managers drew up eleven charges of "high crimes and misdemeanors." For example, Johnson was accused of making reckless, ranting speeches against Congress during the Swing Around the Circle. Johnson's response to these vague charges was quick and furious:

> Impeach me for violating the Constitution! Damn them! I have been struggling and working ever since I have been in this chair to uphold the Constitution they trample underfoot! I don't care what becomes of me, but I'll fight them until they rot! I shall not allow the Constitution of the United States to be destroyed by evil men who are trying to ruin this government and this nation!

The trial began March 30, 1868. After some confusion, the trial managers decided to make a two-pronged attack. They would argue that Johnson's opposition to the Tenure of Office Act was unconstitutional. They would also show that Johnson had abused his office with his remarks about Congress. The testimony of witnesses was not limited to those issues, however. There was testimony on practically any matter that would serve to discredit Johnson, such as his alleged habit of drinking too much.

Johnson was defended by William Maxwell Evarts, a New York lawyer highly regarded throughout the North. Joining him was Benjamin R. Curtis, a former Supreme Court justice. Other lawyers, such as Attorney General Henry Stanbery, assisted. All of Johnson's lawyers felt strongly enough about the importance of the case that they worked free of charge.

Senate Republicans Foil Johnson's Defense

Johnson's attorneys offered to produce witnesses who could testify that Johnson had objections to the Tenure of Office Act long before he quarreled with Stanton. Chief Justice Chase ruled that such evidence could be admitted. However, the Senate repeatedly voted to prevent this.

The second prong of the attack on Johnson concerned his public statements. The defense argued that the Senate could hardly impeach Johnson for exercising the right of free speech which the Constitution gives every American. Butler's response made little legal sense, but it played well with the anti-Johnson faction in the North:

> Is it, indeed, to be seriously argued here that there is a constitutional right in the President of the United States, who, during his official life, can never lay aside his official life, can never lay aside his official character, to denounce, malign, abuse, ridicule, and condemn, openly and publicly, the Congress of the United States . . . ?

President Andrew Johnson Impeachment Trial: 1868

Consciences of Seven Republicans Save Johnson

Throughout the two-month-long trial, Johnson's defense lawyers repeatedly saw their arguments obstructed by political forces. However, seven Republican senators were disturbed by how the trial had been manipulated. Only one side of the case had been presented. Senators William Pitt Fessenden, Joseph S. Fowler, James W. Grimes, John B. Henderson, Edmund G. Ross, Lyman Trumbull, and Peter G. Van Winkle defied their party and public opinion. They voted against impeachment.

The Senate met on May 26, 1868, for the final vote. The shift by the seven Republicans proved critical. The result was thirty-five to nineteen in favor of impeachment. This was one vote short of the two-thirds majority necessary to convict Johnson, and he was acquitted. However, his political career never recovered. Later in 1868, the war hero General Ulysses S. Grant was elected the next president of the United States.

Suggestions for Further Reading

Gerson, Noel B. *The Trial of Andrew Johnson.* Nashville and New York: Thomas Nelson, 1977.

FROM RAGS TO RICHES

Andrew Johnson was born in Raleigh, North Carolina. He never attended school, but went to work as a tailor's apprentice. He rose to become a successful businessman before learning how to read, write, or do mathematics—skills his wife later taught him. When he entered politics, he was committed to representing other poor and working people like himself. He served as both a U.S. representative and a senator from Tennessee.

Paul, M. "Was Andrew Johnson Right?" *Senior Scholastic,* Teachers' Edition (November 1982): 26.

Simpson, Brooks D., Leroy F. Graf, and John Muldowny. *Advice After Appomattox: Letters to Andrew Johnson.* Knoxville: The University of Tennessee Press, 1987.

Smith, Gene. *High Crimes & Misdemeanors: The Impeachment and Trial of Andrew Johnson.* New York: William Morrow, 1977.

Trefousse, Hans L. *Andrew Johnson, a Biography.* New York and London: W. W. Norton, 1989.

The Teapot Dome Trials: 1926–1930

Defendants: Albert B. Fall: Trials 1, 3, and 7; Edward L. Doheny: Trials 1 and 8; Harry F. Sinclair: Trials 2, 3, and 4; Henry Mason Day: Trial 3; William J. Burns: Trial 3; Sherman Burns: Trial 3; Robert W. Stewart: Trial 6

Crimes Charged: Conspiracy to defraud the U.S. government: Trials 1 and 4; contempt of the U.S. Senate: Trials 2 and 5; contempt of court for jury shadowing: Trial 3; perjury: Trial 6; accepting a bribe: Trial 7; giving a bribe: Trial 8

Chief Defense Lawyers: Frank J. Hogan, Wilton J. Lambert, Mark B. Thompson, Martin W. Littleton, G. T. Stanford, R. W. Ragland, George P. Hoover, and William E. Leahy

Chief Prosecutors: Owen J. Roberts, Atlee W. Pomerene, Peyton C. Gordon, Leo A. Rover, and Neil Burkinshaw

Judges: Adolph A. Hoehling, William Hitz, Frederick L. Siddons, and Jennings Bailey

Place: Washington, D.C.

Dates of Trials: November 22–December 16, 1926; March 3, 1927; December 5, 1927–February 21, 1928; April 16–21, 1928; May 31–June 14, 1928; November 12–20, 1928; October 7–25, 1929; March 12–22, 1930

Verdicts: 1: not guilty; 2: guilty; 3: guilty; 4: not guilty; 5: not guilty; 6: not guilty; 7: guilty; 8: not guilty

Sentences: Trial 2: three months imprisonment and $500 fine. Trial 3: Sinclair, six months; Day, four months; Sherman Burns, $1,000; William Burns, fifteen days. Trial 7: one year and $100,000

SIGNIFICANCE: Teapot Dome became the key example of corruption in government and marked the first time an officer in a president's cabinet was convicted of a felony and served a prison sentence.

Oil for the U.S. Navy mixed with the greed of men in power to produce the Teapot Dome trials of the 1920s. American naval ships had been converted from coal to oil power before World War I. In 1909, President William Howard Taft had set aside public lands containing oil as Naval Petroleum Reserves in case of war. One such area was Teapot Dome in Wyoming.

Civilian use of oil was expanding rapidly. Throughout President Woodrow Wilson's Democratic administration (1913–1920), multimillionaire oil barons tried unsuccessfully to obtain leases from the government to drill on the naval reserves. They argued that valuable oil was draining into private fields nearby. Finally, in 1920, Congress gave the secretary of the Navy broad powers to lease the naval reserves. The recovered oil would be sold or exchanged for supplies or construction the Navy needed.

Shortly afterward, Warren G. Harding was elected president. He appointed his friend, Albert Bacon Fall, with whom he had served in the Senate, as secretary of the interior.

The Senate Public Lands Committee investigated the activities of the Secretary of the Interior, Albert Fall.

Fall Owed Eight Years' Back Taxes

Fall had been elected as New Mexico's first senator when the former territory was admitted to the Union in 1912. Born in 1861, he was a self-educated lawyer who had worked as a cowboy and a prospector. Now he owed eight years' back taxes on his ranch in Three Rivers, New Mexico. He had recently sold his interest in the *Albuquerque Journal* to raise cash. Nearly broke, he was ready to quit the Senate. He took the cabinet post without hesitation.

Fall firmly believed that the government's lands—particularly the Naval Petroleum Reserves—should be privately owned, so he changed an executive order, taking away Navy control over the reserves. He did this to make it possible for the lands to be leased without the Naval secretary's approval. He recommended that the Navy accept oil certificates instead of cash for income generated by sales of oil from the leased reserves. Oil certificates could then be used to pay for construction done for the Navy.

By early 1922, Fall played on fears that oil in the reserves was draining away. He was urging the Navy to develop Teapot Dome. He wanted to build a pipeline to storage tanks on the Atlantic Coast and build more storage tanks at Pearl Harbor in Hawaii. Fall proposed that an associate of his, Edward L. Doheny, become the builder for the Hawaiian project. Doheny and Fall had prospected together in 1886, when Doheny had leased profitable lands in California that made him a millionaire a hundred times over.

Meanwhile, Harry F. Sinclair invited himself to visit Fall at his New Mexico ranch. Sinclair was the head of the Sinclair Consolidated Oil Corporation, and he himself had oil holdings worth $380 million. He and Fall discussed leasing the entire 9,481-acre Teapot Dome reserve to Sinclair's Mammoth Oil Company. Sinclair owned all the stock in Mammoth Oil.

Back in Washington, Fall did not invite others to bid for the lease. Instead, he signed the lease and locked it in his desk drawer. The lease gave Mammoth Oil exclusive rights to Teapot Dome's oil for twenty years. The government was to get 16 to 17 percent of the price of each barrel of oil sold. This percentage, or royalty, was to be paid in oil certificates, which would then be used to buy fuel oil and storage tanks from Mammoth.

Word of the contract leaked out. Fall's neighbors suddenly saw signs of prosperity at his ranch. A race horse and fine cattle arrived. Fall paid $100,000 to buy the ranch next door and built a $35,000 hydroelectric plant. He also paid the taxes he had owed since 1912.

A Channel for Corruption

In February 1922, the *Albuquerque Journal* began running a story exposing the oil scheme. Senator Robert M. La Follette of Wisconsin demanded an investigation. Fall's Interior Department was, he said, "the sluice-way [channel] for ninety percent of the corruption in government." Fall resigned.

The Senate began hearings in October 1923, shortly after Harding's sudden death. Edward Doheny testified that Fall had not profited from his Navy contracts. Doheny declared he had "loaned" Fall $100,000. To prove his claim, Doheny had only a note from which the signature had been torn. Secretary of the Navy Edwin Denby took responsibility for the contract with Mammoth Oil. He had played no part in preparing it, but he had not sought the competitive bids required by law. When questioned, Harry Sinclair refused to say much. The Senate learned nothing more.

"Everything Points to Sinclair"

Fall was called before the Senate investigating committee. He pleaded his Fifth Amendment right not to incriminate himself and declined to testify. President Calvin Coolidge appointed Republican Owen J. Roberts and Democrat Atlee W. Pomerene as special counsels to prosecute oil cases. "Everything about Fall's sudden wealth points to Sinclair as the source," said Roberts.

It was disclosed that Fall, who had earned $12,000 a year in the Senate, had recently spent $140,000 on his ranch. In addition, $230,500 in Liberty Bonds was deposited in his account. They bore the serial numbers of bonds given earlier to Sinclair and Colonel Robert W. Stewart, chairman of the Standard Oil Company of Indiana.

In 1924, Roberts brought lawsuits to cancel the government's lease contracts with Doheny and Sinclair. As grounds for these suits, he alleged that they had been obtained through fraud. He won against Doheny, but lost to Sinclair. On appeal, however, three U.S. Circuit Court of Appeals judges agreed that Sinclair's contracts, too, were obtained through fraud.

In November 1926, Roberts tried Fall and Doheny for criminal conspiracy to defraud the government. Defense lawyer Frank J. Hogan compared his clients' situation to the Crucifixion of Christ. He called on the ghost of President Harding to act "from his sacred tomb in Marion [Ohio]" as a witness for his friend, Fall. After debating all night, the jury acquitted both defendants.

After a one-day trial in March 1927, Sinclair was found guilty of contempt of the Senate for refusing to answer the investigating committee's questions. He was sentenced to three months in jail.

Then Fall and Sinclair were tried for conspiracy to defraud the government with the Teapot Dome lease. Sinclair responded by hiring twelve private detectives from the William L. Burns firm to follow the jurors. One of the jurors was overheard boasting that he expected to make $150,000 to $200,000 for deadlocking the trial by refusing to vote with the majority. Judge Frederick L. Siddons declared a mistrial (a trial terminated and declared void before the return of a verdict). Then he put Sinclair, Henry Mason Day (one of Sinclair's executive employees), and William J. Burns and his son—both of whom worked in the detective agency—on trial. The charge was criminal contempt, or obstructing justice. All were found guilty. Sinclair was given the stiffest sentence: six months in jail.

A fourth trial took place in April 1928. Fall and Sinclair were charged with conspiracy to defraud the government. Fall was excused when doctors reported that he was dying. Sinclair admitted giving Liberty Bonds and cash to Fall. But the jury still acquitted Sinclair.

A fifth trial connected with the scandal took place that May. Colonel Robert W. Stewart was charged with contempt of the Senate. He told the investigating committee that he did not know where the suspicious Liberty Bonds came from. He also testified that he had not profited by passing them along to Fall. But when he appeared before the committee a second time, he changed his story. This time he gave the full account of the bonds and revealed his share in the profits. The jury found Stewart, too, not guilty.

Stewart was tried again, this time for perjury (lying under oath) because he had altered the story he told the Senate. The jury acquitted him on this charge, too. But in the meanwhile, in June 1929, the U.S. Supreme Court upheld Sinclair's conviction for jury tampering. He was sent to prison.

In October 1929 Fall was tried for accepting a bribe from Doheny. By that time Fall was in a wheelchair, frail and gasping for breath. He heard his lawyer declare that he would be cleared "before he passes into the Great Beyond." The jury found Fall guilty, but recommended mercy. Judge William Hitz sentenced Fall to one year in jail and a $100,000 fine.

When Judge Hitz tried Doheny in March 1930 for bribing Fall, a different jury heard the same evidence about the alleged crime. Hogan played up Doheny's patriotism by emphasizing that Doheny was a builder of Navy tanks. The jury found Doheny not guilty.

The Teapot Dome Trials: 1926–1930

THE HARDING SCANDALS

Teapot Dome was the most famous of what came to be known as "the Harding Scandals." In another case, officials were charged with stealing millions of dollars that were supposed to go to Veterans Administration hospitals. In yet another scandal, Attorney General Harry Daugherty was involved in fraud concerning the return of German assets seized during World War I. Daugherty avoided conviction by claiming his Fifth Amendment right not to testify against himself.

Fall appealed his conviction for a year. The District of Columbia Court of Appeals upheld his bribery conviction. Then the U.S. Supreme Court refused to review his case. President Herbert Hoover turned down several requests for a pardon. On July 18, 1931, Fall was taken by ambulance to a prison in Santa Fe, New Mexico. He was the first cabinet officer ever convicted of a felony and sent to jail. He was released in May 1932, after serving less than a year. His $100,000 fine remained an unpaid judgment against him until he finally died twelve years later at age eighty-three.

Aftermath

As a result of the cancellation of the Teapot Dome lease, the Navy got more than $12 million from Sinclair. The cancellation of the Doheny leases brought in $35 million. The Naval Petroleum Reserves were used during World War II, and have continued to be bring in money for the government.

Edward Doheny died at age seventy-nine in 1935. Harry Sinclair was eighty when he died in 1956. Owen J. Roberts, who stayed with the Teapot Dome prosecutions for six and a half years, was appointed a justice of the Supreme Court in 1930. He died in 1955 at the age of eighty.

Suggestions for Further Reading

Hargrove, Jim. *The Story of the Teapot Dome Scandal.* New York: Children's Press, 1989.

Morrison, Samuel Eliot. *The Oxford History of the American People.* New York: Oxford University Press, 1965.

Werner, M. R. and John Starr. *Teapot Dome.* New York: Viking Press, 1959.

The Teapot Dome Trials: 1926–1930

Isabel Perón Trial:
1981

Defendant: Isabel Perón

Crimes Charged: Fraud, corruption

Chief Defense Lawyer: Julio Isaac Arriola

Chief Prosecutor: No information available

Judge: Federal Judge Pedro Carlos Narvaiz

Place: Buenos Aires, Argentina

Date of Trial: March 20, 1981

Verdict: Guilty

Sentence: Eight years' imprisonment and lifetime prohibition against holding public or political party office

---

SIGNIFICANCE: Argentine military leaders used corruption charges against deposed (removed from a high position) president Isabel Perón to diminish the strength of the powerful Perónist Party.

Former Argentine president Juan Domingo Perón returned from exile in Spain on June 20, 1973. His supporters expected him to restore order to the chaotic Argentine political scene but before he could do so, he died on July 1, 1974. Leadership of the nation passed to Perón's vice president and third wife, María Estela, called Isabel.

For decades, control of the Argentine government had gone through cycles of civilian rule and miliary dictatorship. It was just such changes that first brought Juan Perón to power in 1943 and then forced him out

Argentine president Juan Domingo Perón, husband of Isabel Perón.

in 1955. Exiled and widowed after the death of his second wife, Evita, Perón met "Isabelita" in a Panama City night club, where she was performing as a dancer. They were married in 1961. She stayed with him in Spain until the political climate in Argentina shifted his way, and she went with him to Argentina in 1973.

Chaos In Argentina

Economic instability and political violence rocked the country even before Perón returned to power. Under Isabel's administration, the situation grew far worse. Inflation soared to 700 percent. Political murders and bombings occurred daily. Left-wing terrorists and right-wing death squads attacked each other constantly. The new administration seemed unable to stop the chaos. Many Argentines expected and even hoped that the military would take over and restore order.

A coup (violent overthrow of government) finally came on March 24, 1976. After a night spent resisting the efforts of military leaders to get her to resign, Isabel Perón boarded a helicopter that was supposed to take her to her official residence. Instead, she was flown out of Buenos Aires to a mansion in a remote part of the country and put under house arrest (confinement under guard to quarters other than a prison).

Corruption Charges

The power of the Perón name in Argentina was strong enough to prevent the military leaders from prosecuting the ousted president on political grounds. She escaped the fate of thousands of other less fortunate Argentines who were kidnapped during what came to be known as the "dirty war." Often such political opponents were tortured and murdered. Yet the military leaders were determined to destroy the Perónist Party that had grown up around Juan and Evita in the 1940s. To do this, they focused on the greatest scandal of Isabel Perón's last year in office.

Isabel (Eva) Perón faced charges of fraud and corruption on March 20, 1981.

Juan Perón died of a heart attack in 1974, at which time Isabel took over the presidency. As president, Isabel Perón was chairwoman of a charity controlled by the Perónist Party. The agency gave away the profits of a national lottery to social welfare projects. On July 26, 1975, the Argentine national bank received a check from the charity for nearly $750,000. It was signed by Perón. The check was not used to pay for medical equipment or some other worthy cause. Instead, it was deposited into the late Juan Perón's estate account, which his widow controlled. Bank officials questioned this curious request. Within days, the check was withdrawn by Isabel Perón's secretary. The president called the deposit an honest mistake.

Perón's opponents immediately moved to make political use of Perón's "mistake." Her allies managed to stop an congressional investigation, but a government inquiry by federal Judge Alfredo Noscetti Fasolino proceeded to investigate the deposit. On December 31, allegedly under political pressure, Fasolino cleared Perón of criminal liability. He did, however, issue arrest warrants for several of her assistants. They were by then living in exile.

Two years later, however, the Perónist Party was in disarray and the military was back in power. Isabel, already under house arrest, was indicted for the check scandal. On May 6, 1976, she was formally charged with mishandling public funds for personal gain.

If found guilty, Perón faced a possible ten-year prison sentence. Despite the military's desire to remove her from Argentine politics, however, there was no clear idea of how to dispose of the former president without stirring up her supporters. The answer was found in new fraud charges. On October 25, Perón was found guilty of embezzling half a million dollars in charity funds. She was kept at a naval base. Her personal assets, amounting to $400,000 in cash and real estate, were frozen by the court.

The Military's Dilemma

Yet the military leaders still could not quietly get rid of their hostage. One week after her conviction, a federal appeals court ruled that Perón should not be held liable for the original fraud charge. Perón was moved to one of her late husband's country estates. Four years went by, and no legal action was taken against her. She was not seen in public until early 1981, when she was back in court.

Argentine federal judges were responsible both for deciding guilt and handing out penalties in such cases. On February 4, 1981, Perón was acquitted of one corruption charge. On March 20, she was not so lucky. On the one hand, she was acquitted of misusing presidential funds and of accepting a gift of $14,000 worth of jewelry from a bank. On the other hand, she was found guilty of taking $1 million from charity funds for her own use. She was also found to be criminally liable for the 1975 transfer of charity funds to her husband's estate.

The two convictions earned Perón a sentence of eight years in prison. The time she had already spent under house arrest made her eligible for parole within a month. The military leaders could not decide whether to put her in jail or let her leave the country. They decided instead to bring two more charges against her. She was accused of giving the Perónist Party ownership of a government building and of using presidential funds to buy personal possessions and make home repairs.

WAR IN THE FALKLANDS

The Argentinean *junta* (HOON-tah—a revolutionary, ruling committee) that opposed Isabel Perón was brought down in part by the 1982 war over the Falkland Islands, known in Argentina as the *Islas Malvinas*. The British had ruled these small South Atlantic islands since the 1830s. However, the territory was also claimed by Argentina. The islands possessed virtually no economy outside of sheep-raising and were home to only 1,813 people in 1980. In 1982, Argentina seized the Falklands, but the British soon reclaimed them in the war.

On June 24, the court found that there was not enough evidence to convict Perón on the second charge. She was, however, declared guilty of illegal transfer of property. A second eighteen-month sentence was to run at the same time as the one she was already serving.

Parole and Voluntary Exile

The military's scheme failed to add time to Perón's imprisonment. International pressure for her release grew. The Perónist Party began to regain strength, and the military began to suspect that they had made Perón into a martyr (one who chooses suffering or death instead of giving up their religion or principles) instead of a criminal.

Perón had already served two-thirds of her sentence. She was paroled and released on July 6, 1981. The conditions of her release barred her from participating in or speaking openly about politics. She was granted permission to visit Spain. Perón settled in Madrid and never returned to Argentina.

The military leadership that had deposed Perón did not last long after her exile. The economy continued to do poorly. In 1982, Argentina lost the Falkland Islands war to Britain. Much of the Argentine population also hated the military for bringing about the other "dirty war" against the Argentine people. The leaders were left with little choice but to hold free elections in 1983.

As a gesture towards the Perónists, President Reynaldo Bignone pardoned Isabel Perón for the fraud convictions. She was now free to run for public office. Bignone, however, did not deliver his pardon until the Perónists had already selected their presidential candidate. But the Perónists elected Isabel president of their party and immediately set about planning her return from Spain.

The Perónists did not immediately regain control of the country. Their candidate lost to Raúl Alfonsín, who became president on December 10, 1983. The Perónist Party eventually did come back into power, but without Isabel. She resigned as party leader in February 1985 and went back to her life in Madrid. "Isabelita" was gone, but Argentine politicians continued to bring her up whenever they needed the image of a heroine or fallen leader to dramatize their speeches.

**Isabel Perón
Trial:
1981**

Suggestions for Further Reading

Rudolph, James D., ed. *Argentina: A Country Study.* Washington, D.C.: The American University, 1986.

Schumacher, Edward. "Argentine Government Frees Mrs. Perón After Five Years." *The New York Times* (July 7, 1981): 1.

Schumacher, Edward. "5 Years a Captive, Mrs. Perón Is Still a Rallying Point." *The New York Times* (May 12, 1981): 2.

Simpson, James and Jana Bennett. *The Disappeared and the Mothers of the Plaza.* New York: St. Martin's Press, 1985.

Oliver North Trial: 1989

Defendant: Oliver Laurence North

Crimes Charged: Obstruction of justice, corruption, perjury

Chief Defense Lawyers: Barry Simon and Brendan V. Sullivan Jr.

Chief Prosecutors: Michael Bromwich, John Keker, and David Zornow

Judge: Gerhard Gesell

Place: Washington, D.C.

Dates of Trial: January 31–May 4, 1989

Verdict: Guilty, three counts; not guilty, nine counts

Sentence: $150,000 fine, two years probation, 1,200 hours of community service

SIGNIFICANCE: Soldiers facing disciplinary action have always excused themselves by saying, "I was only following orders." The trial of Oliver North added a new twist, as a nation wondered, "Just who did issue those orders?"

In 1985 the administration of President Ronald Reagan was anxious to gain the release of American hostages being held in Iran. To achieve this goal, the administration illegally sold arms to Iran. The proceeds of these sales were then sent to the Contra guerrillas, who were trying to overthrow the leftist government in Nicaragua. When news of this deal broke in 1986, a congressional hearing followed.

One of the primary witnesses was Oliver North, who agreed to testify in exchange for immunity (the promise that he himself would not be prosecuted). North was a Marine Corps lieutenant colonel and a member of Reagan's National Security Council (NSC). He told the investigating committee about the U.S. government's role in the arms for hostages deal. His emotional performance before the television cameras filming the hearings brought him great public attention. It also left doubts about his truthfulness. A grand jury later charged him with lying to Congress, obstructing justice, and receiving kickbacks (a return of a part of the sum received) from the arms sales.

Liar or War Hero?

The case opened February 21, 1989. Chief Prosecutor John Keker laid out the government's case against North. He said that North had shredded documents and changed computer records he knew were important to the Iran-Contra investigation. Then North went to see Attorney General Edwin Meese III. There, he "met with the attorney general and some of his top assistants, and when they asked him questions about something very important [that they needed] to know, he lied. . . . The evidence in this

National Security briefing in the Oval Office with Oliver North sitting at the rear, second from left.

case is going to show that these were crimes, and the reason for these crimes was that Colonel North was covering up crimes he had already committed."

North's defense attorney responded simply and directly. He said that his client "never broke the law. He acted within the law at all times. He followed the instructions of the highest ranking officials of the United States of America. He protected the secrets that he was ordered to protect, to save the lives of many people, many sources, many relationships. That's what he was ordered to do, and he followed his orders as any Marine Corps officer and any officer that worked at the National Security Council [would do]." Sullivan painted a moving portrait of North as a Vietnam War hero whose courage under fire led to many promotions.

Unhelpful Witnesses

The biggest problem facing the government was that most of their witnesses admired North. Their testimony made clear which side they were really on. Contra leader Adolfo Calero was typical. "He [North] became sort of a savior. . . . The Nicaraguan people have a tremendous appreciation of this man. So much so . . . that they're going to erect a monument for him once we free Nicaragua." Seldom has a prosecution witness been more helpful to the defense.

Former NSC advisor Robert McFarlane, who was North's boss, took the stand. He had himself already plead guilty to four separate charges of withholding information from Congress. McFarlane was far from straightforward. He answered questions in such a complicated way that no one really knew what he was saying. One of his clearer responses came when Keker asked, "Do you ever recall hearing the president of the United States, Ronald Reagan, instruct you or anyone else in your presence to lie to . . . Congress?"

"No," McFarlane replied.

"About anything?"

"No," McFarlane insisted.

The witness people most wanted to hear testify was Fawn Hall, North's secretary. She told of deliberately shredding documents at North's request. She also explained how she had smuggled documents from his office. "I . . . placed them inside the back of my skirt so they were secured there." Some journalists were hoping for more testimony like this, but it did not come. Hall was another witness who seemed loyal to North. She said nothing further to harm him.

When North testified, he did so with the same confidence that had served him well at the congressional hearing. The first part of his testimony consisted of a shortened version of a speech he was used to making. He had given that speech in a number of locations, charging $25,000 each time as part of his effort to increase his legal defense fund. He painted a picture of the United States under assault at every border. He explained how only his efforts and those of others engaged in the cold war (the term used to define the struggle for power and prestige between the Western powers and the Communist bloc from 1945—the end of World War II—to 1989) kept the Western world safe from Communism. Sullivan asked him how he saw himself. North responded in the emotion-choked voice that became his trademark: "I felt like a pawn in a chess game being played by giants."

Oliver North Trial: 1989

Missing Funds

The prosecution was determined to keep the jury's attention focused on the charges. They did not want jurors to be swayed by appeals to their emotions. They began by asking North about $300,000 in travelers checks that had passed through his hands. "Where would you keep careful track of it, in what kind of book?" asked Keker.

"In a ledger."

"Is that ledger still around?"

"No. . . it was destroyed."

"Do you know who destroyed it?"

"Yes."

"Who?"

"I did," North admitted.

The prosecutors were also curious about the source of $15,000 in cash which North kept in his home. He insisted that it came from his pocket change. He said he had deposited it in a metal box every Friday evening over the course of twenty years.

Keker was astounded. "The change in your pockets grew to $15,000?"

"Yes."

In building their case, the government compiled a thick file on North that listed a number of times that he had been less than truthful. Their work paid off. Over four days of cross-examination, Keker repeatedly

NICARAGUA AND THE CONTRAS

One of the most controversial aspects of the Iran-Contra hearings was the secret U.S. financing of the "Contras." Contras is short for the Spanish word for counter-revolutionaries. The revolution in question took place in 1979. The Nicaraguan dictator Anastasio Somoza-Debayle was overthrown by the Sandinist National Liberation Front. The "Sandinistas," as they were known, nationalized (invested control of in the national government) banking, mining, and other industries. This alienated them from the United States, as many U.S. corporations had investments in Nicaraguan industry. As a result, the United States financed the Contras' war on the Sandinista government. But, as the Oliver North trial showed, this financing was illegal. It was conducted by the National Security Council and financed by illegal arms sales to Iran. It was not authorized by the U.S. Congress. Nevertheless, the U.S.-financed Contra war against the Sandinista government continued for several years.

trapped North in lies and contradictions. The falsehoods often concerned money. When North left the witness stand, he had been changed from a selfless patriot into a clever manipulator.

Sullivan managed to restore some of North's glory. He returned to and expanded on the theme of North as victim: "I draw the conclusion that the president was using Ollie North as a scapegoat." Sullivan ended with a Biblical reference: "'Greater love hath no man than he be willing to lay down his life for another.' That's Ollie North, that's the kind of man he is."

Now it was up to the jury. They retired on April 20. Twelve days of deliberation resulted in not guilty verdicts on all but three counts. This was a long way from the clear message the prosecution wanted to send. Their disappointment only increased as Judge Gerhard Gesell announced North's sentence: a $150,000 fine, two years' probation, and 1,200 hours of community service. The prosecution had been expecting at least some jail time. North's supporters rushed to pay the fine, but they were too late. On July 20, 1990, the U.S. Court of Appeals overturned North's conviction. The evidence used against him, the court said, had been obtained while North was covered by immunity. He was no longer a felon.

Hero or villain? Oliver North's personal appeal and the immunity rule pulled him through. Whether that makes his actions right is still open to debate.

Suggestions for Further Reading

Bradlee, Ben Jr. *Guts and Glory.* New York: D. I. Fine, 1988.

Meyer, Peter. *Defiant Patriot.* New York: St. Martin's Press, 1987.

North, Oliver L. and William Novak. *Under Fire.* New York: HarperCollins, 1991.

Toobin, Jeffrey. *Opening Arguments.* New York: Viking Press, 1991.

Manuel Noriega Trial: 1991–1992

Defendant: Manuel Antonio Noriega

Crimes Charged: Drug trafficking, racketeering, conspiracy

Chief Defense Lawyers: Jon May and Frank A. Rubino

Chief Prosecutors: James McAdams, Myles Malman, and Michael P. Sullivan

Judge: William M. Hoeveler

Place: Miami, Florida

Dates of Trial: September 6, 1991–April 9, 1992

Verdict: Guilty

Sentence: Forty years imprisonment

SIGNIFICANCE: This trial marked the first time a former head of a foreign government faced criminal charges in an American court.

At forty-five minutes past midnight on December 20, 1988, U.S. armed forces began their costliest and deadliest arrest mission. Twenty-five thousand American troops invaded Panama, all looking for one man— General Manuel Antonio Noriega. Noriega was the dictator of Panama and a suspected drug kingpin. The U.S. government believed him to be a major dealer of the cocaine finding its way to America. After holing up in the Vatican embassy in Panama for two weeks, Noriega surrendered. He was then flown to Miami, Florida, to face charges of drug trafficking.

Dictator On Trial

Former Panamanian dictator Manuel Noriega is booked in Miami on drug racketeering charges, January 4, 1990.

As part of its war on drugs, the American government had been trying for five years to remove Noriega from power. His trial in a U.S. court finally opened on September 6, 1991. After one week spent selecting a jury, Michael Sullivan opened for the government. He mocked Noriega as a "small man in a general's uniform." Noriega, Sullivan claimed, gave his "permission, authorization, and encouragement to a scheme to transform his nation into an international cocaine trafficking and manufacturing center."

In a surprise move, defense counsel Frank Rubino did not deliver an opening statement to the jury. He wanted to wait until the prosecution revealed its case against Noriega before deciding on a strategy for defending his client.

After some introductory testimony about Panamanian history, the prosecutors began with Lieutenant Colonel Luis del Cid on the stand. Cid had been a close aide to Noriega for twenty-five years. Like many of the government witnesses, he was himself facing drug charges and agreed to testify against Noriega in exchange for a lighter sentence. Cid described himself as Noriega's "errand boy, bodyguard and bagman." He told of suitcases stuffed with cash arriving from Columbia, either as payoffs to Noriega or to be "laundered" by Panamanian banks so that it could not be traced. An extraordinary moment came when Cid was asked to identify the defendant. As Noriega stood up, Cid leapt to attention. Those in court half expected the witness to salute.

Cartel Contacts Revealed

Floyd Carlton, Noriega's personal pilot, described how two important members of the drug monopoly in Medellin, Colombia, approached him through a third person. Pablo Escobar and Gustave Gavira wanted him to "go and talk with Noriega" about Carlton flying cocaine to Panama under the general's authority. Carlton testified that Noriega "told me he didn't want his name involved in this type of problem." Further, Noreiga told him "if something happened he would know nothing about it." Then Noriega added, "Nothing is to be done without notifying me." According to Carlton, the Medellin group originally offered Noriega between $30,000 and $50,000 for each transport of cocaine. When he relayed this information to Noriega, the general exploded: "Either they're crazy or you are! Not for that kind of money. I won't allow it to happen for less than $100,000 a flight." Carlton estimated that over the years Noriega received $5 million in payoffs.

Rubino questioned Carlton about the alleged meetings. He mentioned that no one else was present. "Mr. Rubino, this was a cocaine deal, we weren't talking about cookies!" the witness snapped back. Defense lawyers did somewhat better getting Carlton to admit that Noriega had been angered to learn that some of the flights had illegally carried drug money destined for Panamanian banks.

By far the most important witness against Noriega was Carlos Ledher Rivas. He was the only founding member of the Medellin group ever to face charges in an American court. Ledher Rivas had been convicted in 1988 for drug trafficking and was serving a sentence of life plus 135 years. He testified that Noriega offered the Medellin group a cocaine pipeline to the United States. In addition to paying the general $1,000 for every kilo of cocaine that passed through Panama, the group agreed to pay Noriega 5 percent of all profits deposited in a Panamanian bank. Other witnesses judged that this sum often amounted to $60 million a week.

Ledher Rivas explained why the Medellin cocaine cartel (a group that limits competition or fixes prices for a particular item) made such a bargain: "We were desperately looking for new routes. We had no point of trans-shipment for the cocaine that was piling up in Colombia." Under questioning by prosecutor Guy Lewis, Ledher Rivas also discussed Noriega's alleged involvement with Cuban dictator Fidel Castro. Ledher Rivas said that Castro, too, was dealing with the Medellin cartel. Much of what Ledher Rivas had to say seemed beside the point, and the defense team began to suspect that Ledher Rivas was prepared to blacken Noriega's name in hopes of getting his own jail sentence reduced.

Rubino established that such a bargain had been struck. Then he challenged Ledher Rivas about Medellin involvement with the right-wing Nicaraguan Contras, who were trying to overthrow their leftist government. This line of questioning clearly upset Ledher Rivas. With great reluctance he said, "To the best of my recollection, there was some contribution to the Contra anticommunist movement." When Rubino pushed him for an exact amount, Ledher Rivas tried to dodge the question. Finally, he said, "It could have been around $10 million." Rubino was prevented from pursuing this line of questioning, however. The U.S. government, which had also been funding the Contras, could have been embarrassed by further revelations.

Judge Falls Ill

The defense case was put on hold when Judge William Hoeveler had to undergo heart surgery. After more than a six-week delay, Noriega's defense team finally got its turn. However, they provided few surprises and none of the bombshells that had been expected. Attorney Jon May portrayed Noriega as one of America's greatest allies in the fight against drugs. The level and quality of help he had given the United States, May said, was "unprecedented among the leaders of Central and South American nations. . . . Over and over the U.S. came to General Noriega for assistance." He added that this only happened when it was in "our national interest to use that relationship in times of crisis."

Some support for May's claim came from Thomas Telles, former head of the Drug Enforcement Agency's Panamanian office. He said that Noriega had promised to help the United States identify cartel members' bank accounts, monitor the movement of their money, and seize the chemicals used to make cocaine.

Noriega's ties to the United States were emphasized by Donald Winters, who had been the Central Intelligence Agency (CIA) station chief in Panama from 1984 to 1986. He said that over a period of fifteen years, Noriega provided Washington with information about Fidel Castro. This information was believed to be so valuable that William Casey, then director of the CIA, made a personal visit in 1984 to thank the Panamanian dictator. Asked to describe the meeting, Winters said, "I would describe it as something more substantial than a courtesy call."

THE PERILS OF COCAINE

The drug that Manuel Noriega was convicted of helping to smuggle into the United States was cocaine. Cocaine comes from the leaves of the coca plant, which is found primarily in the highlands and on the mountain slopes of South America. It also grows in Africa, India, and Australia. Coca is grown commercially in Sri Lanka, Java, and Taiwan to make a cocaine-free extract of the leaves that is used in some cola drinks. Processing cocaine into powder form vastly increases its effects of euphoria, hallucinations, and a temporary increase in physical energy. Cocaine is highly addictive. Its long-term use can cause a general physical deterioration.

Throughout the trial, Noriega remained silent. He did not take the stand in his own defense. After almost seven months, closing arguments finally began on March 31, 1992. Assistant U.S. Attorney Myles Malman described Noriega as "nothing more than a corrupt, crooked, and rotten cop [who] sold his uniform, his army, and his protection to a murderous criminal gang called the Medellin cocaine cartel." He added that Noriega had been responsible for fouling the streets of the United States with "tons and tons of a deadly white powder." Malman admitted that many of the prosection witnesses were also guilty, but said that law enforcement must use "small fish" to catch "big fish." Noriega was "the biggest fish of all."

Frank Rubino bitterly condemned this argument. "This indictment stinks," he told the jurors. "It stinks like dead fish. It smells from here to Washington." The case against Noriega, he said, was based solely on the theory that "if you throw enough mud against a wall, some of it will stick." He zeroed in on the more than twenty prosecution witnesses who had already been convicted of drug offenses. "They are the scum of the earth. These people are disgusting. What kind of morals do these people have?" He saved his most negative remarks for Carlos Ledher Rivas.

The jury deliberated over five difficult days. At one point, one stubborn juror threatened to hold out and cause a mistrial (a trial terminated and declared void before the return of a verdict). But on April 9 they found Noriega guilty on eight charges, while acquitting him of two. Two months later, Judge Hoeveler sentenced Noriega to forty years' imprisonment.

In political, criminal, and economic terms, the trial of Manuel Noriega is without equal. By some estimates, it cost $168 million to convict him. More certain is the expense in American lives: twenty-five were killed during the invasion of Panama.

Suggestions for Further Reading

Booth, Cathy. "The Trial Of Manuel Noriega." *The Los Angeles Daily-Journal* (April 7, 1992): 6ff.

Dinges, John. *Our Man in Panama.* New York: Random House, 1990.

Kempe, Frederick. *Divorcing the Dictator.* New York: G. P. Putnam's Sons, 1990.

Koster, R. Medellin and Guillermo Sanchez. *In the Time of the Tyrants.* New York: W. W. Norton, 1990.

McDonald, Marci. "Threat Of the Beast." *Maclean's* (September 16, 1991): 22ff.

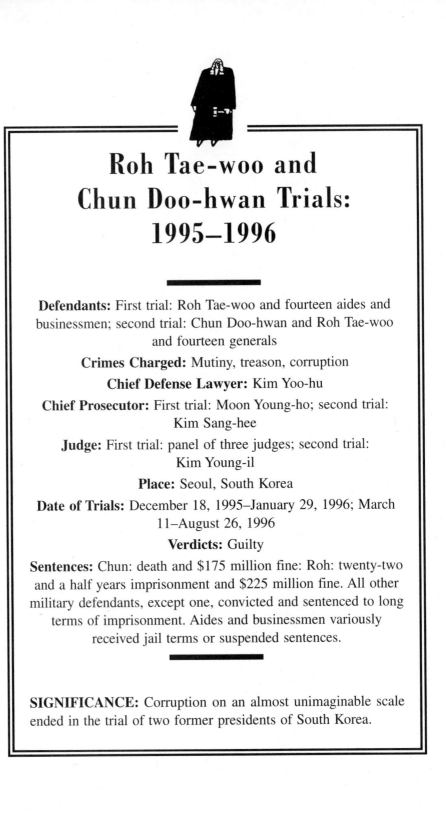

Roh Tae-woo and Chun Doo-hwan Trials: 1995–1996

Defendants: First trial: Roh Tae-woo and fourteen aides and businessmen; second trial: Chun Doo-hwan and Roh Tae-woo and fourteen generals

Crimes Charged: Mutiny, treason, corruption

Chief Defense Lawyer: Kim Yoo-hu

Chief Prosecutor: First trial: Moon Young-ho; second trial: Kim Sang-hee

Judge: First trial: panel of three judges; second trial: Kim Young-il

Place: Seoul, South Korea

Date of Trials: December 18, 1995–January 29, 1996; March 11–August 26, 1996

Verdicts: Guilty

Sentences: Chun: death and $175 million fine: Roh: twenty-two and a half years imprisonment and $225 million fine. All other military defendants, except one, convicted and sentenced to long terms of imprisonment. Aides and businessmen variously received jail terms or suspended sentences.

SIGNIFICANCE: Corruption on an almost unimaginable scale ended in the trial of two former presidents of South Korea.

In the past few decades South Korea has become one of the world's economic powerhouses. The cars, TVs, VCRs and other electronic goods that it exports have brought prosperity to this once-poor nation. Much of the reason for this success lies in the close connection between industry and government. This success also has its dark side. Bribery, for example, is commonplace.

October 19, 1995, was the day when opposition politician Park Key-dong stood up in the South Korean Parliament and made a startling charge. He said that, while in office from 1988–1993, former president General Roh Tae-woo had gathered an illegal slush fund (money collected for unlawful political purposes) totaling $492 million. The money, said Park, had come from some of the country's biggest businesses, including Samsung and Daewoo.

The nation was stunned. It was even more shocked when just over one week later, Roh appeared on Korean television and tearfully admitted the charge. The sixty-three-year-old former president gave an impressive display of remorse, offering to take all the blame and calling for clemency (mercy) for the businessmen who gave him the money. Yet the public mood was unforgiving. Besides allegations of corruption, Roh also found himself facing charges of mutiny (resistance to lawful authority) and rebellion arising from the military coup (attack) that swept him and General Chun Doo-hwan into power in December 1979. It was a brutal takeover, particularly in the south of the country where in May 1980 army troops killed at least 200 pro-democracy protesters. This came to be known as the "Kwangju Massacre."

Crowds Mob Courthouse

First, though, Roh had to deal with the corruption charges. On December 18, 1995, 1,000 riot police encircled the courthouse in Seoul. There hundreds had braved freezing cold temperatures for hours, standing in line for a chance to watch the disgraced president go on trial. In order to satisfy the intense public interest, TV networks broadcast live coverage of Roh's twenty-five-minute trip from the prison where he had been held. The cameras caught his tense expression as he entered the court, handcuffs hidden under the baggy sleeves of his white tunic. Quickly, the first major South Korean politician ever to face criminal charges took his place on a wooden bench in front of the three-judge panel. Also on trial were five former aides and nine business leaders, including the chairman of Samsung, the nation's largest company.

POLITICAL CORRUPTION

In a barely audible voice, Roh answered more than 200 questions from prosecutors over many hours. He insisted that he had not received bribes, only donations from businessmen. This was a long-standing practice of past governments. Asked if he received money from thirty-five business groups, he said, "Yes, but I can't remember exactly where, when, and from whom. When I privately met them, I thought this was the practice." Eventually, under strong cross-examination, he did admit to receiving $32 million from Samsung.

Then, in a surprise move, the defense lawyers withdrew many witnesses, to avoid "unnecessary friction" with the government. Senior prosecutor Moon Young-ho made his closing argument. "This case is a typical power-associated bribery scandal," he said, "which gave an unmeasurable feeling of despair to our people." Moon urged the court to demonstrate that all people are equal before the law. He said, "The defendants say the provision of money was unavoidable, but they willfully corrupted public servants to benefit themselves and win favors, thereby providing cause for close links between politics and business."

After only three sessions spread over more than a month, the hearing was adjourned. The court decided to defer judgment until after Roh's second trial.

Roh's second trial, along with that of his predecessor in office, former president Chun Doo-hwan, opened on March 11, 1996, and aroused even more hostility than the first. Outside the courtroom a furious mob called for blood while others charged $400 per seat to witness the proceedings. Upon seizing power in 1979, Chun had begun an iron rule, ruthlessly suppressing any opposition and jailing thousands of opponents. Alongside the two ex-presidents were fourteen other retired generals, all accused of treason and mass murder in connection with the 1979 coup. At one point a fight broke out in the public gallery as relatives of the victims of military rule traded insults and blows with wealthy relatives of the defendants. Unlike Roh, Chun showed no signs of being sorry and maintained this arrogance throughout the trial. At a pre-trial hearing, he said, "It is true that I received many millions, but all the money was political funds with no strings attached. I never issued orders to give special favors or disfavors to any given firm." Besides charges of treason and rebellion, Chun also stood accused of accepting $275 million in bribes from dozens of businessmen.

Some of Chun's defiance rubbed off on Roh. Mostly he responded to questions with a flat "I don't know anything about it," but when Judge Kim Young-il ordered him to answer more fully, he snarled, "You can't order me around. . . ." The military takeover of the country had been necessary, he declared, because student protests would have driven the nation into anarchy (disorder) and might have encouraged South Korea's Communist-controlled enemy North Korea to attack. "We believed that the government had limited power to settle the turmoil," said Roh. "So we thought that an extension of martial law [the law administered by military forces by a government in an emergency when civilian law enforcement agencies are unable to maintain safety and order] was required."

The facts of the coup could not be argued. Chun declared martial law and named himself "interim president" without calling an election; Roh helped him. Both men claimed that the country would have collapsed in chaos if they had not taken over.

Massive Corruption

It was the sheer scale of corruption that really dominated the proceedings. According to one estimate, Chun had amassed up to $4 billion by asking firms for donations to "off-budget" funds. Every major company in Korea was asked to contribute. When the chairman of Korean Air offered just $150,000, Chun's angry threat to investigate that firm's foreign currency dealings brought about an immediate increase in Korean Air's "contribution."

It was also alleged that Chun took millions of dollars from a charitable foundation set up after a failed bomb attack on his life in 1983 by North Korean commandos that left seventeen of his staff dead. Despite the fact that even primary school children were asked to open their piggy banks for the fund, relatives of the bomb victims saw almost none of this cash, most of which is believed to have been used to build a retirement villa for Chun.

In closing, chief prosecutor Kim Sang-hee said, "This case represents an anti-national crime which plunged the wheel of history into an abyss of disgrace and retrogression." Such evil, he argued, deserved the maximum penalty—death for Chun and life imprisonment for Roh.

When the court announced its verdict on August 26, 1996, senior judge Kim Young-il admitted to having "a heavy heart." Chun, he said, had employed "illegal means which inflicted enormous damage on the people," while both defendants had "put down popular resistance to clear the way for their rise to power, and used martial law for their political purposes."

Because the court felt Chun had been the driving force behind the coup, his penalty was death. Roh, considered to be less to blame, was

A DIVIDED NATION

South Korea, whose official name is the Republic of Korea, was
formed in 1948, when the former single nation of Korea was divided into two parts—the northern half occupied by Soviet
troops, the southern half occupied by U.S. troops. From 1950 to
1953, the two Koreas were at war, resulting from North Korea's
invasion of South Korea in an effort to reunify the country. Meanwhile, in 1948, South Korea had elected Syngman Rhee as its
first president. In 1960, however, Rhee was forced out of office
by a popular uprising against his dictatorial rule. In 1961, General Park Chung Hee and his military *junta* (HOON-tah—a revolutionary ruling committee) seized power in South Korea, establishing a regime that maintained near-total dictatorial control
over the nation by 1975. In 1979, Park was assassinated, and
Lieutenant General Chun Doo Hwan soon assumed control of
South Korea in another military coup. This was the coup that
also brought General Roh Tae-woo to power.

jailed for twenty-two and a half years. Both were also convicted of corruption and were ordered to pay fines totaling $400 million.

Thirteen other former generals also received prison terms ranging
from four to ten years for their roles in the coup and the Kwangju Massacre. Only one, Park Jun-byung, was acquitted. The fourteen former
presidential aides and businessmen convicted at the first trial were given
prison terms—some suspended—ranging from ten months to more than
two years.

The shockwaves from these trials undermined the very fabric of
South Korean life, and in a land where great value is placed upon honor,
few could understand the greed that had brought such shame and disgrace
upon their nation.

—*Colin Evans*

Suggestions for Further Reading

Jun, Sun-Hoon. *South Korea.* Hove: Wayland, 1996.

The Nando Times. [Online] Available http:\\www.nando.net, August 26, 1996.

Shin, Paul. "Seoul Transfixed As Roh Goes to Trial Today." *The News-Times* (December 1995).

Suh, Sang-won. "All Falling Down: Two Presidents, 7 Tycoons–Who's Next?" *Asiaweek* (December 15, 1995).

**R o h
T a e - w o o a n d
C h u n
D o o - h w a n
T r i a l s :
1 9 9 5 – 1 9 9 6**

Index

Italic type indicates volume numbers; **boldface** indicates main entries and their page numbers; (ill.) indicates illustration

Note: Trial names have been treated as titles, so that *In the Matter of Baby M* falls under "I" and "John Brown Trial" is listed under "J," while John Brown himself is listed under "B"—Brown, John.

Bizos, George *3:*773
Black, Hugo L. *1:*33, 37, 136, 213
Black, William P. *2:*404
Black Consciousness Movement *2:*468, 470
Black Hand *2:*303, 307
Black Local Authorities Act *2:*486
Blackard, Pamela *1:*53
Blacklist *1:*132, 134
Blackmun, Harry A. *1:*39, 41, 47, 89, 93-94
Blair, Montgomery *1:*15, 19
Blake, Timothy *2:*454
Blakeney, Ben Bruce *3:*814
Blanck, Max *1:*249, 252
Blasphemy *3:*608, 610
Blatman, Yonah *3:*829
Bleeding Kansas *3:*706
Blewett, George Francis *3:*814
Bligh, William *3:*588-592, 588 (ill.)
Bliss, Theodore *2:*386
Bloch, Alexander *2:*364, 366-367
Bloch, Emanuel H. *2:*364, 366
Bloom, Molly *1:*126-127
Blow, Peter *1:*16
Blow, Taylor *1:*19
Blowers, Sampson Salter *2:*381, 386
Blunt, Anthony *1:*150
Blythin, Edward C. *2:*439, 442-444
Boda, Chen. *See* Chen Boda
Boda, Mike *2:*423, 426
Bodart, Philippe *2:*354
Bodkin, Archibald *3:*718
Boer War *2:*471
Bogart, Humphrey *1:*131
Bokassa, Jean-Bédel *2:*491-495, 492 (ill.)
Boleyn, Anne *3:*660, 665, 670
Bollingen Prize for Poetry *3:*752
Bolsheviks *2:*309, 313; *3:*730-733, 745
Bolt, Robert *3:*663
Bonaparte, Napoleon. *See* Napoleon Bonaparte
Bonfield, John *2:*406
Book of Daniel *2:*370
Booth, John Wilkes *2:*517
Borah, William E. *2:*297, 300
Borgerhoff-Mulder, W. G. Frederick *3:*814
Bormann, Martin *3:*807, 811, 823
Boston massacre *2:*381-391, 382 (ill.)
Boston Massacre Trials **2:381-391,** 382 (ill.)
Bostwick, Charles S. *1:*249, 252
Bothwell, earl of. *See* Hepburn, James (earl of Bothwell)
Botts, Lawson *3:*704, 707
Bounty *3:*587-592
***Bounty* Mutineers Court-Martial** **3:587-592,** 588
  (ill.), 590 (ill.)
Bradford, William *1:*105, 107
Bradley, Daina *2:*508
Bradley, Richard *1:*105, 109, 168, 170
Bradshaw, John *3:*684-685, 687, 689
Brain death *1:*227, 229
Branch Davidians *2:*505
Brandeis, Louis D. *1:*81, 118
Brando, Marlon *3:*591
Brandt, Willy *2:*373, 375, 463
Brannon, John *3:*814
Branton, Leo Jr. *2:*446, 449-451
Braun, Harland W. *1:*233, 237-238
Breach of confidence *1:*148, 151
Breach of office *2:*516
Brennan, William J. Jr. *1:*39, 41, 47, 89, 95, 101,
  136-137, 137 (ill.), 139
Brewer, David J. *1:*29
Brewer, James *2:*388-389
Brewer, Roy *1:*130
Bribery *1:*260; *2:*374, 528, 549-550
Bridges, R. R. *1:*199, 201
Briseno, Theodore J. *1:*233-234, 238

Brisset, André *3:*710, 713
Britano, Jacob *3:*631
British Board of Trade *1:*256
British Broadcasting Corporation (BBC) *2:*321
British Commonwealth *3:*814
British North America *1:*168
British Parliament *1:*75, 110, 206; *2:*383
British rule *1:*80, 205; *2:*328, 333, 457
British Security Service *1:*148-150
Brodsky, Joseph *1:*196
Bromley, Thomas *3:*664, 668
Brooks, Alfred W. *3:*814
Broun, Heywood *2:*428
Brown, Henry B. *1:*29
Brown, J. W. *1:*70-71
Brown, Jim *2:*496-497
Brown, John *3:*704-709, 707 (ill.)
Brown, Linda *1:*34
Brown, Oliver *1:*34, 38
Brown, William *2:*390
Brown v. Board of Education *1:*5, **33-38,** 37 (ill.)
Brownell, Herbert *1:*136
Broz, Josip ("Tito") *3:*764-767
Bruno, Giordano *3:*628-633, 629 (ill.), 630 (ill.)
Bruno Richard Hauptmann Trial **2:431-438,** 432
  (ill.)
H.M.S. *Brunswick* *3:*591
Bryan, William Jennings *3:*648-649, 651, 651 (ill.),
  655
Buback, Siegfried *2:*459, 462, 464
Buchanan, James *1:*20
Buchenwald concentration camp *3:*809
Buck, Carrie *1:*81-88, 86 (ill.)
Buck, Emma *1:*82-83
Buck v. Bell *1:*81-88, 85 (ill.), 86 (ill.)
Buck v. Priddy *1:*83
Buenger, Wilhelm *3:*724, 727
Bukharin, Nikolai *3:*733-734
Burdick, Benjamin *2:*386
Burger, Warren E. *1:*39, 41, 43, 47, 89
Burgess, Guy *1:*150
Burkett, Thomas *3:*587, 590-591
Burkinshaw, Neil *2:*523
Burmeister, Steven *2:*508
Burnett, McKinley *1:*34
Burnham, Margaret *2:*446, 450
Burns, Lucy *1:*191, 194
Burns, Sherman *2:*523
Burns, William J. *2:*523, 527
Burr, Aaron *2:*513, 515; *3:*699-703, 700 (ill.), 701
  (ill.)
Burr, Richard H. III *2:*503,
Burr *3:*702
Burroughs, George *3:*644
Burton, Harold H. *1:*33, 37
Burton, Mary *1:*169-170
"Butcher of Lyons" *3:*837
Butler, Benjamin *2:*520-521
Butler, Eddie *2:*456
Butler, John Washington *3:*649
Butler, Pierce *1:*81, 85
Butler Act *3:*652, 654
Butt, Charles *1:*75, 77
Butterfield, Alexander *1:*42
Byrn, Michael *3:*587, 589, 591

C

Čabrinović, Nedeljko *2:*302-303, 305
Caesar *1:*168-170
Caiaphas *3:*608, 610
Cain and Abel *3:*653
Cajetan, Thomas de Vio *3:*623
Caldwell, James *2:*385
Calef, Daniel *2:*386

Index

Index

Equal Protection Clause of the Fourteenth Amendment *1:*33, 49, 177, 242
Erlichman, John D. *1:*40, 42
Ernesto Miranda Trials *1:***215-220,** 216 (ill.)
Ernst, Morris L. *1:*123-127
Escobar, Pablo *2:*544
Espionage Act *1:*118, 121, 192-193; *2:*371
Estabrook, Arthur *1:*84
Estela, María *2:*530
Esterhazy, Charles *3:*713, 715
Eugenics *1:*82-83
European settlers *1:*10, 208; *2:*471, 489
Euthanasia *1:*244-245
Evans, Peter *1:*204
Evarts, William Maxwell *2:*517, 520
Evolution *1:*87; *3:*648-655
Evolutionists *3:*651, 654
Excessive force *1:*233
Excommunication *3:*621, 626
Executive privilege *1:*39, 43-45
Exile *1:*189; *2:*295, 492, 530, 533-534; *3:*713, 734, 743-744, 772, 788, 790
Ezra Pound Trial *3:***748-752,** 751 (ill.)

F

Fabre, Pierr-Elie *3:*711
Facing Mount Kenya *1:*205
Falangist Party *3:*746
Falck, Dr. *2:*320
Fall, Albert B. *2:*523-528
False report *1:*233; *2:*312
False testimony *2:*485, 487; *3:*605
Farben, I. G. *2:*463
Farmer, Fyke *2:*364
Fascism *3:*746, 749
Fasolino, Alfredo Noscetti *2:*532-533
Fatzer, Harold R. *1:*33, 36
Fawkes, Guy *3:*678, 680-683
Faxian, Wu. *See* Wu Faxian
Fay, David *1:*112
Federal Bureau of Investigation (FBI) *1:*42; *2:*360-361, 365, 367, 437, 448, 506-509
Federal Court of Appeals *1:*36; *2:*479, 481
Federal troops *2:*298; *3:*706
Federalists *1:*3, 113-116; *2:*514-515; *3:*699
Feldbauer, Max *2:*302
Fenton, Elliott *1:*262
Ferguson, Danny *1:*52-54
Ferguson, Helen *2:*418
Ferguson, J. H. *1:*29
Ferguson, John A. *1:*30
Fessenden, William Pitt *2:*521
Field, Alexander M. *1:*15
Field, Marshall *2:*404
Field, Roswell M. *1:*18-19
Field, Stephen J. *1:*29
Fielden, Samuel *2:*404, 406-407, 409
Fifth Amendment *1:*214; *2:*367, 526, 528; *3:*594
Fifth U.S. Army Corps *2:*461
"Final Solution" *3:*811, 824
Finch, Katherine *1:*160
Finerty, John *2:*364
First Amendment *1:*23-24, 26, 50, 110, 119-123, 131, 138, 140, 194; *2:*439; *3:*652, 654-655
The First Circle *3:*790
Fisch, Isidor *2:*435
Fischer, Adolph *2:*404, 407, 409
Fischer, Bram *3:*773, 775-776
Fisher, Bishop *3:*661
Fitts, David *2:*335, 337
Fitzgerald, James *2:*410, 414
Fleming, Silas *1:*34
Flexner, James *3:*584, 586
Florian, Karel *3:*779

Florida Supreme Court *1:*212
Florida's Division of Corrections *1:*212
Florio, Jim *2:*437
Flowers, Robert *1:*89
Floyd, Jay *1:*89, 92
Flynn, Elizabeth Gurley *2:*428
Flynn, John *1:*215
Foley, John *2:*364
Foran, Thomas A. *1:*141-142, 144-145
Forced labor *2:*292; *3:*834
Ford, Gerald *1:*45; *3:*761
Ford's Theatre *2:*517
Fort Benning *3:*593, 594, 597
Fort George *1:*169
Fort Leavenworth *3:*597
Fort Raleigh National Historic Site *3:*676
Fort Ticonderoga *3:*585
Fortas, Abe *1:*212, 213
Fortier, Lori *2:*505-506
Fortier, Michael *2:*505-507, 509
Forzinetti, Ferdinand *3:*711
Foster, Jodie *1:*67
Foster, William A. *2:*404
Foth, Eberhard *2:*459, 464
Fouquier-Tinville, Antoine *2:*392; *3:*695
Fourteenth Amendment *1:*5, 31, 33, 37, 49, 85, 91, 93, 177-178, 180-181, 200, 242, 244; *2:*519; *3:*652
Fourth Home Rule Bill *1:*80
Fowler, Joseph S. *2:*521
Fox, George *1:*166
Fox Libel Act *1:*110
Francis I *3:*694
Franck, Edouard *2:*491, 493
Franco, Francisco *3:*746
Frank, Hans *3:*807, 809, 811
Frank, Leo Max *2:*416-421, 417 (ill.)
Frank, Moses *2:*417
Frankfurter, Felix *1:*33, 37; *2:*364, 428-429
Franz Ferdinand *2:*302-306, 303 (ill.)
Fraud *1:*64; *2:*526, 528, 530, 532-533, 535
Frederick III *3:*623
Free exercise of religion *1:*23, 26
Freedom of Information Act *2:*370
Freedom of the press *1:*105, 110-112, 138, 140, 151; *3:*798
Freeman, Harrop *1:*221
Freikorps *2:*310
Freisler, Roland *2:*320, 323, 325
French and Indian War *2:*382
French Resistance *3:*615, 737, 837, 840
French Revolution *2:*396; *3:*692, 697-699
French War Office *3:*710
Frick, Wilhelm *3:*810-811
Fries, John *2:*515
Fritzsche, Hans *3:*811, 813
Froines, John R. *1:*141, 144-145
Fromm, Friedrich *2:*322-323, 322 (ill.)
Frost, Robert *3:*748, 752
Fuchs, Klaus *2:*365
Fuchs, Senator *2:*291
Fugitive slave law *2:*17 (ill.)
Fuhrman, Mark *2:*497-498, 500-501
Fuller, Alvan T. *2:*428
Fuller, Melville W. *1:*29
Funk, Walther *3:*807, 809, 812
Furness, George *3:*814
Furniss, Robert W. Jr. *3:*748

G

Gahan, H. Sterling *2:*355
Galilei, Galileo *3:*634-640, 636 (ill.)
Galileo Galilei Trial *3:*634-640, 636 (ill.)
Gallinari, Prospero *2:*473, 476-477

H

Index

Index

S

Index

Index

Index